IMAGES
of America

CEMETERIES AROUND LAKE WINNIPESAUKEE

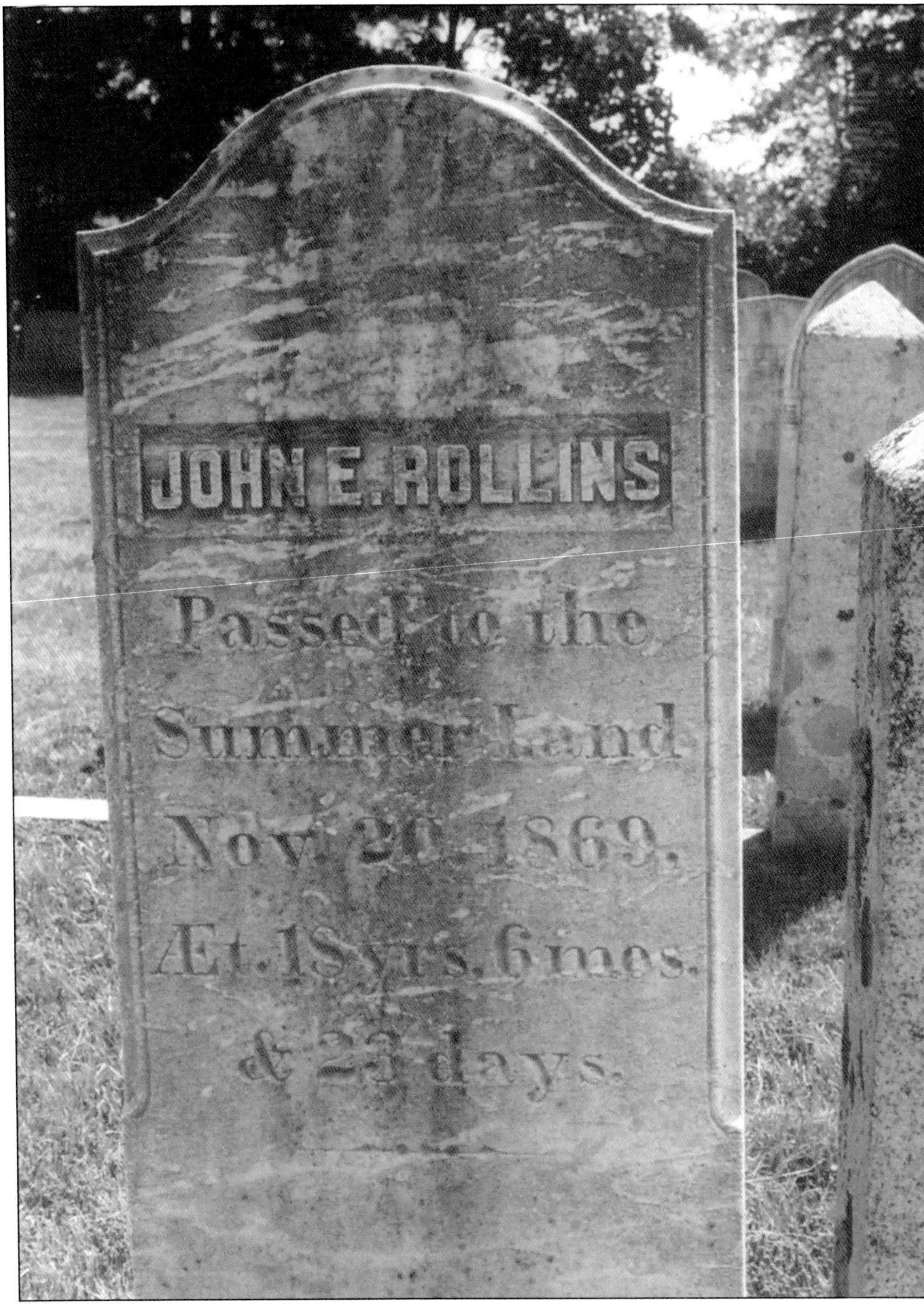

JOHN ROLLINS (1869), MELVIN VILLAGE CEMETERY, TUFTONBORO. The sentiment implied on young John Rollins's gravestone no doubt belies the belief held by many through the years that Lake Winnipesaukee in summer time is as close as one can get to heaven on earth.

On the cover: Please see page 104. (Courtesy Laconia Public Library.)

IMAGES
of America

CEMETERIES AROUND LAKE WINNIPESAUKEE

Glenn A. Knoblock

ARCADIA
PUBLISHING

ISBN 0-7385-3931-7

Published by Arcadia Publishing
Charleston SC, Chicago IL, Portsmouth NH, San Francisco CA

Printed in the United States of America

Library of Congress Catalog Card Number: 2005931675

For all general information contact Arcadia Publishing at:
Telephone 843-853-2070
Fax 843-853-0044
E-mail sales@arcadiapublishing.com
For customer service and orders:
Toll-Free 1-888-313-2665

Visit us on the Internet at http://www.arcadiapublishing.com

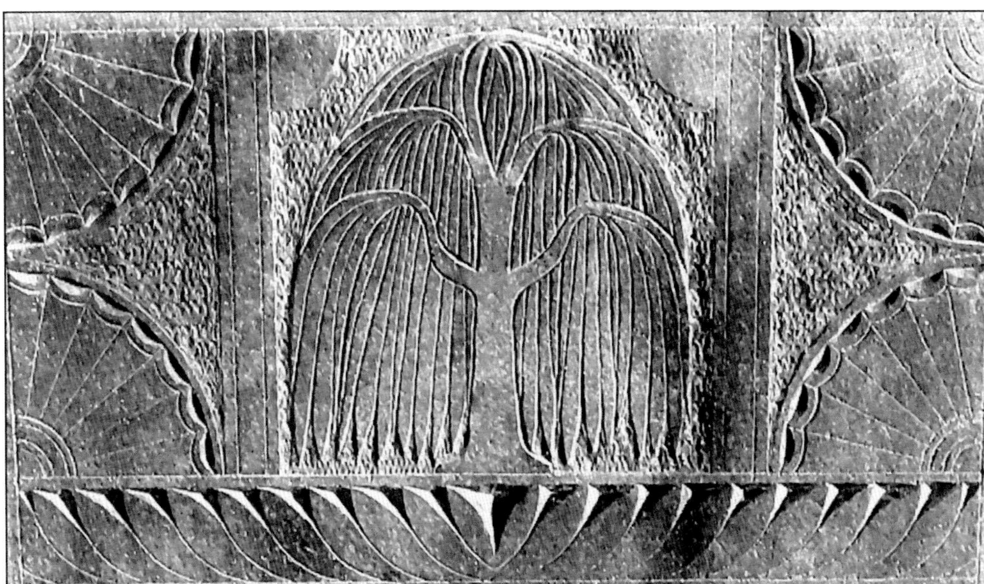

DETAIL, JONATHAN GILMAN (1847) STONE. This gravestone, found in the Smith Meeting House Cemetery in Gilmanton, is for a descendant of the town's founding family.

Contents

Acknowledgments		6
Introduction		7
1.	New Durham and the Altons	9
2.	Wolfeboro	25
3.	Tuftonboro, Melvin Village, and Mirror Lake	39
4.	Moultonborough	51
5.	Sandwich	63
6.	New Hampton and Center Harbor	73
7.	Meredith and Holderness	83
8.	Laconia	97
9.	Gilford and Belmont	107
10.	The Gilmantons	117

ACKNOWLEDGMENTS

In researching cemeteries for this book, I have tried to stick as close to the lake's shore as possible and highlight cemeteries that are either easily visible or easily found with a map. However, some towns and cemeteries, due to their historical nature, could not be ignored even though they did not meet my exact criteria. Thus, I have included cemeteries in the towns of New Durham, Sandwich, Holderness, New Hampton, and Gilmanton. It is with great regret that space did not allow for a full treatment of all towns in this study and excluded such towns as Ashland and Sanbornton. In addition to town histories, published cemetery records, family genealogies, and published New Hampshire state records, the following works were consulted: *History of Merrimack and Belknap Counties, New Hampshire* (1885), edited by D. Hamilton Hurd; *The History of Carroll County* (1889) by Georgia Drew Merrill; *The Register of Soldiers and Sailors of New Hampshire in the War of the Rebellion* (1895) by Augustus Ayling; *Three Centuries on Lake Winnipesaukee* (1936) by Paul Blaisdell; and *New Hampshire Churches* (1856) by Robert Lawrence. For those who wish to find many of the cemeteries in this book, the best map for this purpose by far is DeLorme Mapping Company's *The New Hampshire Atlas and Gazetteer.* While this map is still in print, modern editions do not show cemeteries. However, earlier versions, dated 1988 and before, do show them and can be found online or in used book stores.

As always, I have many people to thank. Foremost is my wife, Terry, who is always supportive of my endeavors and offers steady encouragement. Thanks, too, to my daughter, Anna, who has to put up with her dad's absences. I would also like to thank artist Peter Ferber for allowing me to reproduce his painting *Center Harbor Idyll.* Peter's watercolor paintings are even more impressive in person and are available from the Art Place at 9 North Main Street in Wolfeboro. Last, but not least, the following individuals have been of great help in providing information and/or illustrations for the book: New Durham, Cathy Orlowicz, Crissa Evans, and Rev. James Nason; Alton, Mark Northridge, Tom Hoopes, and Jean Roberts; Wolfeboro, Jim Rogers; Moultonborough, Sandra Barnes, Jane Rice, and Mary Dunn; Sandwich, Rosa Rediger; New Hampton, Lyn O'Callaghan; Laconia, Judith Livingston Loto; Gilford, Dianne Mitton and Joan Nelson; and Belmont, Wallace Rhodes.

All photographs in this book are by the author or from my personal collection unless otherwise noted. This book is dedicated to Jim Maier (1962–1975), "Done too soon," and our family dog, Brownie (1991–2006).

INTRODUCTION

The Lake Winnipesaukee area of New Hampshire has long been an idyllic place for boating and outdoor enthusiasts. However, for those who care to dig a little deeper, the historical aspects of the area's first permanent inhabitants and their settlements are equally compelling. One unique way to experience this history firsthand is to visit the many cemeteries found in the communities that front Lake Winnipesaukee and several nearby lakes.

The earliest inhabitants in this area were Native Americans. While many of their artifacts, some thousands of years old, have been discovered around the lake, their burial grounds remain largely unknown and most were likely destroyed by the area's first white settlers. However, two cemeteries have Native American associations even today. The Melvin Village Cemetery has a marker that denotes the spot where remains were discovered in 1808. Within Wolfeboro's Pine Hill Cemetery was once a cleared area that was long known in local lore as "Indian's Dance," possibly indicating a place of ceremonial importance.

The date of the white-European discovery of Lake Winnipesaukee is uncertain but likely occurred by 1633. The area was mapped by 1677, but it was not until 1727 that the first town on Lake Winnipesaukee, Gilmanton, was incorporated. Like many frontier towns in New England, the time between Gilmanton's incorporation and actual settlement varied greatly. It was not until December 1761 that Gilmanton gained its first true citizens when Benjamin Mudgett and his wife Hannah arrived from Brentwood, having traveled the last 12 miles on foot. Not only is Gilmanton the oldest town surrounding Lake Winnipesaukee, it also has the area's oldest documented cemetery: Smith Meeting House Cemetery, established in 1776.

Following the successful settling of Gilmanton, towns in the area, most granted by Royal Governor Benning Wentworth to groups of proprietors prior to 1767, grew rapidly. These towns, all settled between 1761 and 1785, were third- or fourth-generation settlements in New Hampshire. In older towns such as Hampton or Dover, one of the first things attended to was the procurement of a minister and, soon after, the building of a meetinghouse and establishment of a town burial ground. In the Lakes Region, this pattern changed; people came to the area for economic opportunity and land. Religion, to be sure, was still an important component in the lives of most settlers, but it was not the overriding concern that it once was. Thus, the building of meetinghouses and establishment of public burial grounds around Lake Winnipesaukee did not often come until a later date. The first meetinghouse around the lake was apparently built in East Moultonborough in 1773. The area's oldest town, Gilmanton, did not erect a meetinghouse until 1775, 14 years after its first settler arrived.

So, then, what did early settlers do when it came to the burial of their dead? Many were buried in small family burying places or slightly larger places that served one particular area or group of families. Those family or neighborhood cemeteries that survive today serve as archaeological sites that help to document settlement patterns from a town's earliest beginnings. One interesting example of this is the North Wolfeboro Cemetery. Now located on a dirt road in a heavily wooded area that is lightly traveled, it once served an area known as Dimon's Corner, a community of nearly 200 individuals, complete with its own physician, tavern, stores, and church, that flourished from around 1772 until about 1870. All around Lake Winnipesaukee, there are many such places. Some towns have close to 100 cemeteries, while the average number of cemeteries in most communities is close to 30. In many cases, these cemeteries are the only discernible physical remnants of a now vanished neighborhood or family farm, with only the names on the gravestones to give us a clue as to who once lived in the area.

While cemeteries are found all around the lake, those found on its many islands are surprisingly small in number. Long Island has two, the Brown and Lamprey cemeteries, the latter for descendants of the famed shipbuilding family of the same name. Sleepers Island has a small cemetery, while the Davis Cemetery can be found on Governors Island. Most interesting is Bear Island. It has a simple fieldstone cemetery with nine burials for individuals whose identity is unknown. The island also has the famed "mystery stone," a rock that bears the initials JPH and the date 1873, along with a carving of an anchor. Whether this is a gravestone or the carving of an island visitor is unknown.

The area's cemeteries are similar to many other cemeteries in New Hampshire in layout. Following old English customs from the early days of Christianity, most of the gravestones are facing west, with the deceased lying between the headstone and the footstone facing east toward the rising sun, so as to be able to "see" the dawn of the coming Resurrection. In the earliest days in the Lakes Region, gravestones, if used at all, were made of simple fieldstones found locally that were often unlettered. If lettered, it was simply done, usually with the deceased's name or initials crudely but lovingly carved by a family member or friend. It was not until the 1780s that professionally carved gravestones begin to appear. Most of the earliest gravestone carvers whose work is found in this area, dated before 1810, came from the Merrimack Valley region of Massachusetts, Boston, or the New Hampshire seacoast. One carver of local origins whose work stands out is Matthias Weeks. A native of Gilmanton, this stonecutter later moved to Moultonborough and practiced the art of gravestone-making for many years. The extent of his work is just now beginning to come to light.

Finally one might wonder about how these gravestones themselves came to their final resting places. The answer is simple and is found all around us: Lake Winnipesaukee itself. Gravestones are heavy objects; a large pair can weigh over 600 pounds. While horse- or ox-drawn carts were used, there can be no doubt that stonecutters also utilized shipping on Lake Winnipesaukee, first by ferry or gundalow, then by horse boat, and later by steamships, to get these unique works to their final destination.

One

NEW DURHAM AND THE ALTONS

New Durham was established by a grant in 1749. First called Cocheco Township, it was not permanently settled until 1762, at which time it was also incorporated and given its present name. It has always been, for the large part, a rural community and remains so to this day, with fewer residents per square mile than many other area towns. Because of this, New Durham is unique in this study. All of its older cemeteries are family plots that lie on private land and are inaccessible to the public. It was not until the middle of the 20th century that a public cemetery was established. This rare glimpse at New Durham's private cemeteries is highlighted by the important religious history to be found, for it was here in 1780 that Benjamin Randall established the first Free Will Baptist church in America. One may wonder why it was that Randall, a native of New Castle, chose to settle his family and found his church in such a remote area. However, a drive to the top of Ridge Road, where Randall's church can still be seen, on a bright and sunny day brings one a sense of understanding. With its spectacular view of the surrounding mountains, more pristine even in Randall's time, is it any wonder that he was inspired to found his church here? Some may question New Durham's inclusion in this study; is it really a Lakes Region town? Its location on Merrymeeting Lake, just scant miles from Alton Bay, and its close association with Alton, surely makes it a worthy addition.

The town of Alton, including Alton Bay, West Alton, and East Alton, was originally a part of New Durham and was called New Durham Gore. Though the town did not gain its first permanent inhabitants until 1770, when Jacob Chamberlain and others came to Alton Bay, it was the site of much activity and commerce. A blockhouse for the fur trade with the Pennacooks was built here prior to the French and Indian War. The population of the area grew as its location as a staging point at the southern terminus of the lake grew in importance, and in 1794, it petitioned for incorporation. The name Roxbury was at first suggested, but it was soon changed to Alton, and so it remained. The town's oldest cemetery still in use is Riverview Cemetery, with burials dating to the early 1800s. Most interesting is the Gilman's Corner Cemetery in East Alton. Located a short distance from the historic meetinghouse, it once sat in an open field; now it is surrounded by woodlands and all but inaccessible, except to those who know the area. Like New Durham, Alton has many private family cemeteries, including one on Sleepers Island. Perhaps the most fascinating is the lone burial site of Sarah Glidden. Town legend has it that she was a witch, and it seems only appropriate that her final resting place, if she rests at all, is not too distant from Devil's Den Mountain.

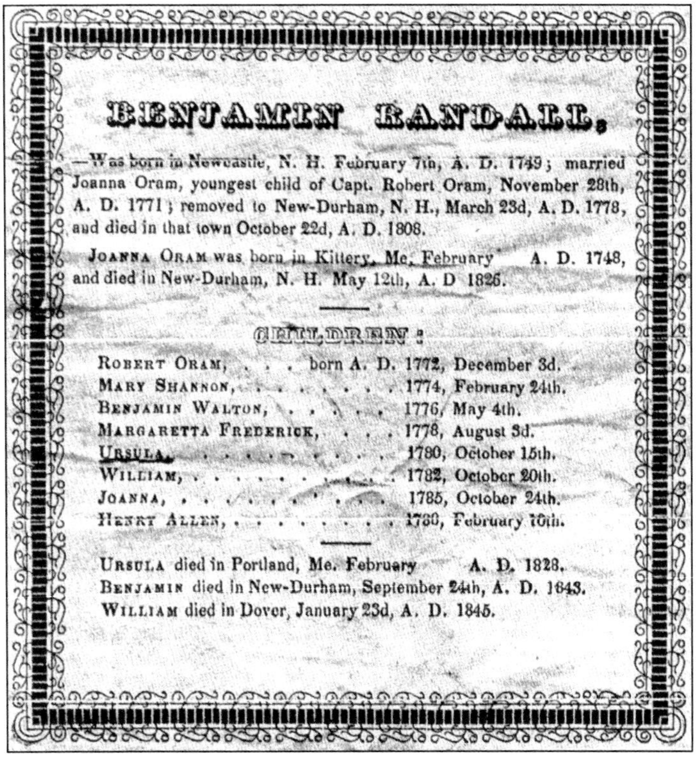

BENJAMIN RANDALL.

—Was born in Newcastle, N. H. February 7th, A. D. 1749; married Joanna Oram, youngest child of Capt. Robert Oram, November 28th, A. D. 1771; removed to New-Durham, N. H., March 23d, A. D. 1778, and died in that town October 22d, A. D. 1808.

JOANNA ORAM was born in Kittery, Me. February A. D. 1748, and died in New-Durham, N. H. May 12th, A. D 1826.

CHILDREN:

ROBERT ORAM, . . . born A. D. 1772, December 3d.
MARY SHANNON, ... 1774, February 24th.
BENJAMIN WALTON, ... 1776, May 4th.
MARGARETTA FREDERICK, ... 1778, August 3d.
URSULA, ... 1780, October 15th.
WILLIAM, ... 1782, October 20th.
JOANNA, ... 1785, October 24th.
HENRY ALLEN, ... 1780, February 10th.

URSULA died in Portland, Me. February A. D. 1828.
BENJAMIN died in New-Durham, September 24th, A. D. 1843.
WILLIAM died in Dover, January 23d, A. D. 1845.

BENJAMIN RANDALL FAMILY DOCUMENT. The Randall family moved to New Durham in 1778. Five years previously, Benjamin changed his religious views on baptism and the idea of salvation and began preaching his own ideals. Deemed a heretic by the Baptist church in Berwick, Maine, Randall was ordained an evangelical preacher in 1780 and organized the First Free Will Baptist Church, the first of its kind in America. (Courtesy Crissa Evans.)

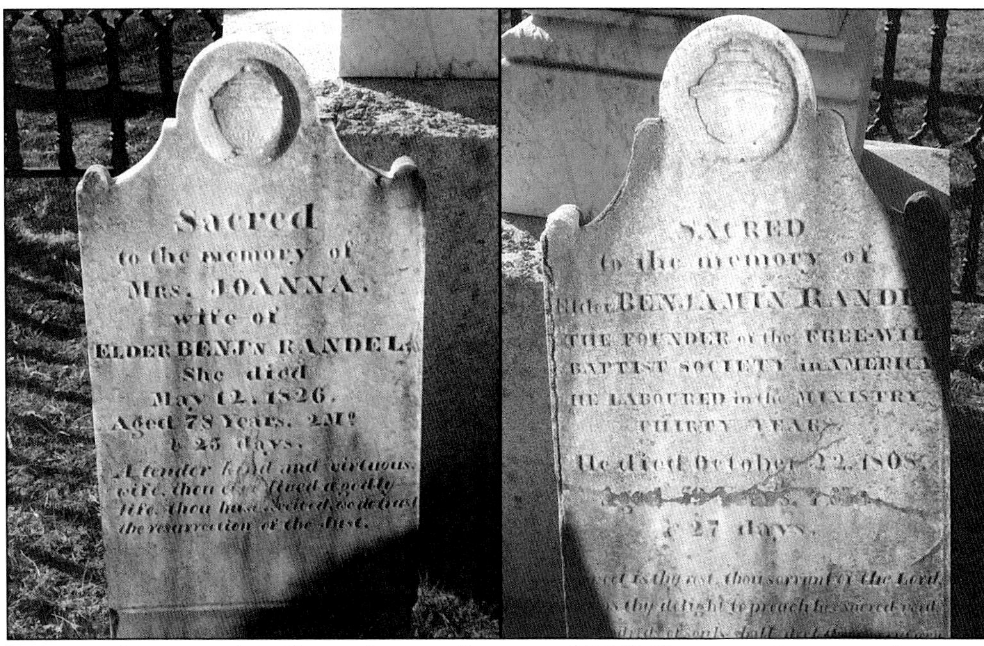

BENJAMIN RANDALL (1808) AND JOANNA RANDALL (1826), RANDALL CEMETERY. Benjamin Randall, a sailmaker and tailor by trade, and his wife, Joanna, together helped build the Free Will Baptist faith from a once-radical ideal to a widely accepted reality by the end of the 18th century. Their gravestones were likely carved by Portsmouth's Samuel Treat, while their burial site is an important and sacred site to today's Free Will Baptists.

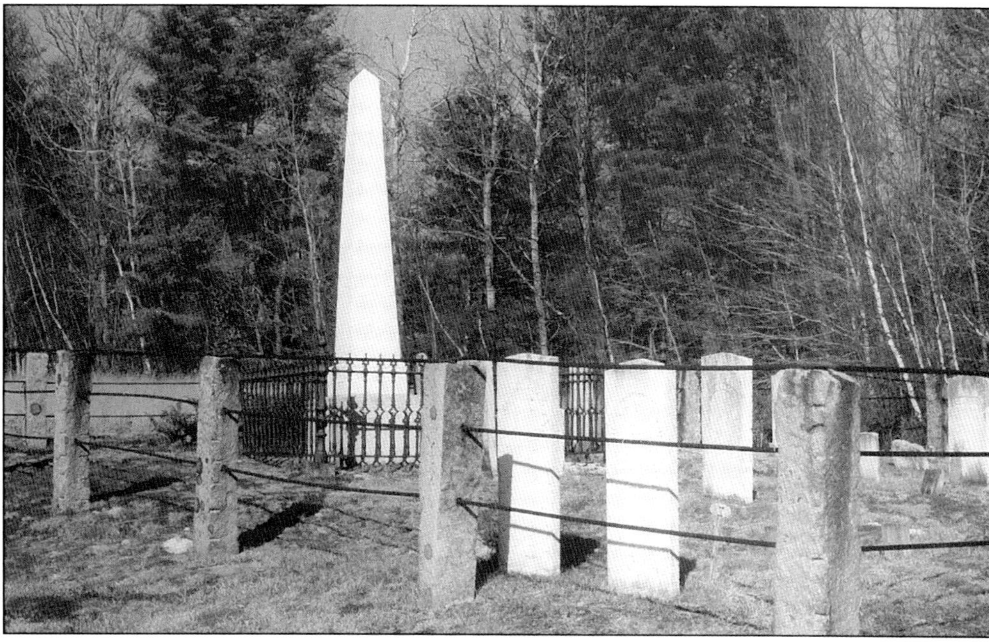

THE RANDALL CEMETERY AND FIRST FREE WILL BAPTIST CHURCH. The Randall Cemetery is located in a field on land once owned by Benjamin Randall and located just a short distance from the church built in 1818–1819, still standing today (below) at the top of Ridge Road. Members of the Randall family, including his parents, are buried here, as are those of his wife, and the Orams, originally of Kittery, Maine. While the original gravestones for Joanna and Benjamin Randall were likely erected soon after Joanna's death in 1826, the marble obelisk, extensively carved with data regarding Randall's career on one side and tenets of the Free Will Baptist faith on the others, was erected some years later in tribute to Randall's lasting contributions. (Right photograph courtesy Crissa Evans.)

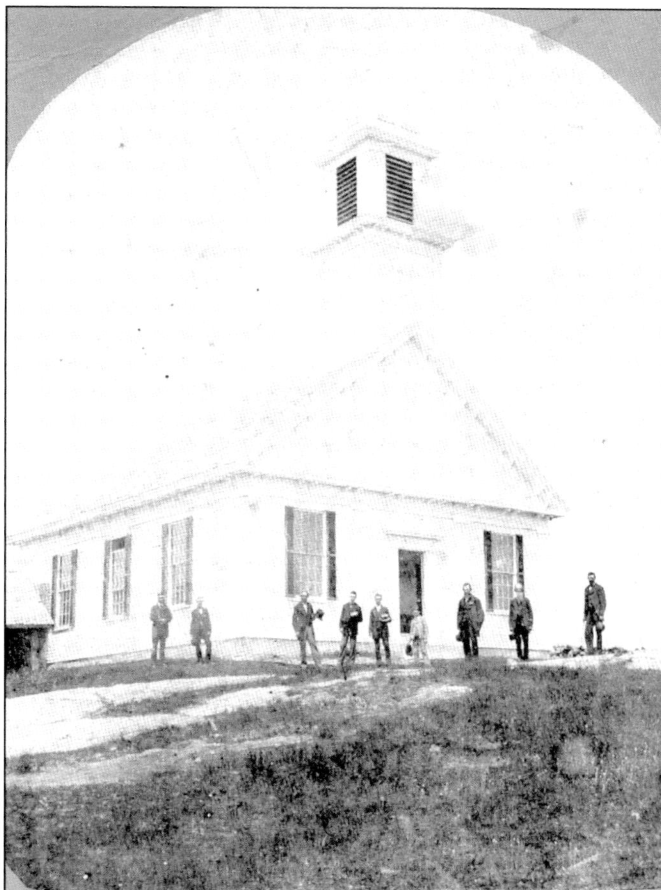

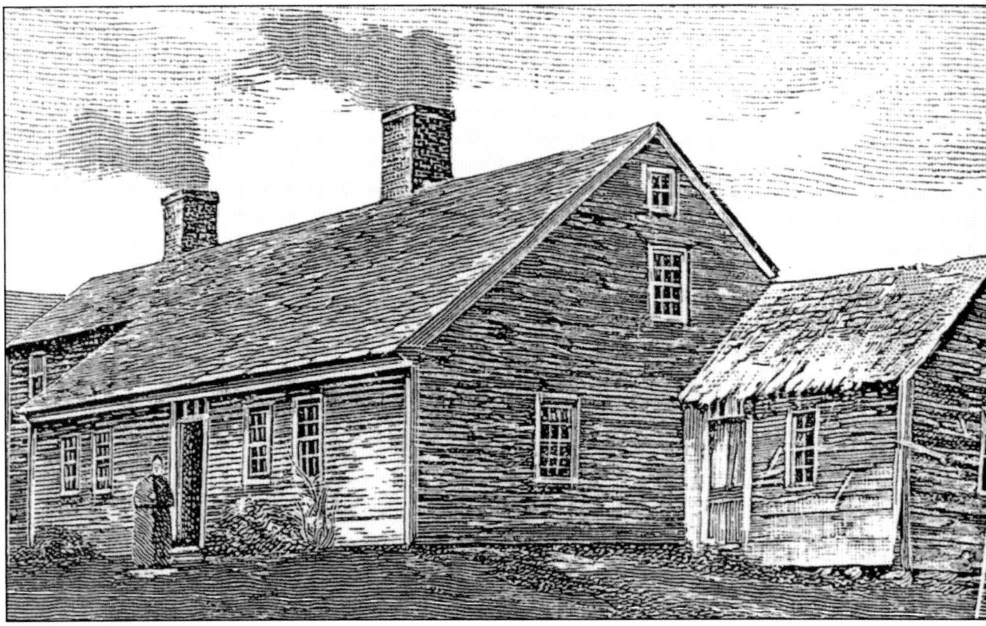

THE BOODEY HOUSE, C. 1892. This, the oldest house in New Durham, was built around 1769 by Zechariah Boodey. Still standing today, it has always remained in the possession of Boodey's family descendants. It was here on June 30, 1780, that the First Free Will Baptist Church was established by Elder Benjamin Randall, Rev. Robert Boodey, Rev. Joseph Boodey, Nathaniel Buzzell, Judith Cartel, and others. (Woodcut from *Centennial Souvenir of the New Hampshire Yearly Meeting of Free Baptists*, 1892.)

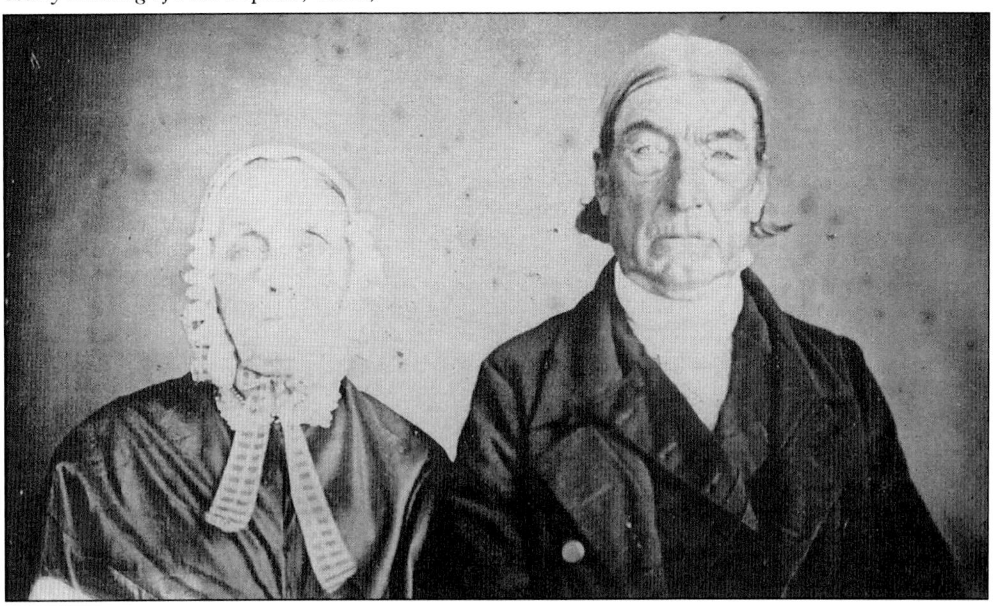

PORTRAIT OF ELDER JOSEPH AND MARCY BOODEY. Joseph, the son of Zechariah Boodey II, was born in the Boodey log cabin on April 12, 1773. Ordained a Free Will Baptist minister in 1799, he worked with his namesake uncle in organizing churches throughout New Hampshire and Vermont. Joseph married Marcy Pike in 1800, and she would remain his companion and helpmate until her death nearly 56 years later. (Courtesy Crissa Evans.)

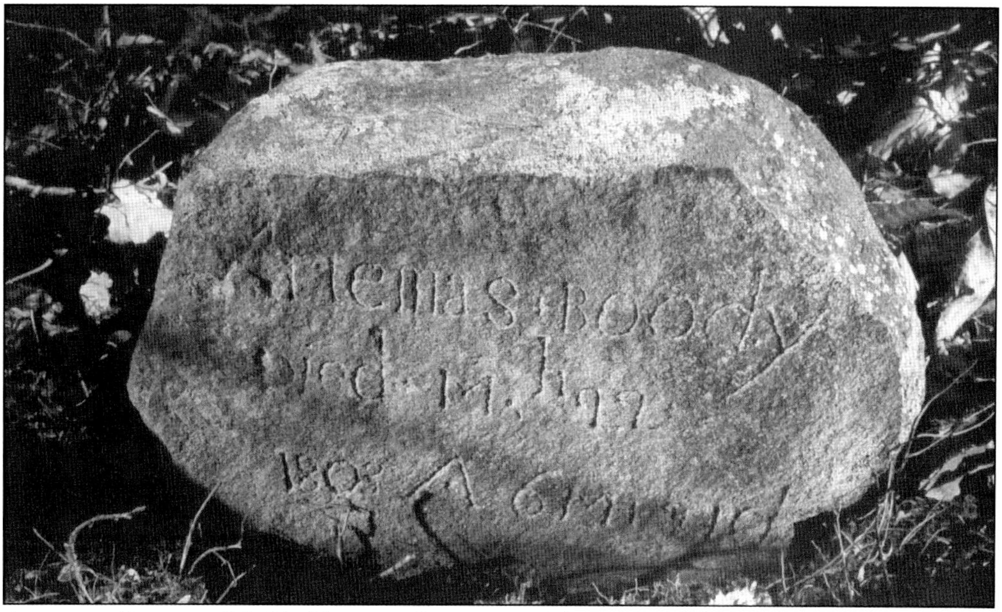

ARTEMAS BOODEY (1803), BOODEY CEMETERY. Like many children during this time, the son of Marcy and Elder Joseph Boodey died at a young age. Artemas was only six months and 21 days old when he died on March 22, 1803, from causes unknown. His simply cut fieldstone was likely carved by Elder Joseph himself and is one of the oldest dated gravestones to be found in all of New Durham.

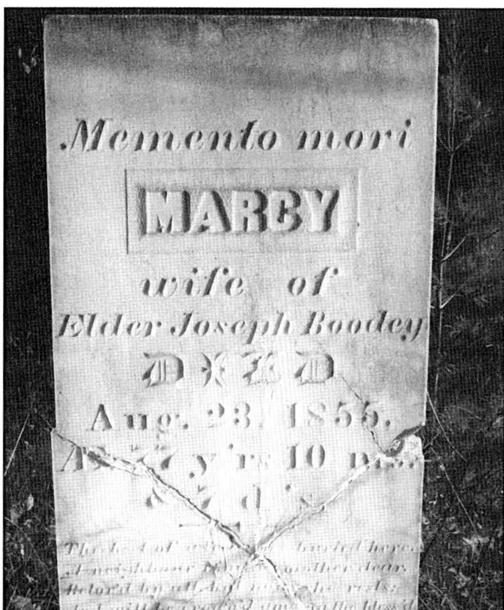

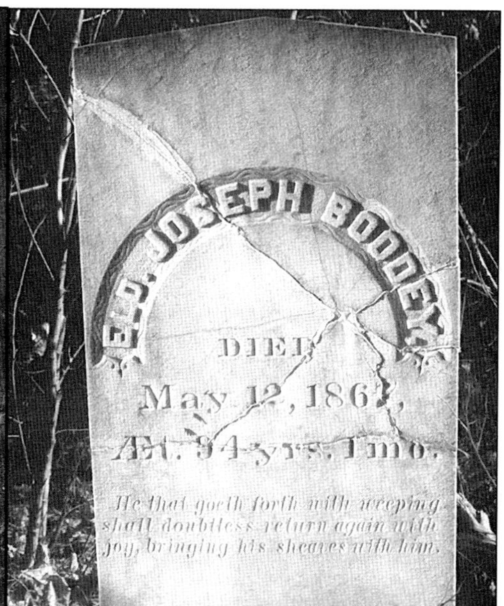

MARCY BOODEY (1855) AND ELDER JOSEPH BOODEY (1867), BOODEY CEMETERY. The Boodey family was a prime mover in the Free Will Baptist faith in New Durham for nearly 100 years. Elder Joseph was one of the most respected men of his time, noted for his integrity as much as his preaching and writing abilities. On the stone for Joseph's wife, there are four lines of verse composed by him.

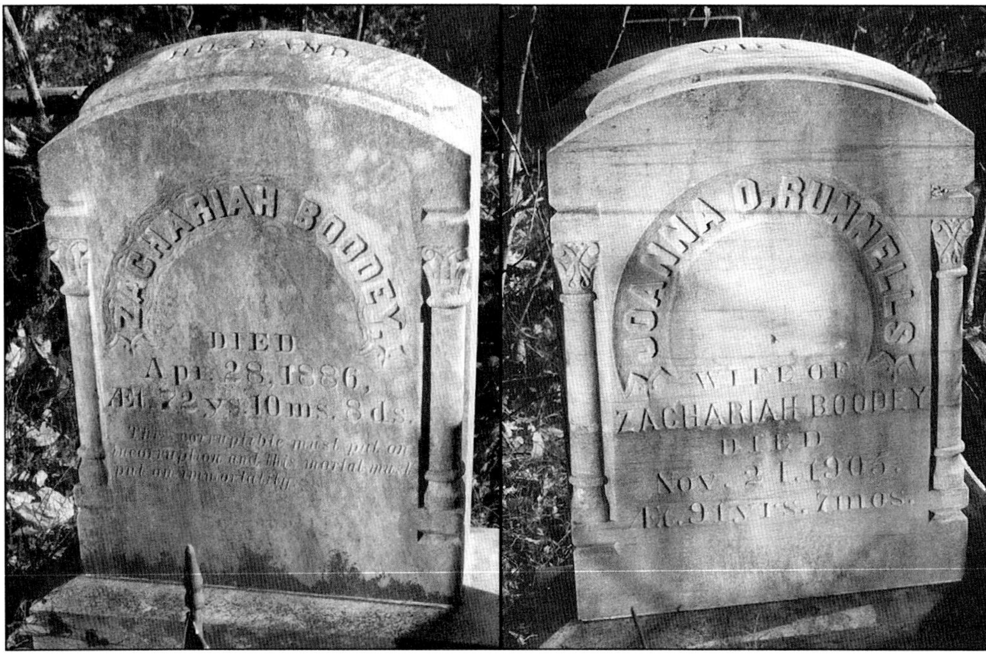

ZACHARIAH BOODEY (1886), AND JOANNA RUNNELLS (1905), BOODEY CEMETERY. Zechariah Boodey was the son of Reverend Joseph and Marcy Boodey. Later residing in Massachusetts, he married Joanna Oram Runnells of Portland, Maine, a granddaughter of Rev. Benjamin Randall, in 1837. After Zechariah's death in 1886, Joanna reverted back to the use of her maiden name, unusual for the times, and a sure sign that she was an independent-minded woman.

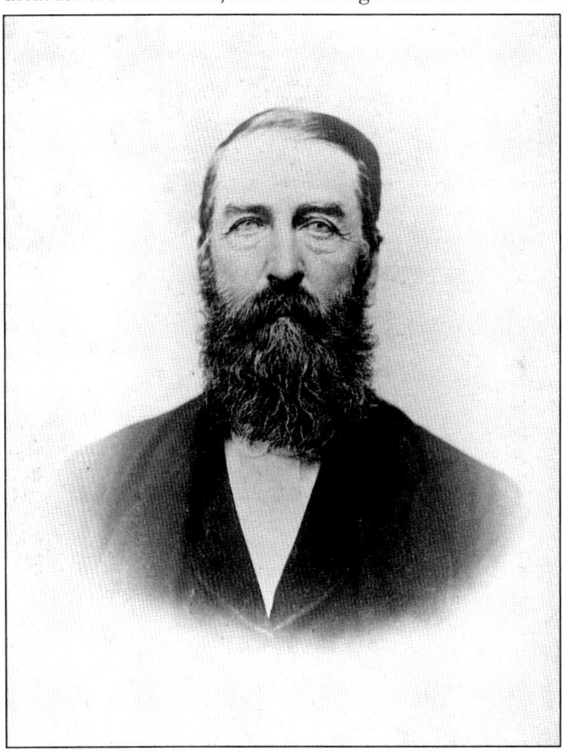

PORTRAIT OF ZACHARIAH BOODEY. Col. Zachariah Boodey was the sixth child of Elder Joseph and Marcy Boodey. A farmer by trade for most of his life, he served in New Hampshire's 33rd militia regiment prior to the Civil War. Residing with his wife Joanna first in New Durham and later in Watertown, Massachusetts, Zachariah also founded a camp in Alton. This portrait was taken at Cochituate, Massachusetts. (Courtesy Crissa Evans.)

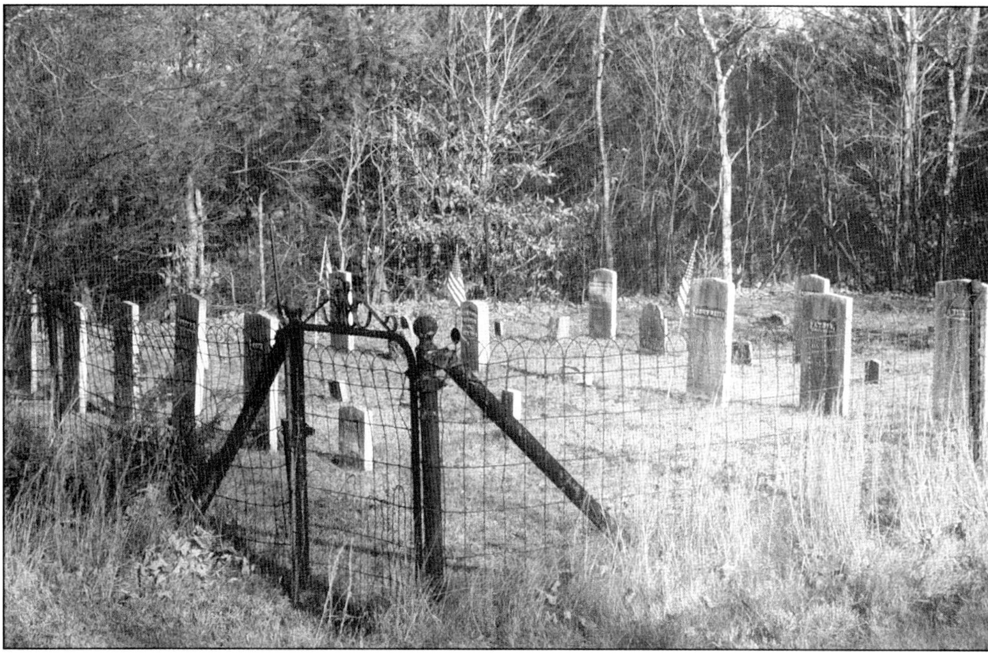

The Davis Cemetery. This family cemetery, well cared for, is located close to Davis Crossing Road in New Durham. The oldest burial is for the head of the family, Revolutionary War seaman John Davis, who died in 1831, while later burials extend into the 20th century.

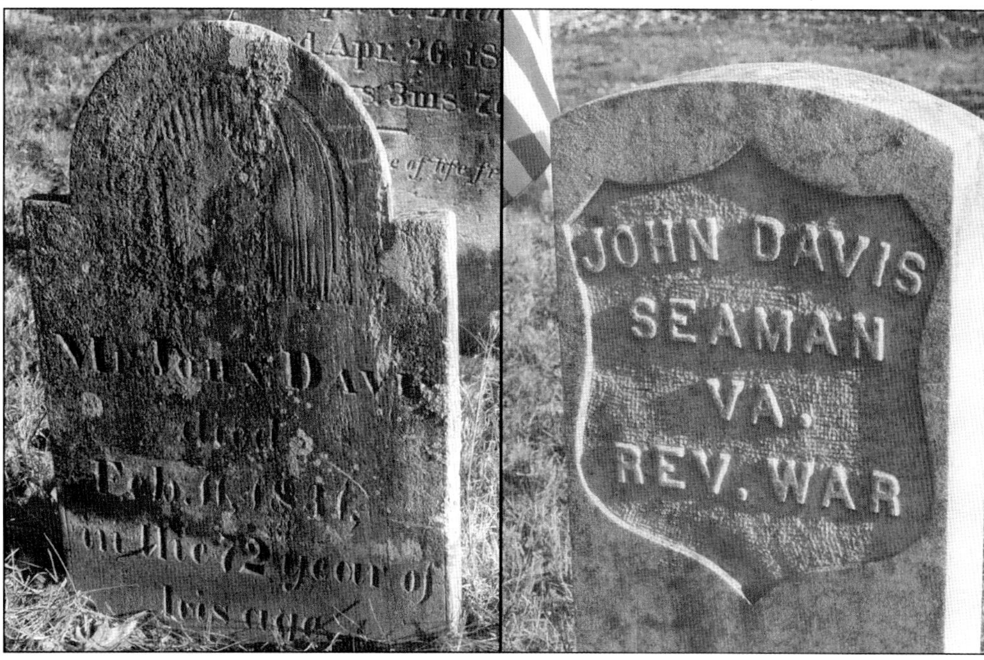

John Davis (1831), Davis Cemetery. John Davis enlisted in the Continental Navy from Kittery, Maine, in October 1779, serving on the Portsmouth-built *Ranger.* He became prisoner-of-war in May 1780, when his ship was captured at Charleston by the British. Eventually released, Davis made his way from Philadelphia to Kittery by August 1780. Davis's original gravestone is at left, while his Revolutionary War marker (right) incorrectly indicates that Davis served for Virginia.

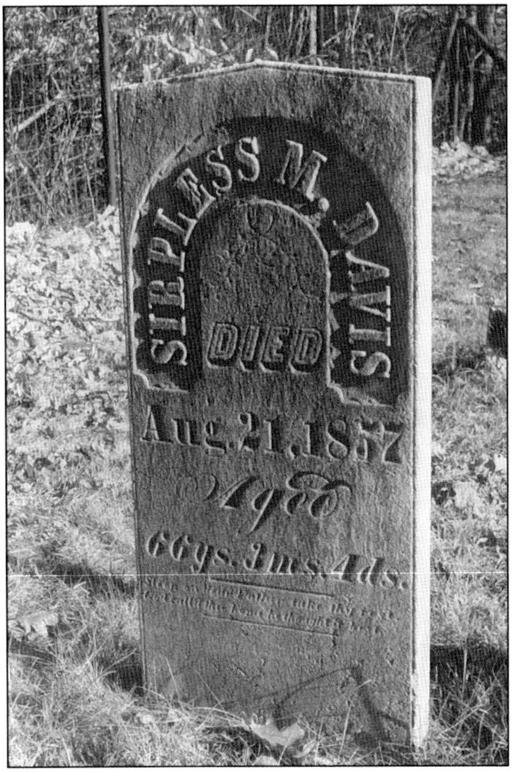

SIRPLESS DAVIS (1857), DAVIS CEMETERY. Sirpless Davis was one of a large number of children in the family and, contrary to the look and sound of his name, did not achieve knighthood or fame abroad. New Durham lore has it instead that Davis received his unusual name simply because the family had a "surplus" of children.

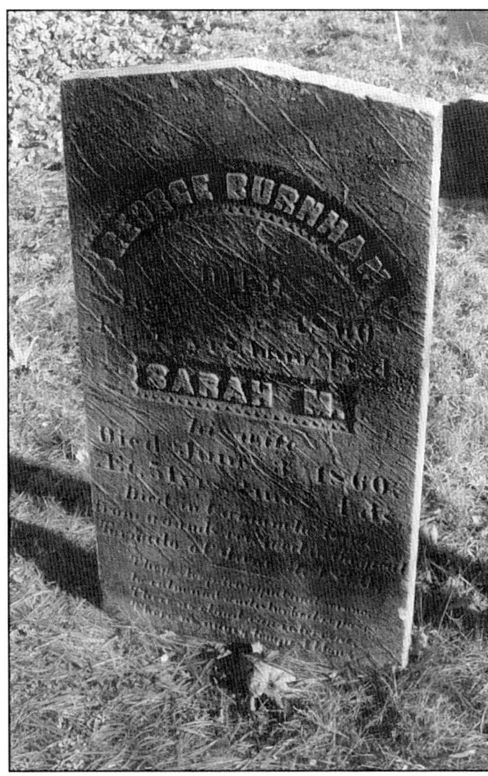

GEORGE AND SARAH BURNHAM (1860), DAVIS CEMETERY. The inscription on this stone tells a sad tale: "Died in Commanche Iowa from wounds received in the great Tornado of June 3, 1860. They sleep tranquil and serene, in calm and undisturbed repose; There no cloud can intervene. There no mighty tempest blows." Sarah Burnham died on the day the tornado struck; her husband died two days later. Rare for the time, their bodies were brought back from Iowa for burial in New Hampshire.

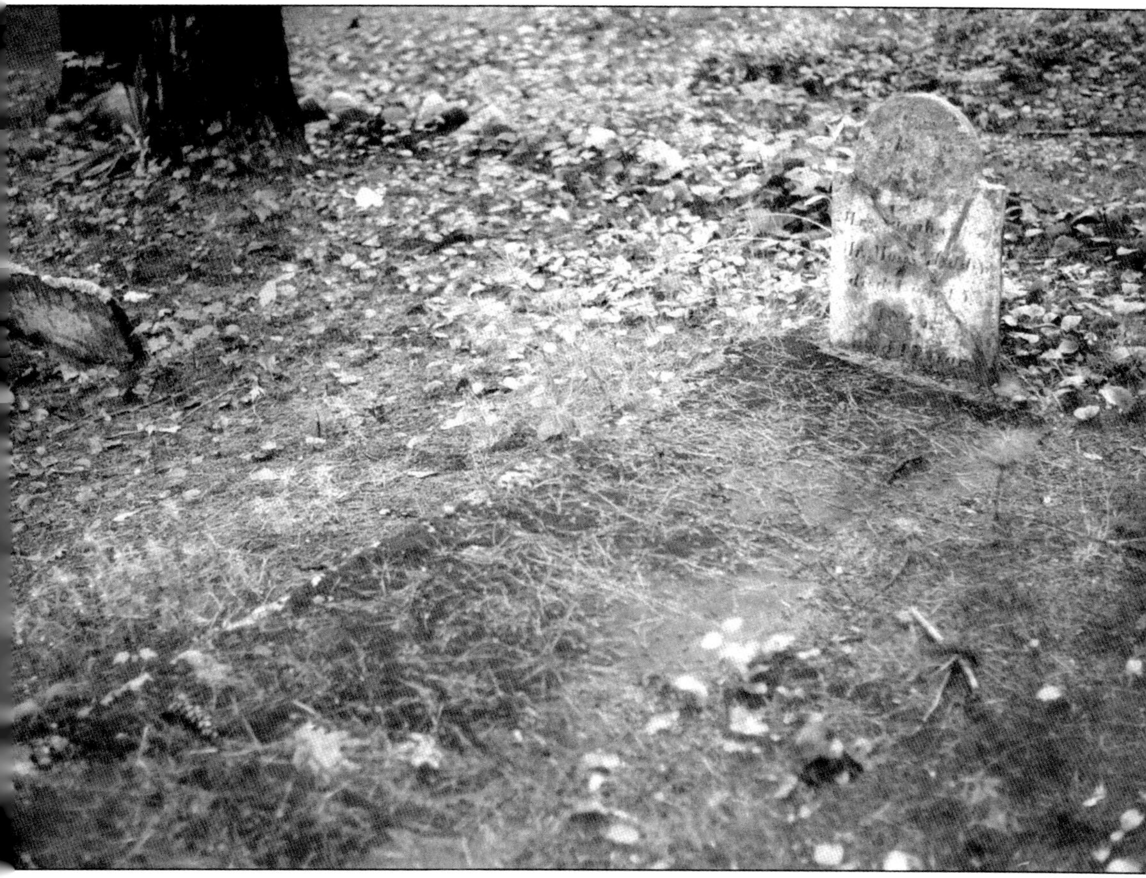

SARAH GLIDDEN (1825), GLIDDEN CEMETERY. This small family cemetery lies in a remote site in East Alton. Church records record that "Brother Moses Glidden's wife was killed by a stream of lightning. The shock was solemn and awful. The people appeared awakened and many who had not prayed many years began to pray the following evening . . . her remains were committed to the house for all living on the Sabbath after in presence of a very solemn assembly." The death of Sarah Glidden at the age of 42 was a shock to this small community. Lore further states that her death occurred in an open field on a bright and sunny day. The legend that Sarah Glidden was a witch is likely based on the fact that she, unlike her husband, was not an active church member and is furthered by the unusual rock slab that covers her grave, said to prevent her from rising out of her grave and bewitching others. Sarah's burial site is located close to Devil's Den Mountain, a curious fact surely noted by her fellow townspeople.

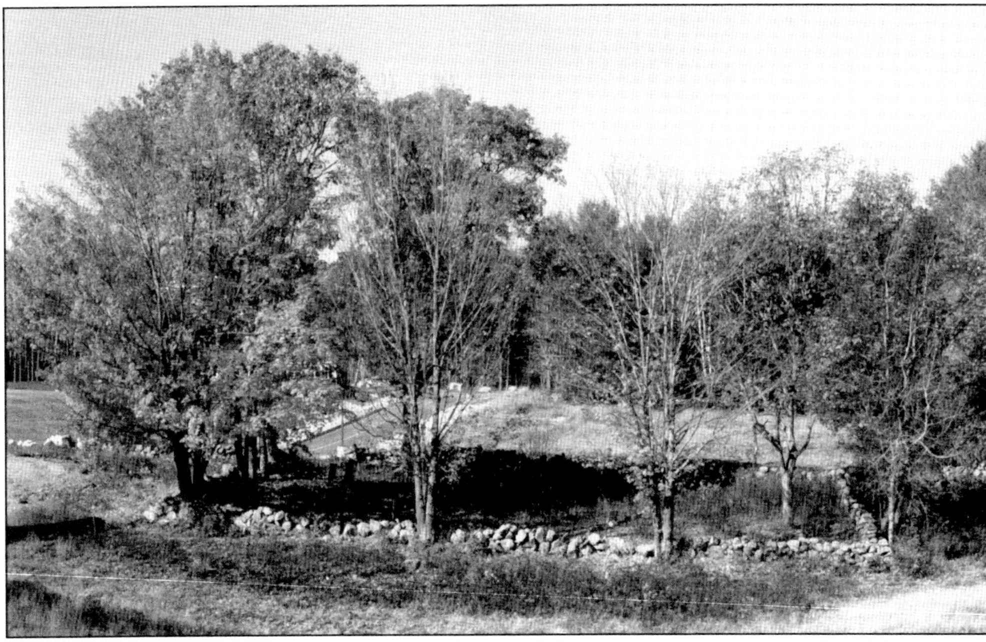

THE KELLEY-CLOUGH CEMETERY, EAST ALTON. This scenic cemetery, enclosed by a stone wall and shaded by rock maple trees, is typical of neighborhood cemeteries found in the Lake Winnipesaukee area. While East Alton residents, for many years, worshipped at the Free Will Baptist meetinghouse at Gilman's Corner, the cemetery sits adjacent to the newly built St. Katherine Drexel Catholic Church.

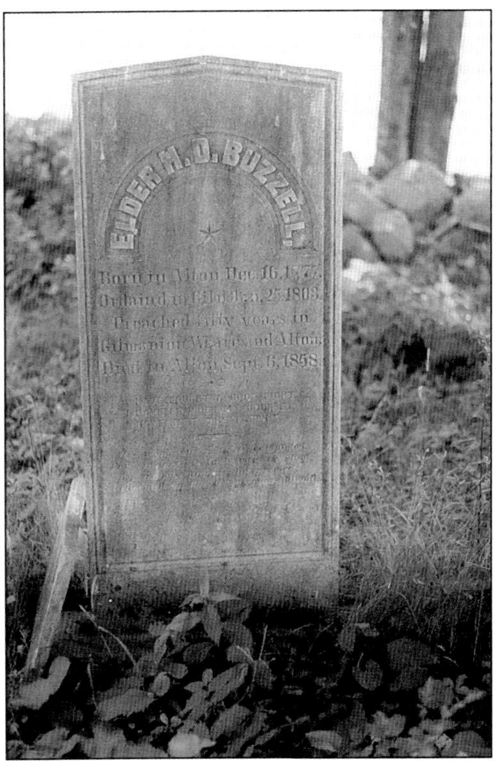

ELDER HEZEKIAH BUZZELL (1858), KELLEY-CLOUGH CEMETERY. Elder Hezekiah Buzzell, a native of Alton, was an active preacher in the Free Will Baptist faith beginning in 1803. The epitaph on the front of his gravestone reads, "I have fought a good fight. I have finished my course. I have kept the faith." On the back it is noted that Buzzell's gravestone was "erected as a tribute of respect" in 1863.

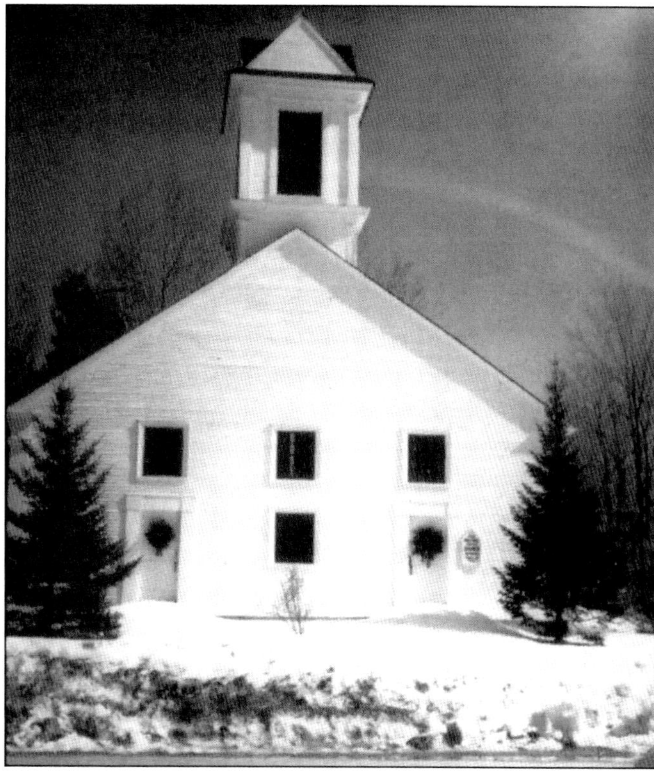

EAST ALTON MEETING HOUSE AT GILMAN'S CORNER. This community church was established in 1803, while the date of the building of its meetinghouse, still standing today, was sometime between 1803 and 1820. Its last regular church service with an established minister was in 1883, and by 1908, the church became extinct when its last member died. Today it is owned by the East Alton Meeting House Society. (Courtesy East Alton Meeting House Society.)

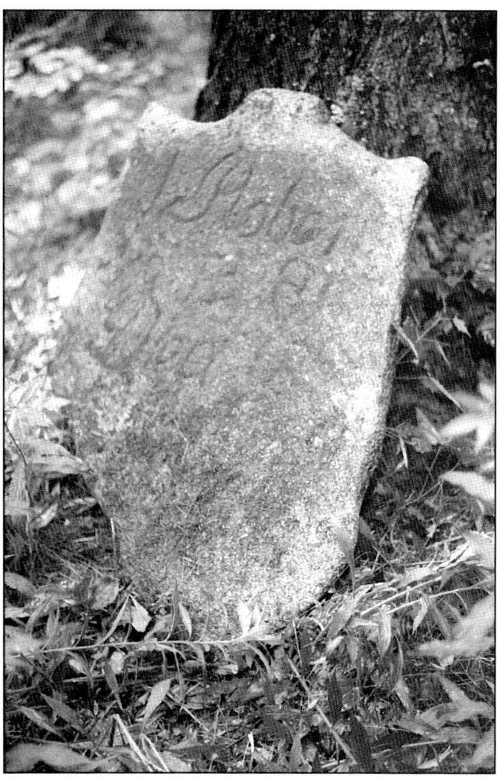

JOSEPH ROBERTS (1810), GILMAN'S CORNER CEMETERY. Joseph Roberts was an early settler in Alton, coming here from Dover in 1775 and living along the lake in an area now known as Roberts Cove. He was a "gentleman-selectman" in town and the first town clerk of New Durham Gore, later to be called Alton. Aged 81 at his death in 1810, Roberts was one of the earliest burials in this cemetery.

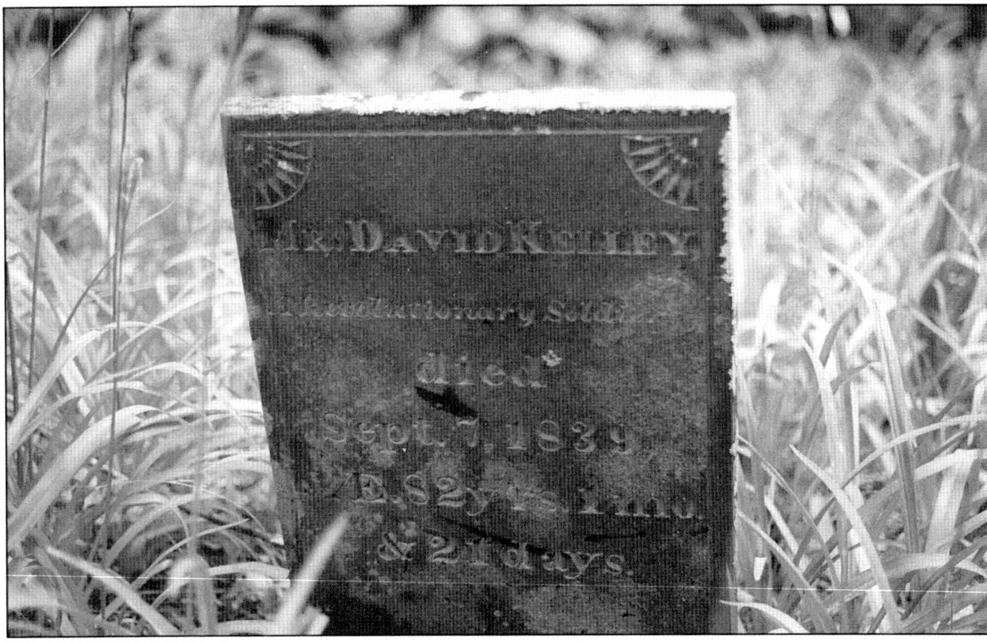

DAVID KELLEY (1839), GILMAN'S CORNER CEMETERY. Born in 1757 and a native of Epping, David Kelley served for 13 months during the Revolution. He first enlisted in the company of Capt. Smith Emerson in 1775, followed by other stints of militia service, including his last in 1776 under Capt. Joseph Badger that took him to Fort Ticonderoga. After the war, he removed to New Durham but attended church in East Alton.

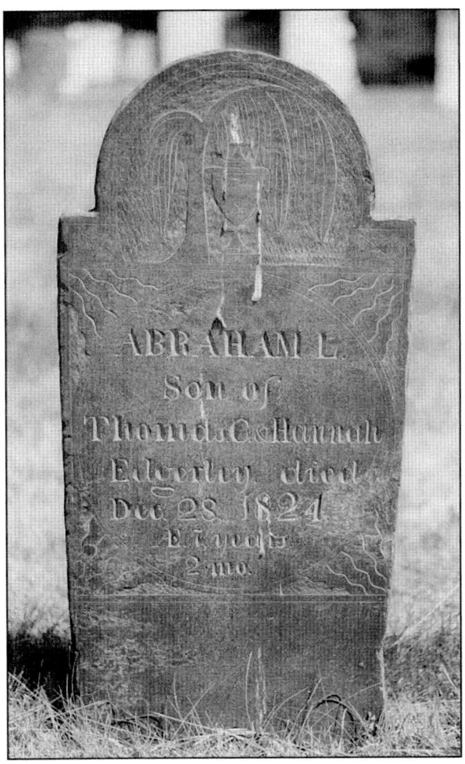

ABRAHAME EDGERLEY (1824), RIVERVIEW CEMETERY, ALTON. Burials in this cemetery date from the 1820s to modern times. However, those gravestones, such as this one from its earliest days, are the most interesting. Hannah and Thomas Edgerley buried three children in less than a year, Esther, and Abrahame and Mary, who died within a month of each other during the winter of 1824–1825, possibly due to a contagious illness.

COL. GEORGE SAVAGE (1883), RIVERVIEW CEMETERY. Born in New Durham in 1818, George Savage became a shoemaker by trade and an accomplished businessman. Later in life, he became the proprietor of the Cocheco House hotel in Alton and a driving influence in the building of the Cocheco Railroad. However, Savage is best known for his service during the Civil War. Enlisting at Alton in 1862, in the 12th New Hampshire Regiment, he was soon promoted to major. On May 3, 1863, Savage was severely wounded during the Battle of Chancellorsville, being shot through the jaw by a rebel sharpshooter. His brother, Capt. Moses Savage, was killed during the engagement. George recovered and continued to serve in his old regiment, nicknamed the New Hampshire Mountaineers. He was promoted to lieutenant colonel (at right) in 1864 for his fine service and discharged several months later.

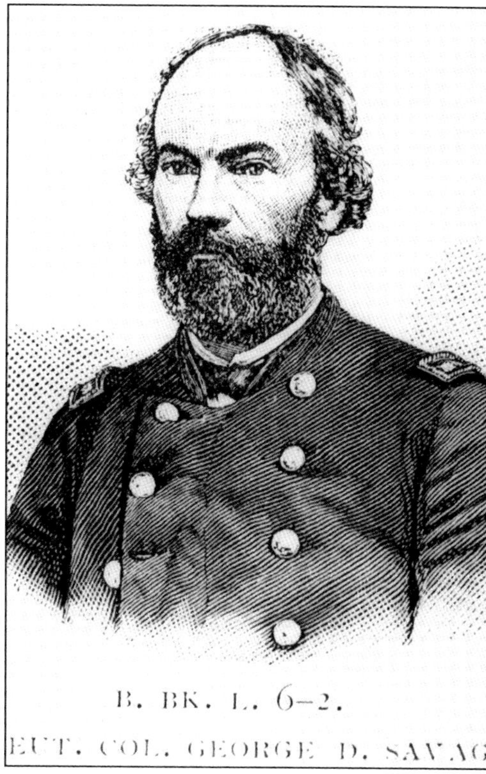

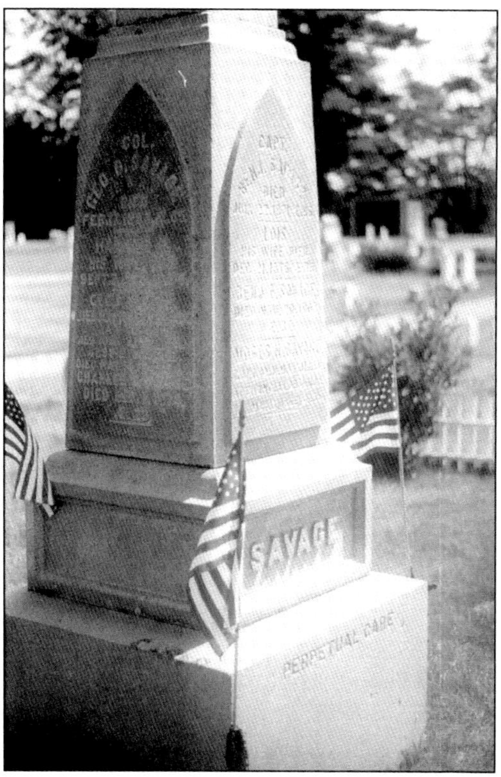

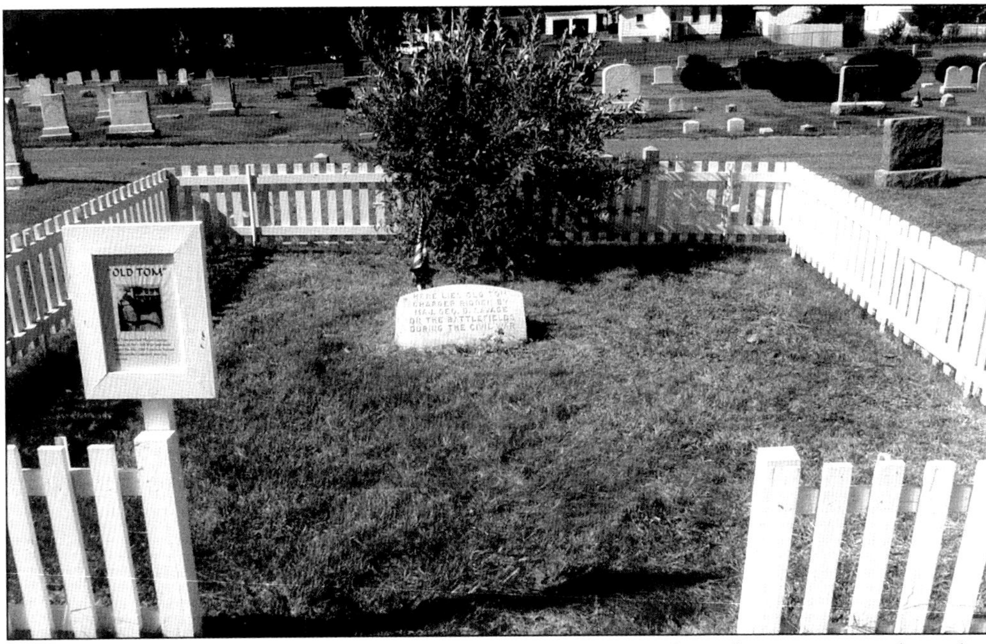

"OLD TOM," RIVERVIEW CEMETERY. One of the most unusual Civil War veterans buried in Alton is "Old Tom," the charger that George Savage rode off to war as his mount. Like his master, Old Tom made it through the war to return home safely. At his death, he was buried close to his master, at the time just outside the confines of Riverview Cemetery but now within its expanded borders.

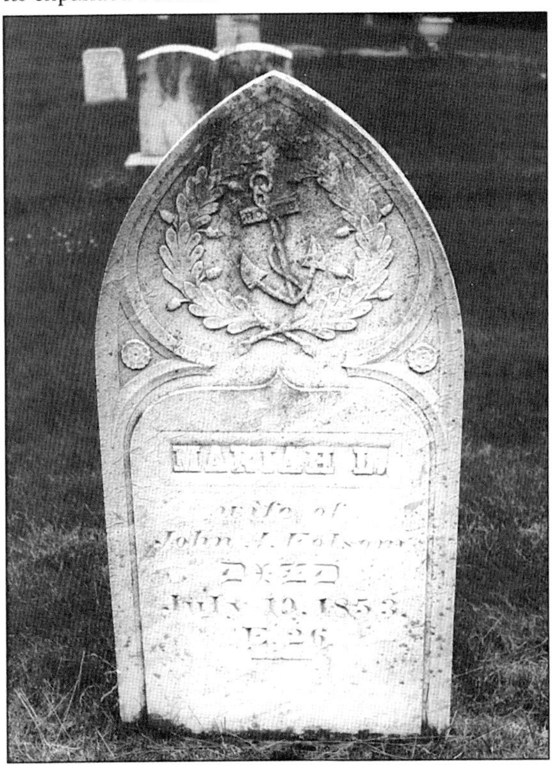

MARIAH FOLSOM (1853), RIVERVIEW CEMETERY. The largest cemetery in the Altons, Riverview has a wide range of stylistic gravestones. This one for the young wife of John Folsom, Mariah, features as its motif the ancient Christian symbol of hope and redemption, the anchor, circled by a garland of oak leaves.

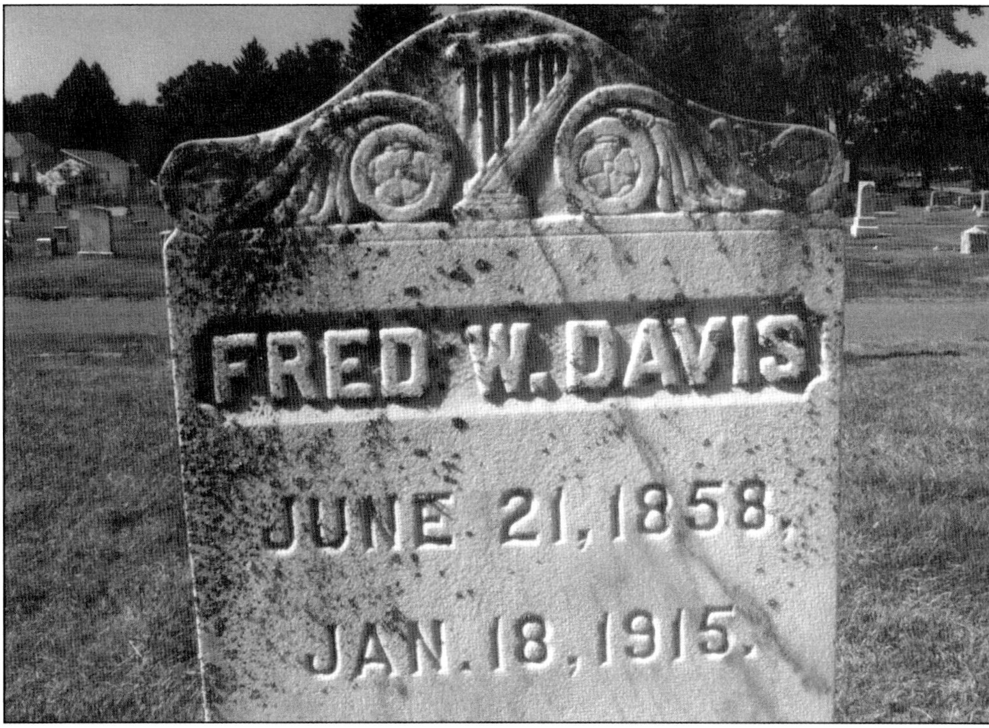

FRED DAVIS (1915), RIVERVIEW CEMETERY. The use of decorative motifs on gravestones in New England waned by the mid-1800s, and by the early 1900s, most gravestones were plain with little or no decoration. This attractive stone for Fred Davis is an exception, featuring a harp flanked by a scrollwork and floral design. While the harp is often a symbol of Irish heritage, it is also a symbol of hope.

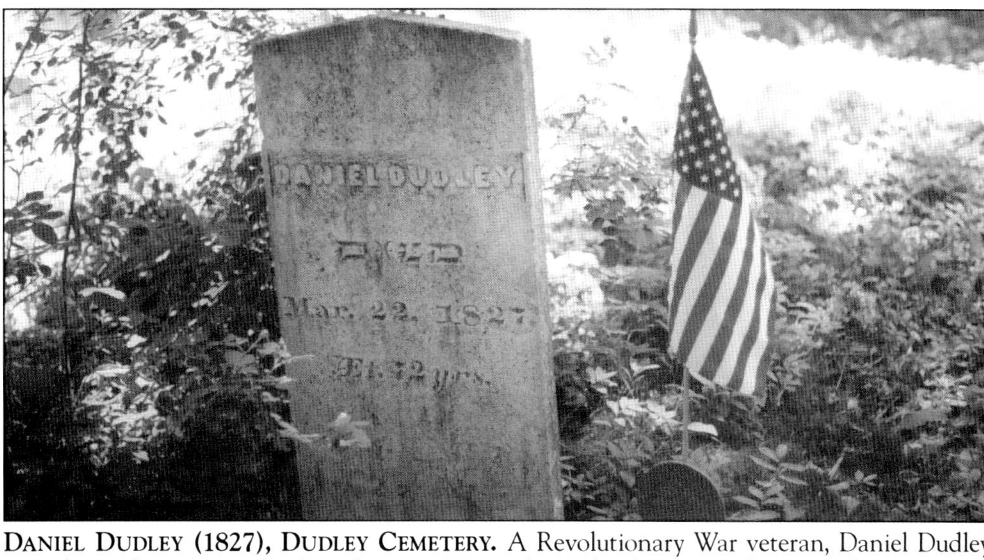

DANIEL DUDLEY (1827), DUDLEY CEMETERY. A Revolutionary War veteran, Daniel Dudley served one short term of militia duty in 1777, under Col. Thomas Stickney. With the rank of corporal, he was in charge of the "public stores" at Fort No. 4 in Charlestown. Later, in 1780, Dudley did further duty for six months in the 3rd New Hampshire Regiment stationed along the Hudson River in New York.

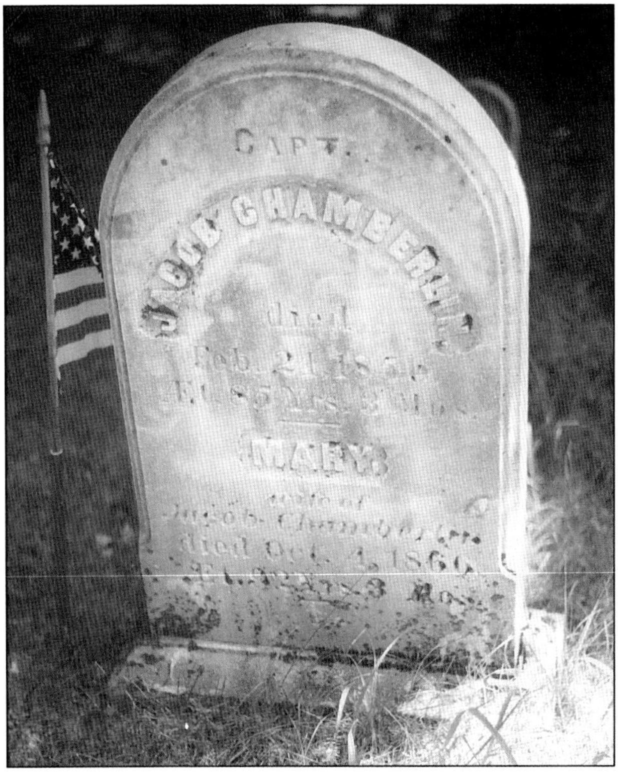

JACOB CHAMBERLAIN (1856), ALTON BAY CEMETERY. Jacob Chamberlain, born in 1771, was likely one of the first children to be born in the township that would later become Alton. His father, Jacob Chamberlain, was one of New Durham Gore's first settlers, establishing a homestead along what is now Alton Bay around 1770. He likely derived his title of "captain" from service in the War of 1812 or in the state militia.

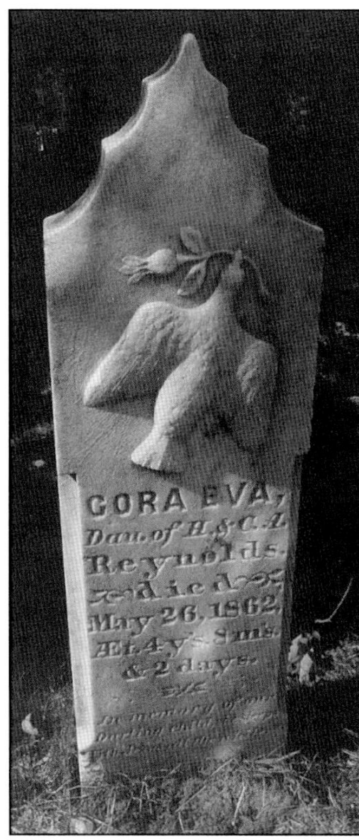

CORA EVA REYNOLDS (1862), ALTON BAY CEMETERY. This touching stone marks the grave of a four-year-old girl. The dove in flight is a symbol of love and purity, very appropriate for a young child, as well as the Holy Spirit. The flower in the beak of the dove flying skyward symbolizes both a young life cut short and a hope of heavenly reward and resurrection.

Two

WOLFEBORO

The town of Wolfeboro was established by grant to a group of men, most from Portsmouth, in 1759. The first attempt at settling the town by Elisha Bryant and his three sons failed in 1765. A renewed attempt at settlement by Benjamin Blake, who began to build a log cabin in the woods in the summer of 1767, was successful in 1768 when Blake moved with his wife Molly to their new home. Wolfeboro's earliest settlers lived close to Rust Pond in South Wolfeboro. However, the number of settlers remained small until Royal Governor John Wentworth came to town. As a proprietor, he drew one lot of land and later gained six other lots, all bordering on Lake Wentworth. In possession of nearly 4,000 acres of land, he resolved to build an English-style country seat here, hoping that others might follow his example in clearing the wilderness and developing New Hampshire's resources. His mansion was finished in several years and Governor Wentworth "set out for his country-seat on Winnipiseogee pond" in July 1770, thus making Wolfeboro America's first summer resort.

One of those settlers enticed to the area was Col. William Cotton, a trader who came to town in 1781 and opened a tavern and store. Because of the predominance of his family and the large amount of land owned by its descendants, the area in North Wolfeboro is still known today as the Cottonboro District. Several Cotton family cemeteries are located in this area, though not easily accessible. Buried in the Dudley Cotton Cemetery is Mary Cotton Redpath (died 1914) who, along with her abolitionist husband James Redpath, is one of the originators of the United States' Memorial Day holiday.

In the early days of Wolfeboro, family cemeteries were the norm. It was not until 1786 that plans to build a meetinghouse in Wolfeboro center were begun. However, it was not completed until 1792. Adjacent to the meetinghouse was the town's first public burial ground following the customs of old. Most notable here are the burial sites of the town's first minister, Ebenezer Allen, who died in 1806, and the large rock that marks the grave of John Marden and his wife, dated 1813.

Wolfeboro has two other public cemeteries of note. Pine Hill Cemetery was established in the mid-1800s, as was Lake View Cemetery. It is interesting to note that Lake View Cemetery, a beautiful spot, was quite the fashionable place to be laid to rest in the late Victorian era. A number of town residents who had previously been buried on their own land were reinterred here, sometimes with their original slate gravestone markers, sometimes with new marble markers, by their descendants. One such example of this practice is Elder Isaac Townsend. He died in 1846 and was buried on his homestead but had donated a lot in Lake View while still alive for use by his Free Will Baptist followers. However, the lot was never claimed, and Townsend and his family were reinterred here around 1898.

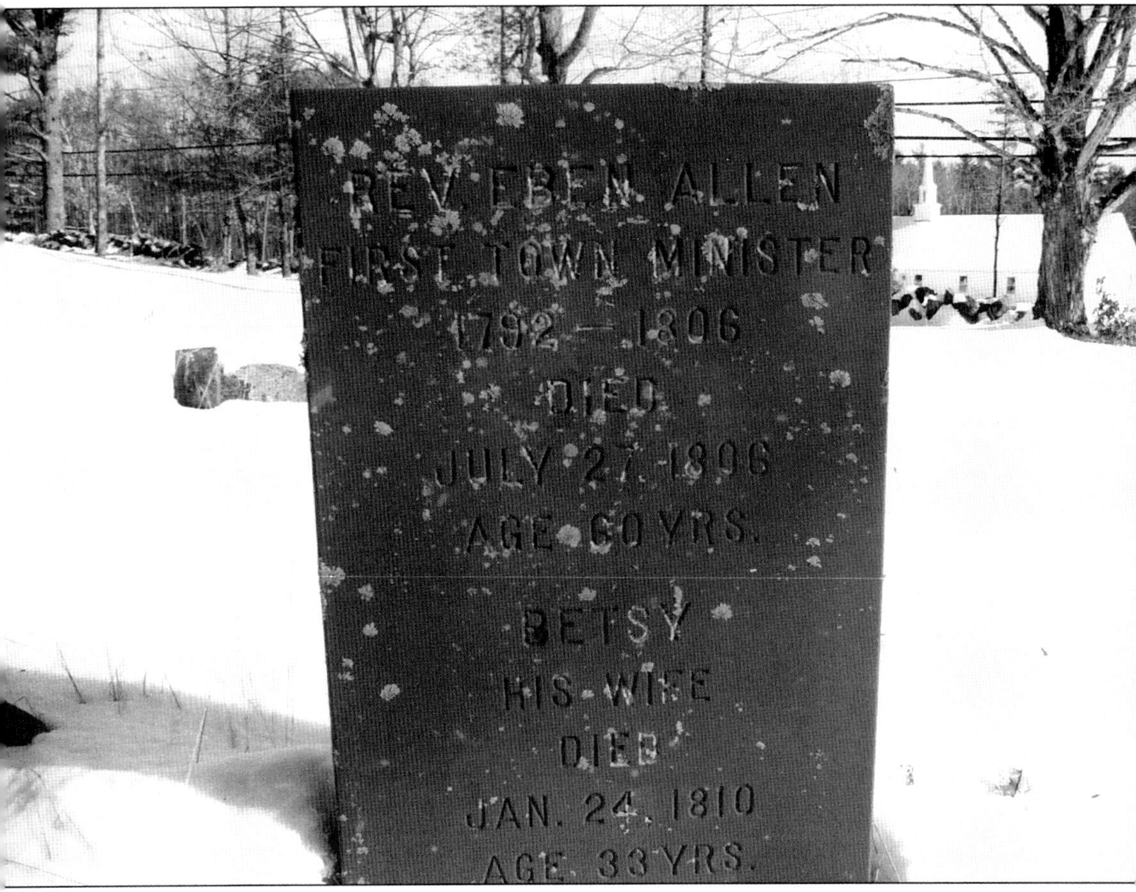

Ebenezer (1806) and Betsy (1810) Allen, Town House Cemetery. Born in 1746 at Vineyard Haven, Massachusetts, and a 1771 Harvard graduate, Rev. Ebenezer Allen was ordained in Wolfeboro in 1792. He was well respected, "though not remarkable for pulpit oratory." Allen was a bachelor until he married Betsy Fernald in 1796. Though their time together was short, they had six children. Allen's salary was £45 a year: one third in cash, two thirds in foodstuffs. He was also to be supplied annually with 25 cords of firewood, though for several years, this part of his salary went unfulfilled. This surely caused a hardship for Allen, who only had a stump for one arm due to a "shooting accident" and, while in the pulpit, wore over it a black silk mitten. Allen died of apoplexy on the Sabbath after having preached earlier. Followed to the grave just four years later by his wife, their burial site for years was neglected, as the cemetery was abandoned. In 1899, the current headstone was set to replace the original, which had been broken.

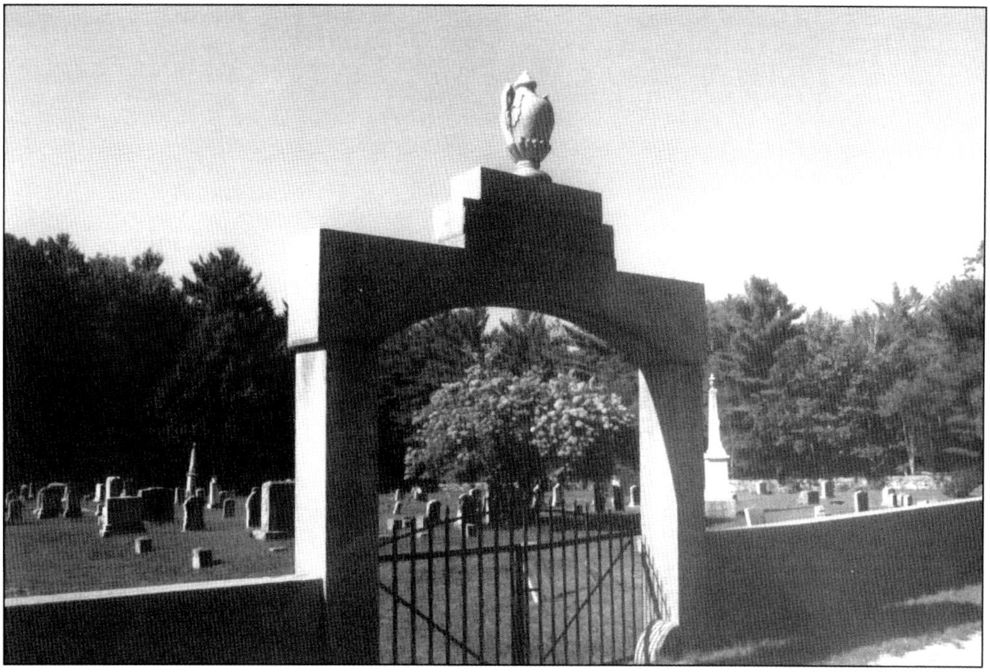

HERSEY CEMETERY. This cemetery is a fine example of one that started out as a family cemetery and grew into a neighborhood cemetery. It is situated on the site of the original College Road that Royal Governor John Wentworth had built from Wolfeboro to Dartmouth. The land in the area was bought by Jonathan Hersey, a settler from Newmarket who became a farmer and land speculator and gained a large fortune.

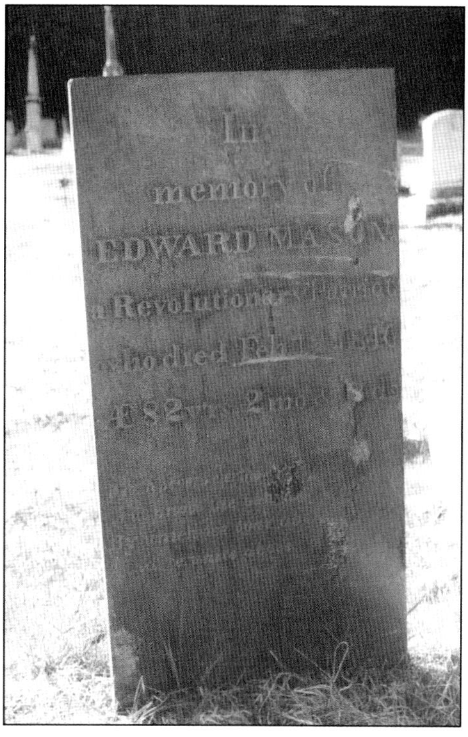

EDWARD MASON (1840), HERSEY CEMETERY. This "Patriot" was born in Stratham in 1757 and came to Wolfeboro after the Revolutionary War. His service in the war was extensive, Edward Mason having first enlisted in 1775 for eight months and again in 1776 for a militia stint. He enlisted for the remainder of the war in the 2nd New Hampshire Regiment in 1778, gaining a promotion to sergeant major in 1780.

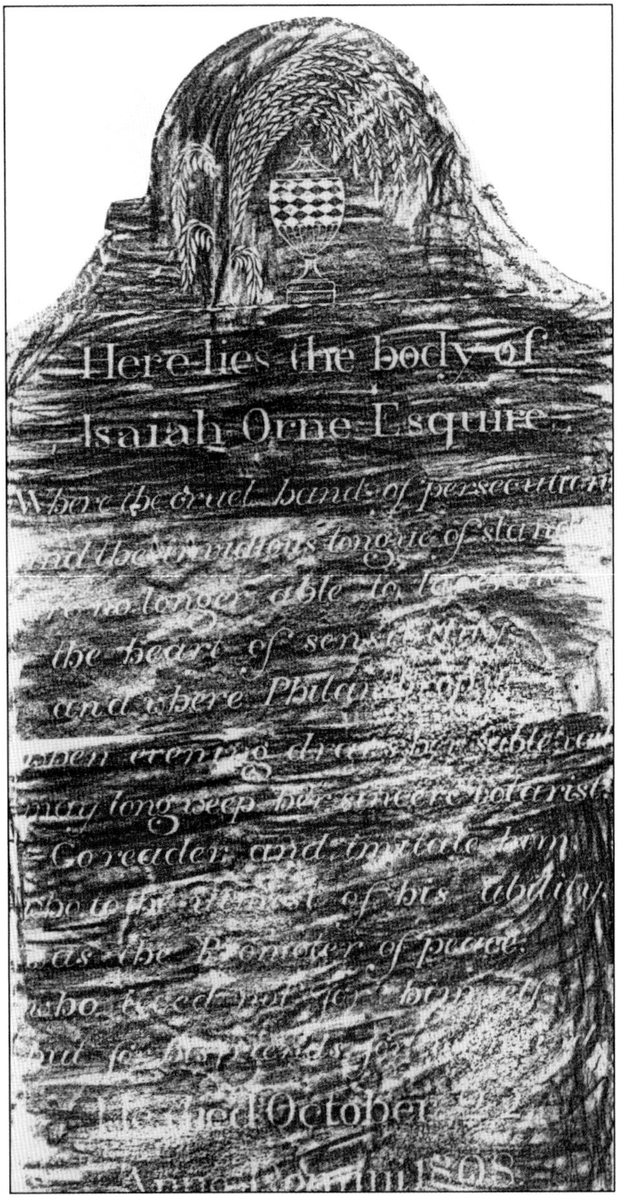

ISAIAH ORNE (1808), ORNE CEMETERY. The Horne family came to Wolfeboro in 1777, when Ebenezer Horne exchanged land in Dover for 1,500 acres in Wolfeboro owned by John Flagg. One of these lots was given to his son, Isaiah, then nearly 21 years old and one who was "most ambitious." By 1782, Isaiah taught school in Wolfeboro, teaching the second term for three months for $33 in silver. His fellow teacher was Dudley Leavitt, the famed almanac maker, whom Isaiah later helped to hire as schoolmaster in 1807 by paying part of his salary. It was Isaiah who, by "legislative enactment," had the *H* dropped from the family name. He married Mary Rust, the daughter of settler Col. Henry Rust, and with her had eight children. Isaiah was active in town and state affairs, serving as a juror, highway surveyor, selectman, town clerk, and state representative. He also was a founder of the town's social library in 1804. The wording on Isaiah's gravestone is quite interesting, surely indicating that he suffered from criticism offered by his fellow townsmen.

WILLIAM COTTON CEMETERY. This family burial site on Cotton Mountain in North Wolfeboro lies on land once owned by William Cotton, a French and Indian War veteran and an officer in the state militia. (Courtesy Wolfeboro Historical Society.)

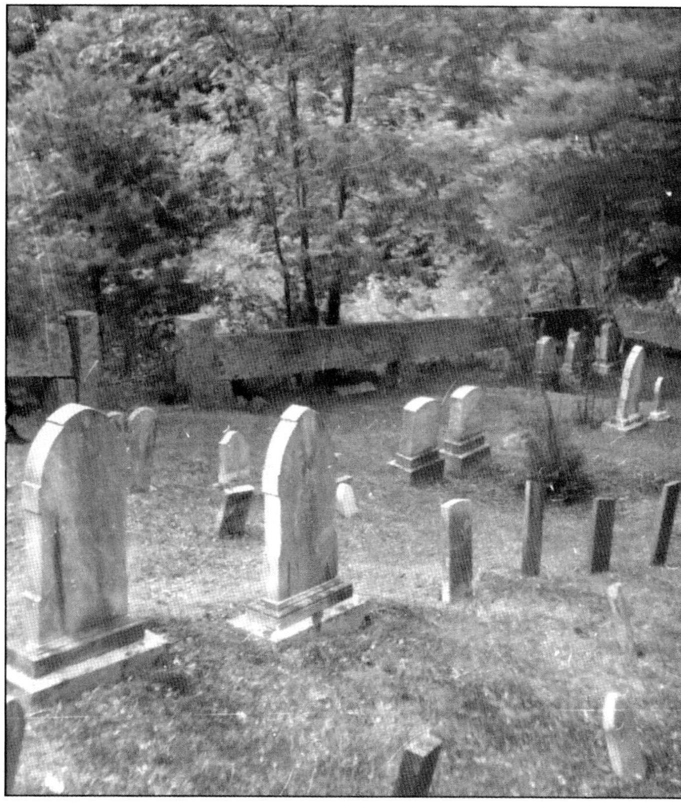

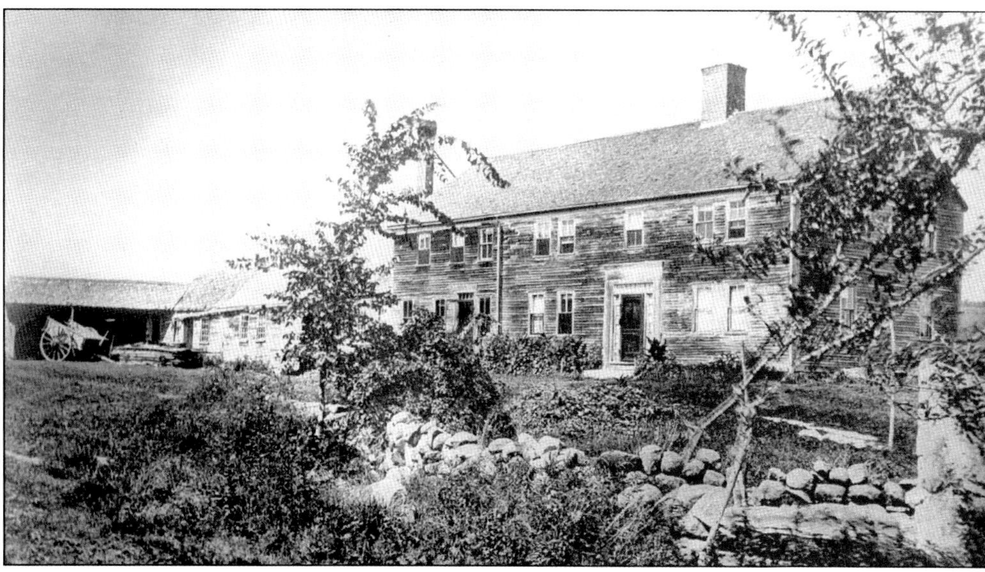

WILLIAM COTTON HOMESTEAD, C. 1900. William Cotton was one of early Wolfeboro's most prominent citizens, arriving in town with his wife Mary and eight children in 1781. He purchased a large tract of land in North Wolfeboro and was a farmer, retailer, and tavern operator. His descendants continued in the area, and at one time, 12 family farms, comprising 1,600 acres, were owned by Cotton family members. (Courtesy Wolfeboro Historical Society.)

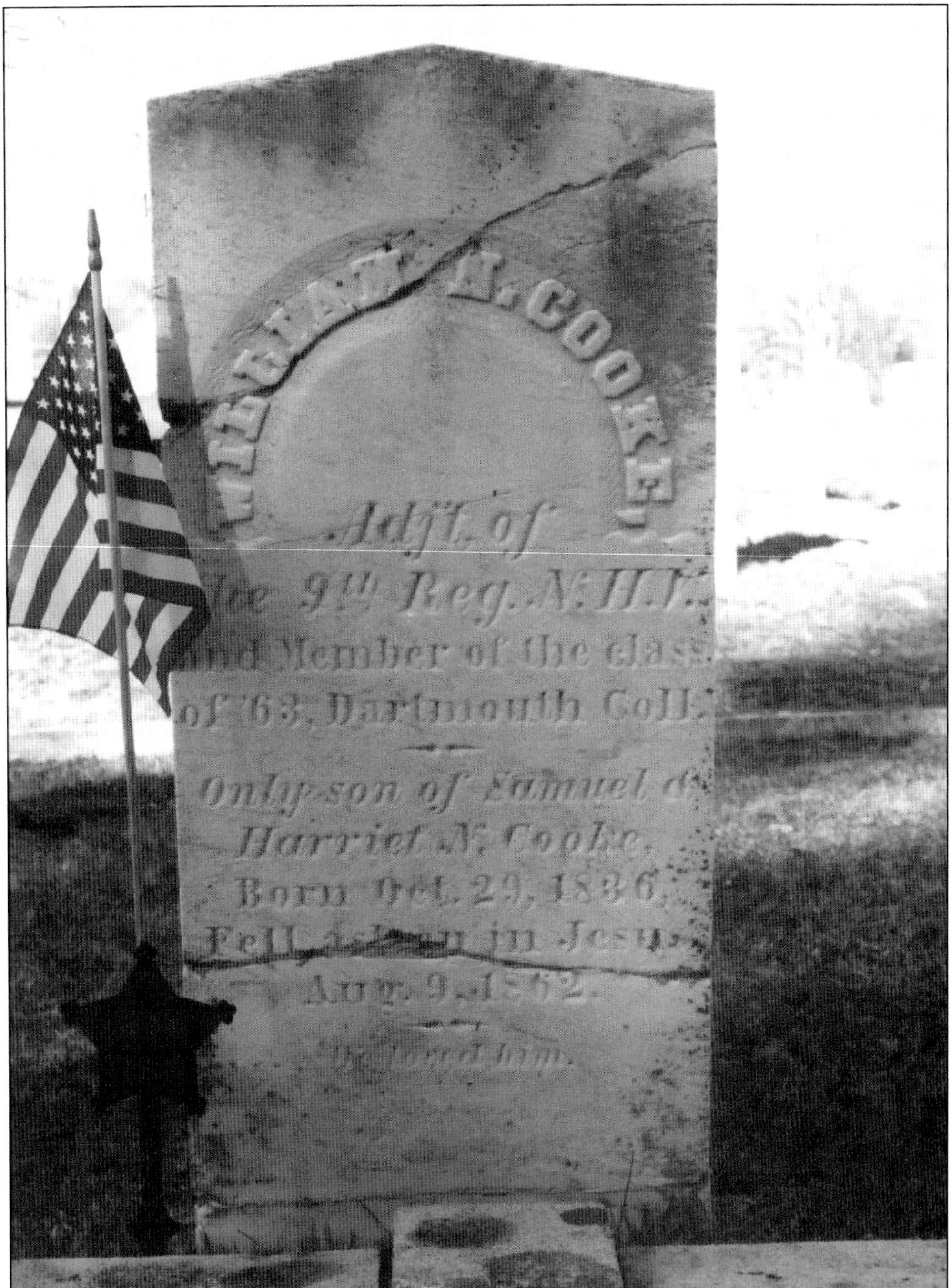

WILLIAM COOKE (1862), PINE HILL CEMETERY. Young William Cooke, like so many men at Dartmouth College, felt a strong urge to go off to war and defend the Union. One group of students even formed their own cavalry regiment. Cooke, however, enlisted in the 9th New Hampshire Regiment in July 1862. Educated and full of promise, he was made adjutant of the regiment but, sadly, never made it to the front lines. He became ill, perhaps of camp fever, while his regiment was still at Dover on the seacoast and subsequently died.

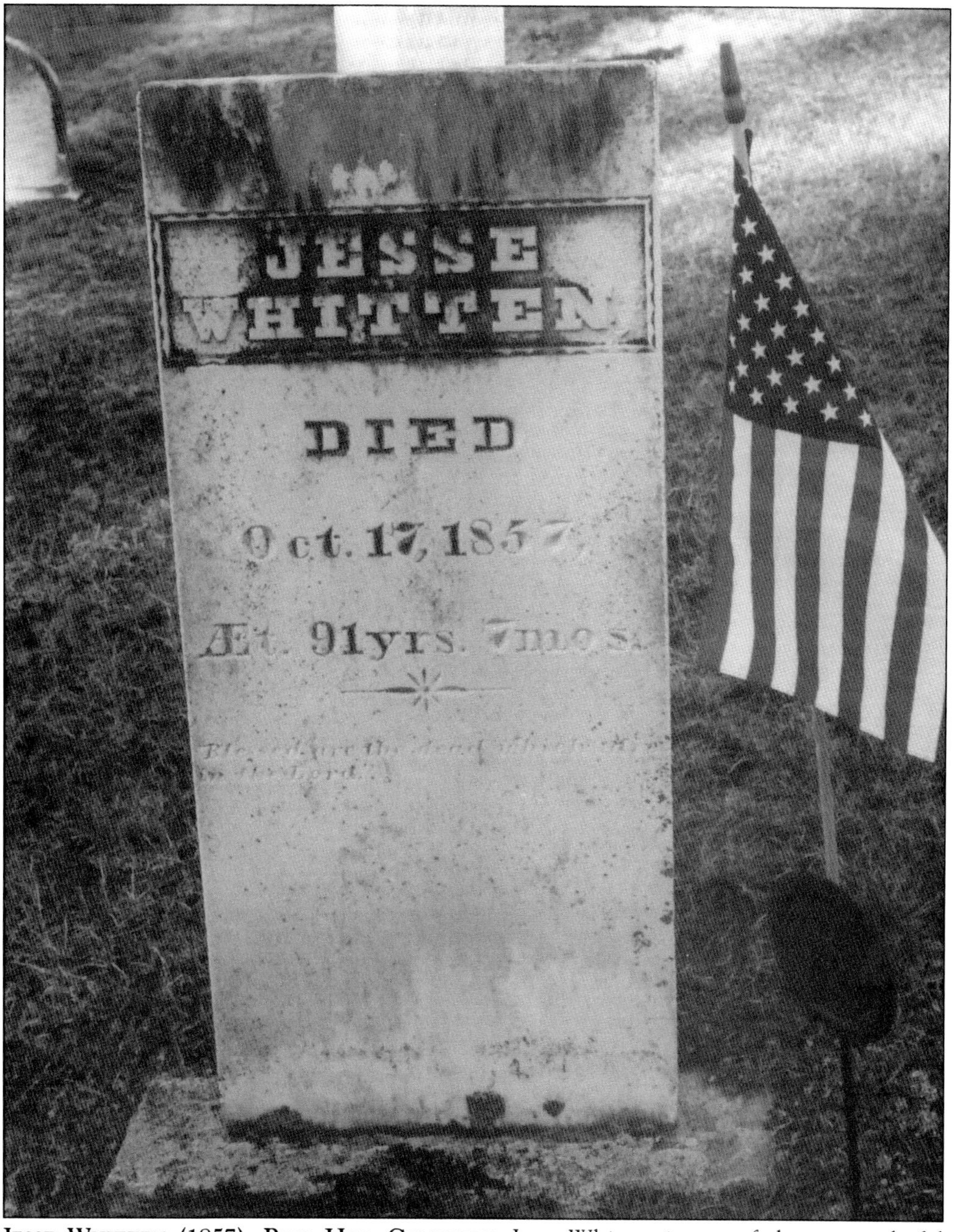

JESSE WHITTEN (1857), PINE HILL CEMETERY. Jesse Whitten is one of the most colorful characters in Wolfeboro town history. Born in 1766, he went to sea at age 16 and served on a privateer at the end of the Revolutionary War. After age 21, he came to Wolfeboro and settled on 50 acres of land along Smith River, later purchasing even more land. One historian calls Whitten "an enthusiastic and quite demonstrative religionist," as he belonged to the Free Will Baptist congregation of Elder Isaac Townsend. Whitten was also a doctor, though without formal training, and was said to be good at catching rattlesnakes on Rattlesnake Island to use their oils for medicinal purposes. Though small in size, Whitten was known for his prowess as a wrestler in his younger days and lived to a ripe old age.

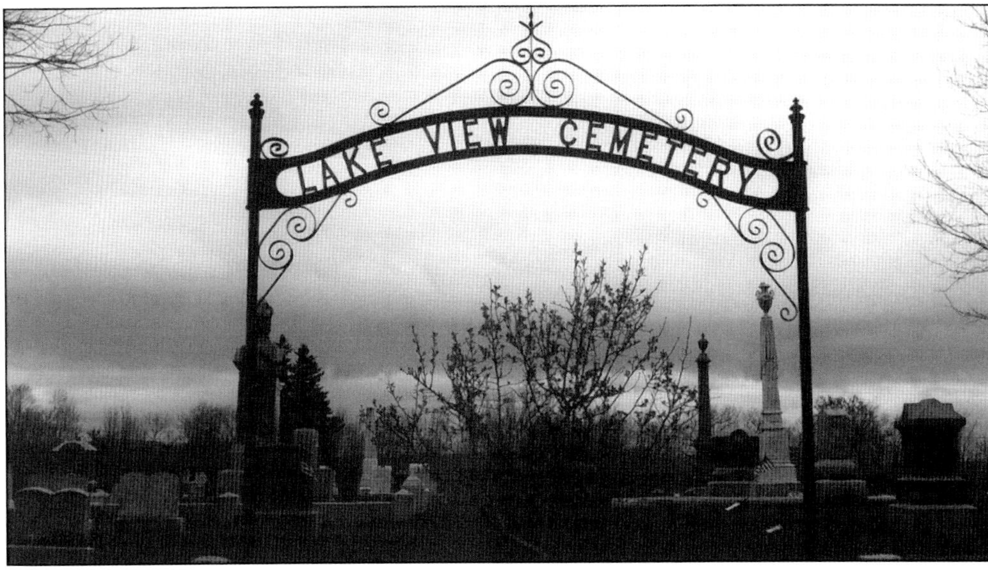

LAKE VIEW CEMETERY. This cemetery is one of the most beautiful cemeteries in Wolfeboro, and also the largest. Though houses now block the view across Main Street, at one time this cemetery had a fine view of Wolfeboro Bay on Lake Winnipesaukee. The earliest burials here date back to the 1820s, but the elaborate and finely wrought cemetery gate did not come along until much later during the Victorian era.

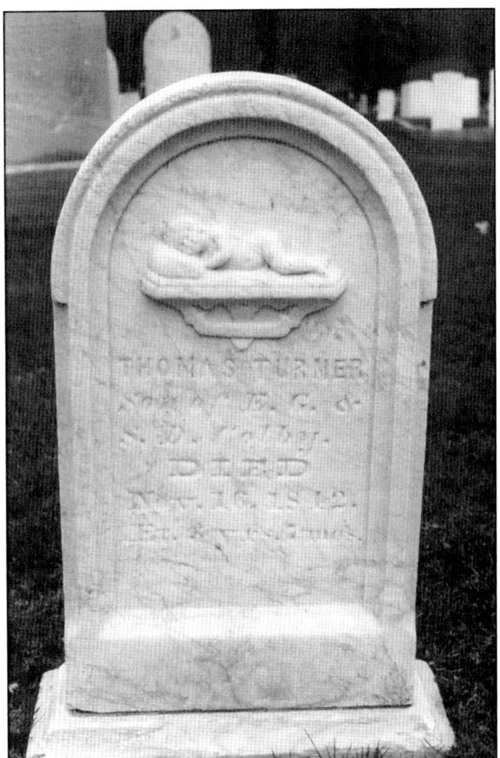

THOMAS TURNER COLBY (1842), LAKE VIEW CEMETERY. One of the most interesting aspects of Lake View is the wide variety of gravestone carvings to be found here. This marble stone for a three-year-old child is both touching and appropriate. The symbolism depicted here, of innocence and eternal rest in heaven, is plain for all to see and surely provided a measure of comfort for grieving parents.

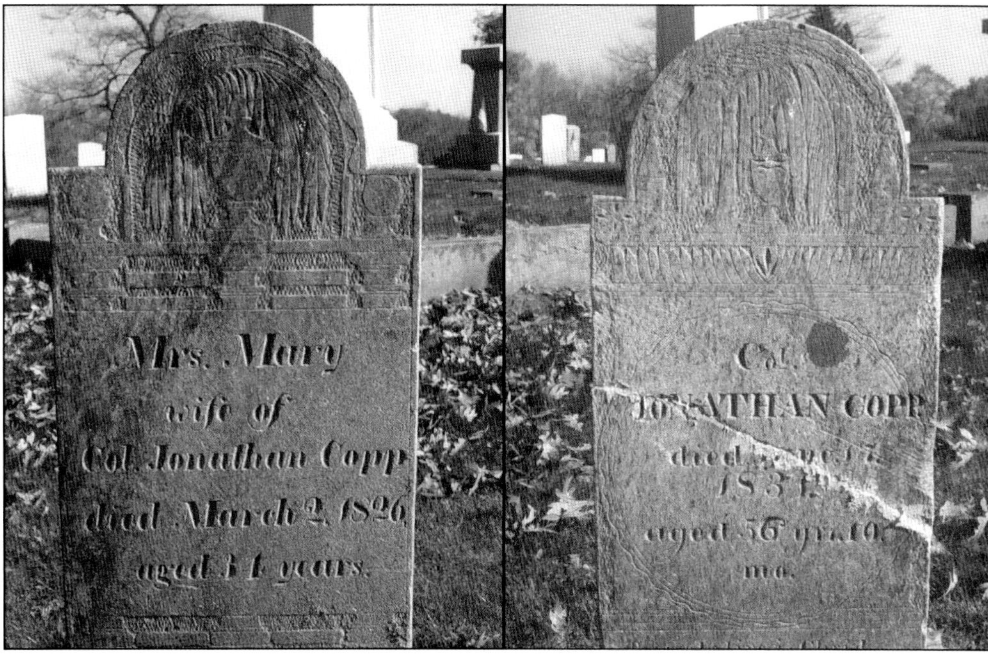

MARY (1826) AND JONATHAN (1831) COPP, LAKE VIEW CEMETERY. Unusual for the times, both Jonathan and Mary Copp were teachers in Wolfeboro. While little is known about Mary's career, Jonathan taught for many years beginning in 1802. The couple also operated Copp's Tavern at Rendall's Corner for a number of years and had a small store. Jonathan's title of colonel came from his militia service, not uncommon for a tavern keeper.

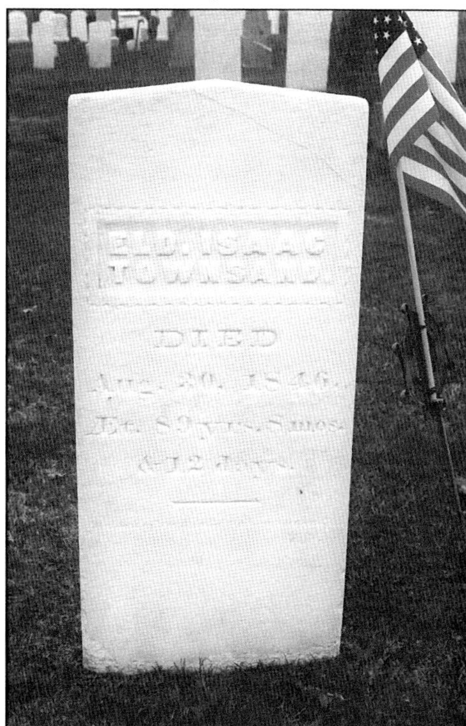

ELDER ISAAC TOWNSEND (1846), LAKE VIEW CEMETERY. A native of Newmarket, Elder Isaac Townsend served in the Revolutionary War on the privateer *Portsmouth*. After the war, he went to New Durham and became a Free Will Baptist convert. He removed to Wolfeboro in 1791 and was ordained a minister on the same date as Ebenezer Allen. A tanner by trade, he had a large farm and, in 1796, married Lydia Evans.

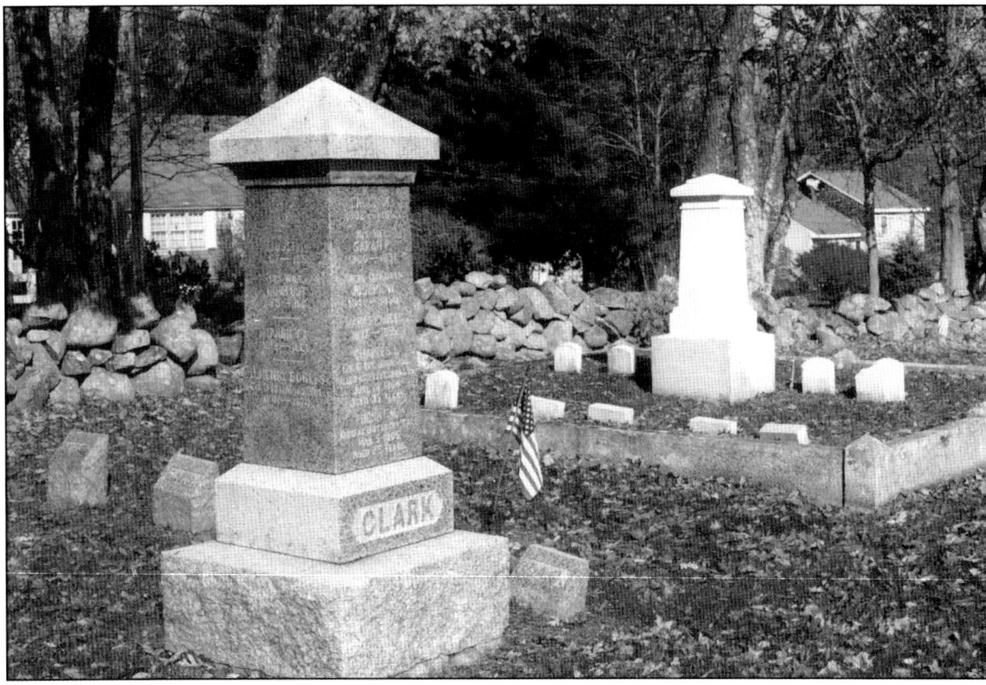

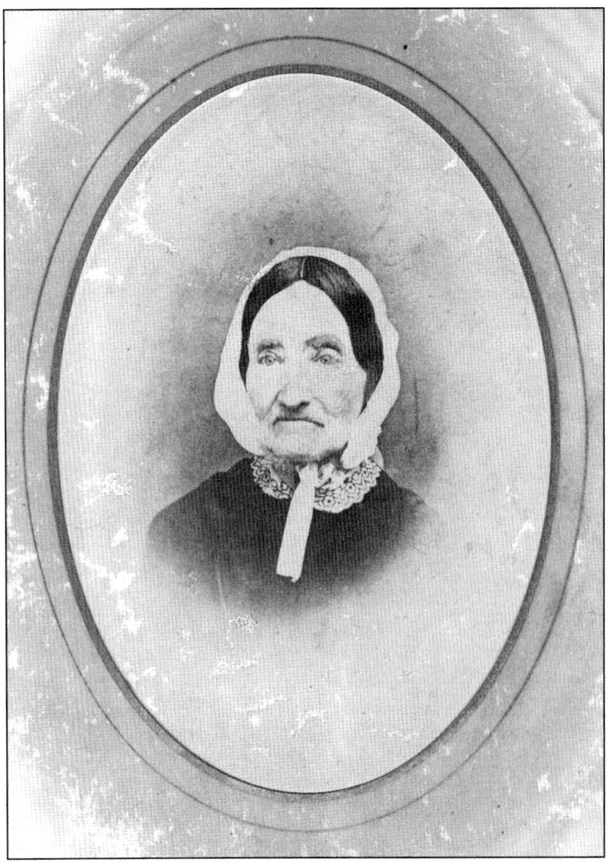

THE CLARK FAMILY PLOT, LAKE VIEW CEMETERY. The Clark family has had a long and distinguished past in Wolfeboro, and to this day, through the Clark Museum complex, provides a unique window through which those alive today can view Wolfeboro's history. Joseph Clark and his wife Comfort (left) arrived in Wolfeboro in 1817 from Greenland, purchasing a house previously built in 1786. They had eight children, but only two stayed in this area. Joseph Clark practiced the trade of a cabinetmaker and died in 1851, while Comfort lived 10 years as his widow. However, the old homestead remained in the family, and the original house eventually passed to his grandson, Greenleaf Clark, and was donated to the town at his death. This house stands today as a centerpiece for the Wolfeboro Historical Society. (Left photograph courtesy Wolfeboro Historical Society.)

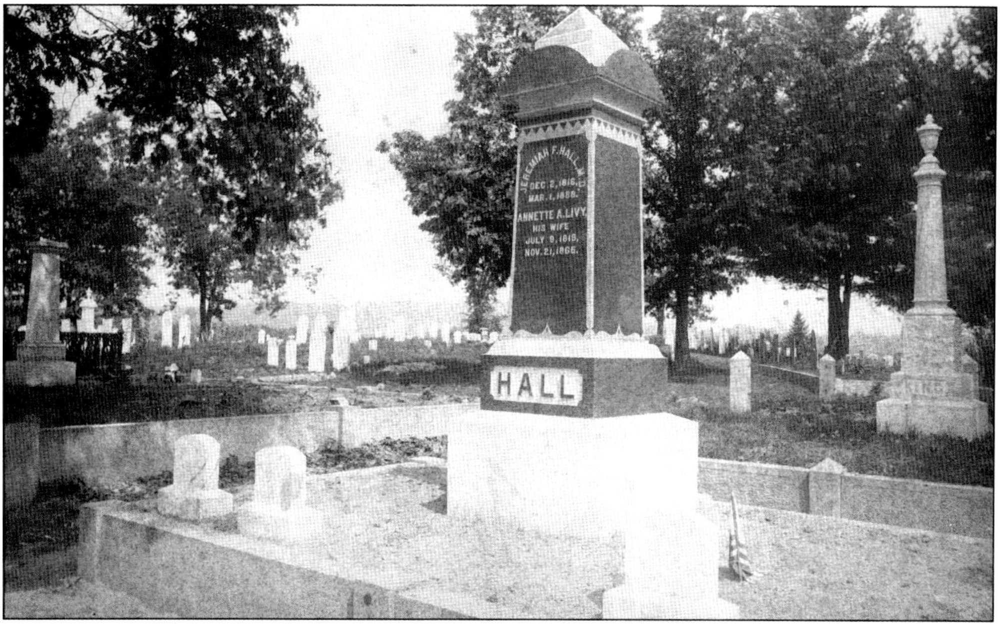

JEREMIAH HALL (1888), LAKE VIEW CEMETERY. Jeremiah Hall was a prominent doctor in Wolfeboro for 30 years. A native of Northwood, he first practiced medicine with Dr. David Livy and married his daughter Annette. During the Civil War, he served as a surgeon in the 15th New Hampshire Regiment. After the war, now widowed, he removed to Portsmouth and was actively involved in statewide medical affairs. (Courtesy Wolfeboro Historical Society.)

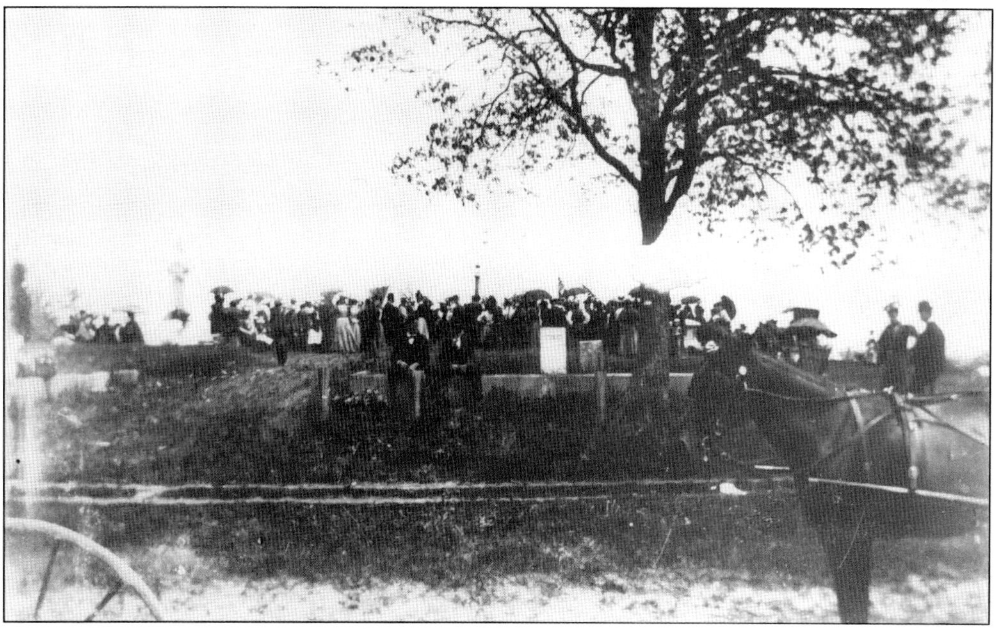

A FUNERAL SERVICE, C. 1900. This unusual photograph depicts a funeral service in progress, probably at Wolfeboro's Lake View Cemetery. Photographs such as this are rare for the time, indicating that the deceased was someone important in town affairs. Note the men at far left, possibly the driver or undertakers accompanying the horse-drawn hearse whose wheel is just visible at lower left. (Courtesy Wolfeboro Historical Society.)

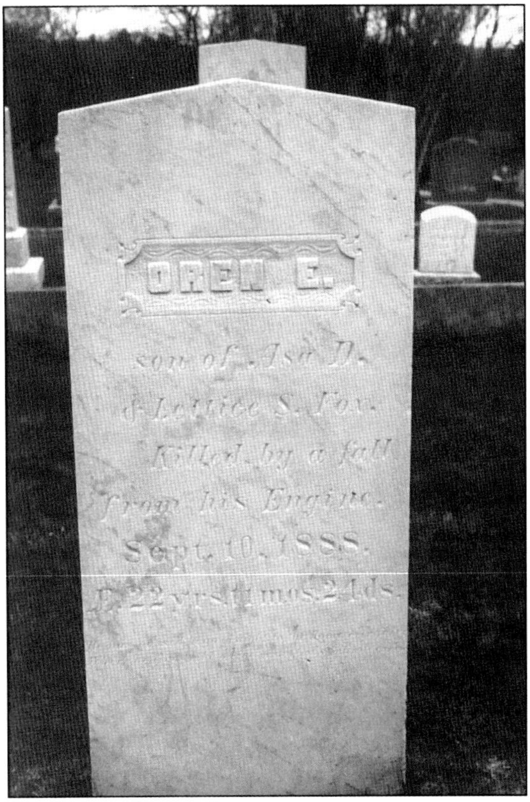

OREN FOX (1888), LAKE VIEW CEMETERY. This marble gravestone is one of the most unusual in all of Lake View Cemetery for the fact that the circumstances of death are noted. Unfortunately, the full details of Fox's death are unknown, as is his position, perhaps engineer or coal-passer, in the train crew. However unusual it may appear, railroad-related deaths during this time were not uncommon. The railroad came to Wolfeboro in August 1872 and was instrumental in opening up the town to the outside world and further building up its status as a summer resort. Though the railroads were the glamorous transportation of the times, to the men who operated such trains (below), the work was both dirty and dangerous. (Bottom photograph courtesy Wolfeboro Historical Society.)

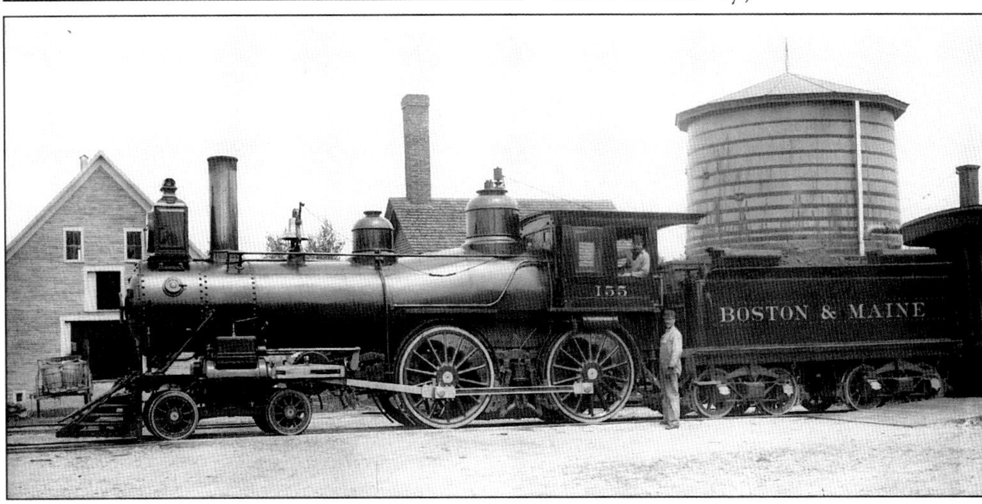

JOHN KANE (1865), LAKE VIEW CEMETERY. The crossed cannons on John Kane's gravestone well illustrate his service in the 1st New Hampshire Heavy Artillery Regiment. Little is known about Kane from New Haven, Connecticut, who enlisted at age 20 in September 1864 and died five months later. It is unknown if he is the same John Kane hailing from Quebec who enlisted for Laconia in early 1864 but deserted days later in Concord.

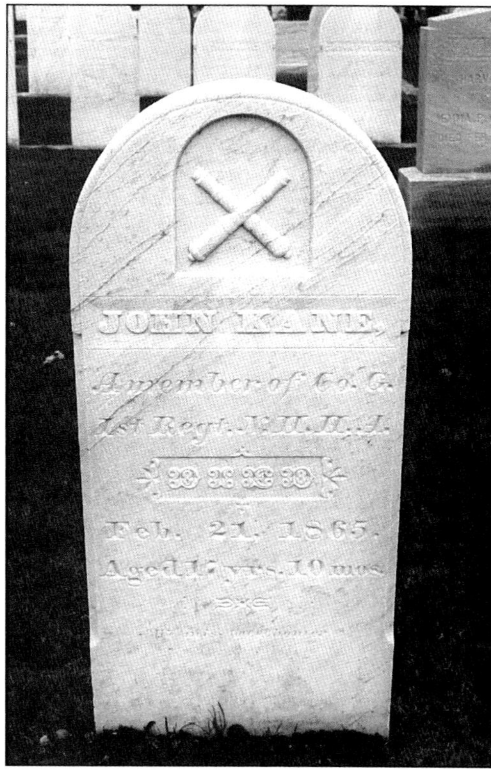

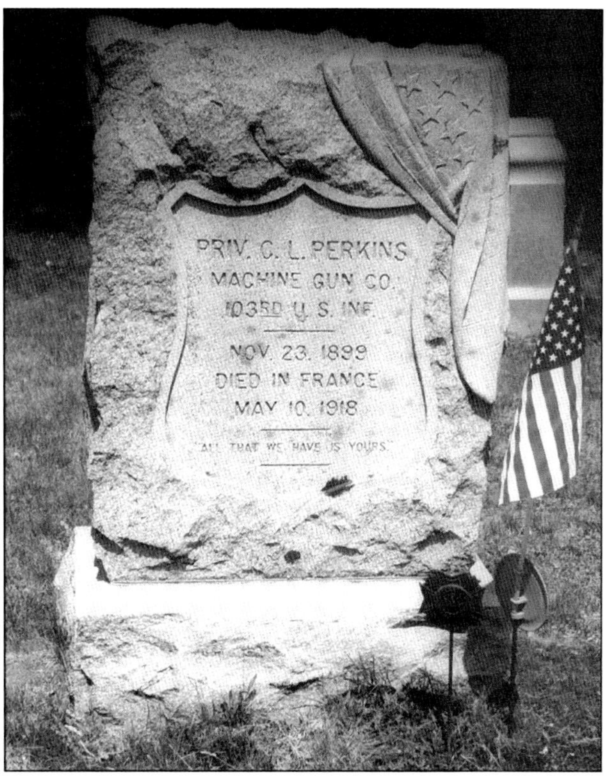

C. L. PERKINS (1918), SOUTH WOLFEBORO CEMETERY. Often forgotten are the veterans of World War I, "the war to end all wars," The Lakes Region had a number of men who went off to fight in this bloody conflict, a number of them serving, as C. L. Perkins did, in the 103rd U.S. Infantry Division. This granite marker, with its shield and draped flag carved in stone, is a true work of art.

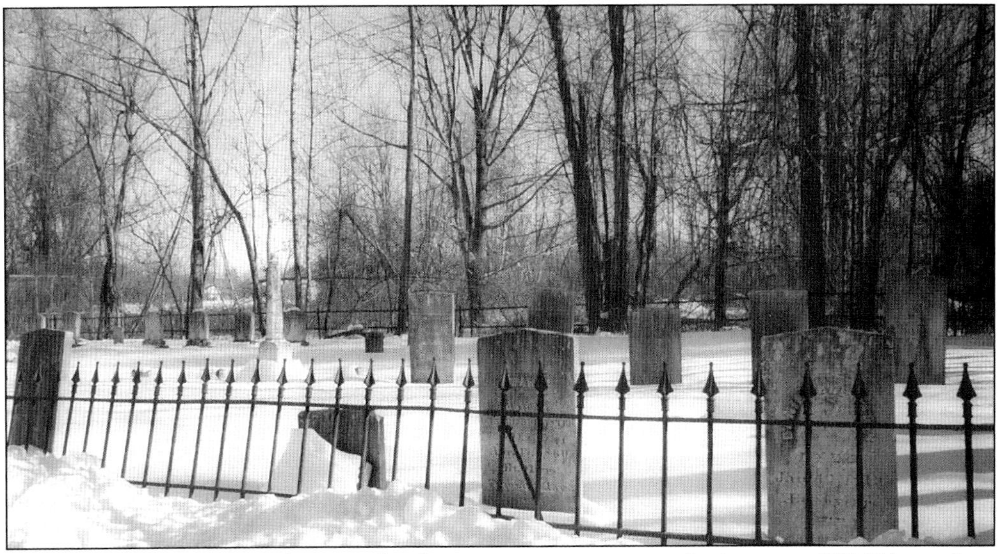

BREWSTER CEMETERY. Perhaps no family is more prominent in the history of Wolfeboro than the Brewsters. The first in town was Daniel Brewster, who arrived here before 1792. Daniel Brewster had two sons, George and Daniel, both of whom are buried in the Brewster Cemetery (above). One of George's children, John Brewster, born in 1812, left home at age 16 to teach school in nearby Milton. John never again lived in Wolfeboro but visited from time to time and made a fortune as a businessman. At his death in 1886, he left a $10,000 annual bequeathal to the Wolfeborough and Tuftonborough Academy, made on the condition that the name of the academy be changed to the Brewster Free School or Academy (below) and that there be no restrictions in regards to age, sex, or race. John also provided for the building of a town hall and the establishment of a free library in Wolfeboro. (Bottom photograph courtesy Wolfeboro Historical Society.)

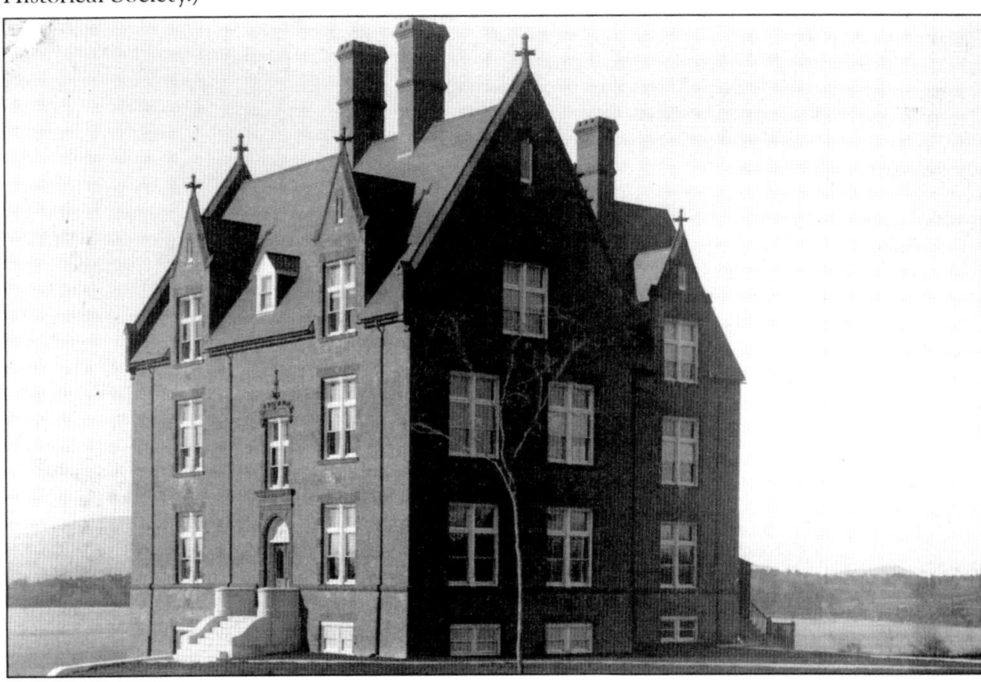

Three

TUFTONBORO, MELVIN VILLAGE, AND MIRROR LAKE

The town of Tuftonboro, which encompasses the communities of Mirror Lake and Melvin Village, was first granted to John Tufton Mason prior to the American Revolution. The proprietor of the largest amount of land in town after the Revolution was Portsmouth's Woodbury Langdon. By 1782, when Langdon petitioned the legislature for a tax abatement, only five families were in town. However, enough settlers moved here so that in 1795, the town was incorporated.

In 1810, the town voted to build a townhouse in Center Tuftonboro where town meetings could be held. It is interesting to note that this was to be a purely secular structure, in keeping with the changing times, and was not for religious services. However, nothing was done, and town meetings continued to be held in private residences until around 1820, when the town house was finally built. Nearby, the Town House Cemetery, the first public cemetery in town, was established. While burials continue in this cemetery, those who walk to its far end can easily discern where the first burials took place, most marked by plain fieldstones. Two other family cemeteries in this part of town also merit discussion. The Hoyt-Ladd-Remick Cemetery is the final resting place for William Mallard, one of the petitioners for the town's incorporation in 1795, as well as John Stockbridge, Melvin Village's fourth postmaster who, at his death, was said to weigh 500 pounds. The French Cemetery beside French's Brook is noteworthy as the final resting place of Thomas French. It was at his house, in 1820, that the First Christian Church of Centre Tuftonborough was organized. French, called a "man of means," had the first mill-operated turning lathe in the area and was known for his chair-making skills. Perhaps some of the chairs he made, with "seats made of basket stuff," are still in use today in Tuftonboro.

In regards to other cemeteries within Tuftonboro's boundaries, the Melvin Village Community Church Cemetery is one of the most beautiful of any found around Lake Winnipesaukee. Located just behind the Melvin Village Community Church, and established at the same time as its building in 1866, its view of Moultonborough Bay is spectacular. Other interesting cemeteries located very close to the lakeshore are the Edgerly-Blake Cemetery overlooking Nineteenmile Bay, and Thomas Cemetery on Tuftonboro Neck, where may be found the final resting place of Augustus Wiggin, for years captain of the famed *Mount Washington* steamship. It should come as no surprise, really, why Wiggin chose this spot to be buried. A resident of Tuftonboro, he steamed within a mile or two of this location during his many voyages over the years between Wolfeboro Bay and Center Harbor. Perhaps the spirit of Captain Wiggin, even to this day, if one believes in such things, is happy to hear the whistle off in the distance of the new *Mount Washington* as it comes to and from Wolfeboro Bay and continues the cycle of voyages that he made so popular and successful over 100 years ago.

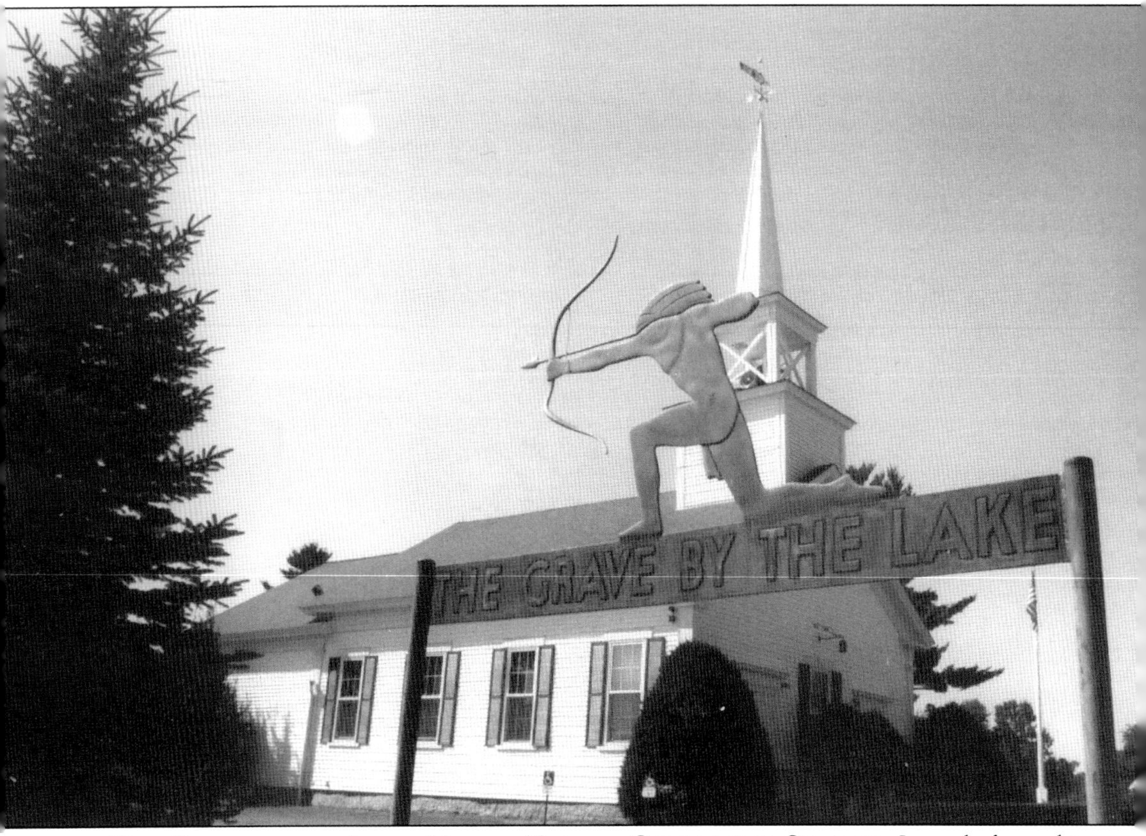

The Grave by the Lake, Melvin Village Community Church. Long before white men came here, Native Americans inhabited the shores of Lake Winnipesaukee. The most celebrated of their remnants was the 1808 discovery here of a large skeleton said to be of a large man, probably a tribal chief, nearly seven feet tall and accompanied by a large headstone. This discovery was later made famous by poet John Greenleaf Whittier in his poem "The Grave by the Lake," which reads in part:

> Where the Great Lake's sunny smiles
> Dimple round its hundred isles,
> And the mountain's granite ledge
> Cleaves the water like a wedge,
> Ringed about with smooth, gray stones,
> Rest the giant's mighty bones.

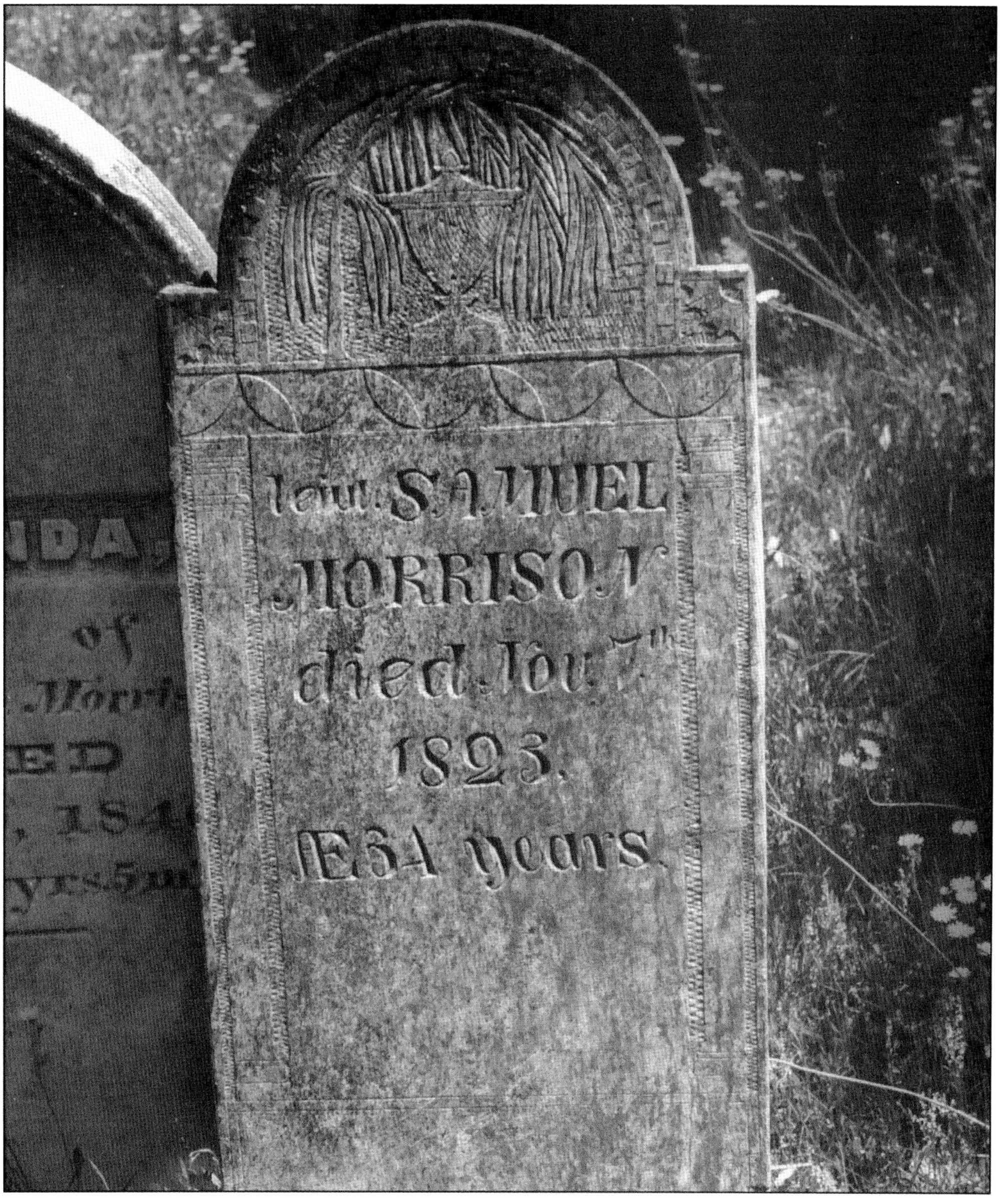

SAMUEL MORRISON (1823), EDGERLY-BLAKE CEMETERY. Buried in this scenic cemetery overlooking Nineteenmile Bay, little is known about Lt. Samuel Morrison. His military title may have been earned during the War of 1812 or possibly due to local militia service. Morrison did serve as a town selectman for one year, just prior to his death, in 1822. The date of his arrival in Tuftonboro is uncertain, but he may be the same Samuel Morrison that resided for a time in Gilmanton and was an ardent church attendant who strictly upheld the ideal of not working on the Sabbath. Morrison's gravestone is a nice example of the earlier work of carver Matthias Weeks during his time in Gilmanton. Characteristic of his carving work is the petal border above the deceased's name and the spiderweb design on the squared shoulders. Also unique is Weeks's lettering of the military title of the deceased carved in lowercase letters and abbreviated incorrectly. If Morrison was indeed from Gilmanton, it is very likely that he and carver Weeks knew each other well.

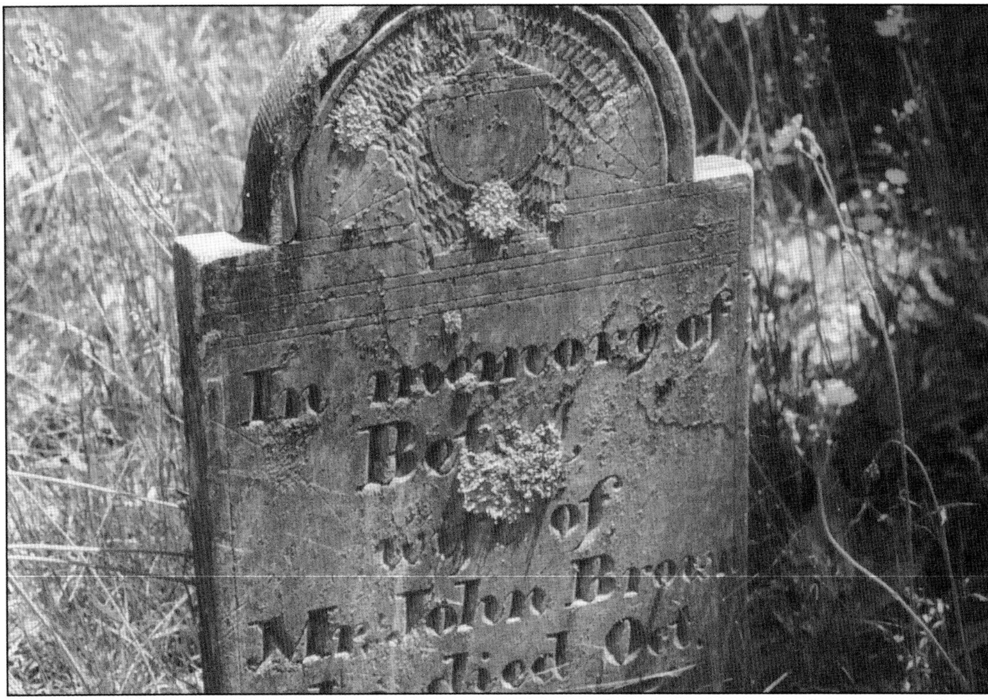

BETSEY BROWN (1827), EDGERLY-BLAKE CEMETERY. Though in poor condition overall, the Edgerly-Blake Cemetery is notable for its fine collection of early slate gravestone carvings. Many of these were carved by Matthias Weeks, including this one for the wife of John Brown, Betsey. Though diminutive in size, this stone is notable among Weeks's work for its simplicity, a funeral urn flanked by two sunburst designs.

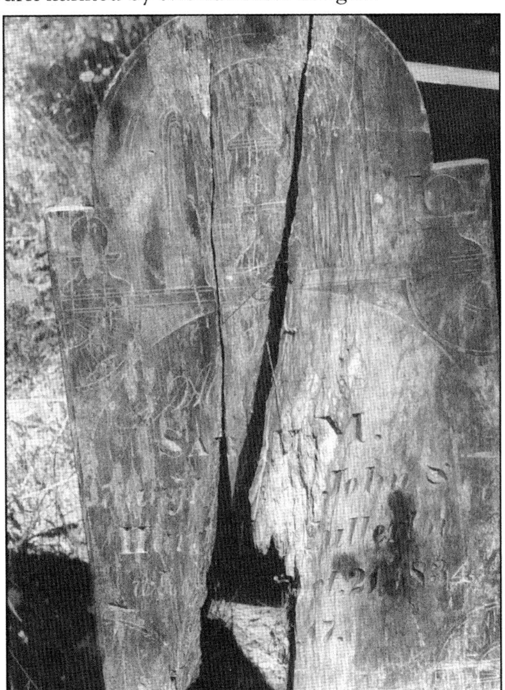

SARAH FULLERTON (1834), EDGERLY-BLAKE CEMETERY. This gravestone for the daughter of John and Hannah Fullerton, Sarah, will soon be lost forever unless properly repaired. Though broken into several pieces, the former beauty of this carving by Matthias Weeks is easily visible and contains many of his hallmark tendencies, including the sunburst designs flanking the circular inset. Sarah was likely the granddaughter of Wolfeboro Revolutionary War soldier Sgt. John Fullerton.

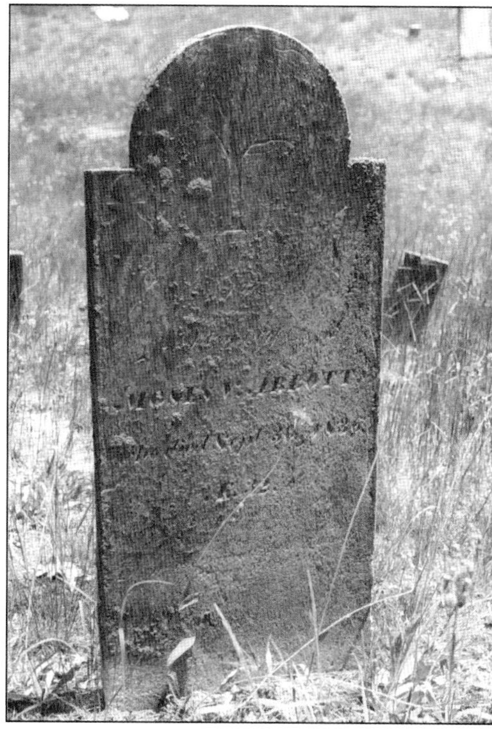

MOSES ABBOTT (1836), EDGERLY-BLAKE CEMETERY. Moses Abbott was likely the son of Tuftonboro's Samuel Abbott and his wife Anna Abbott (née Varney) from Wolfeboro, married in December 1789. Like many others in this rural town, Moses was likely a farmer, the land being well suited for this purpose. His gravestone is another of Matthias Weeks's carvings after he moved to Moultonborough, perhaps aided by his son Franklin, who also became a stonecutter.

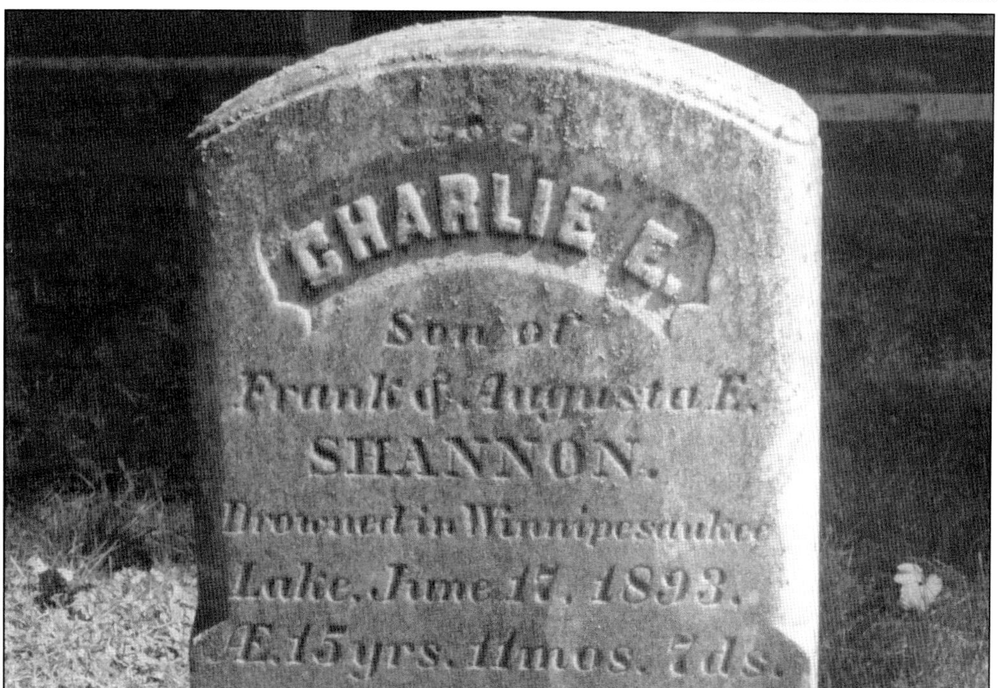

CHARLIE SHANNON (1893), EDGERLY-BLAKE CEMETERY. Though beautiful, the lake has also claimed its share of drowning victims over the years. As this gravestone shows, young Charlie Shannon, on the verge of manhood, "drowned in Winnipesaukee Lake" on an early summer day in 1893. Area residents still place flowers on Shannon's grave, even today.

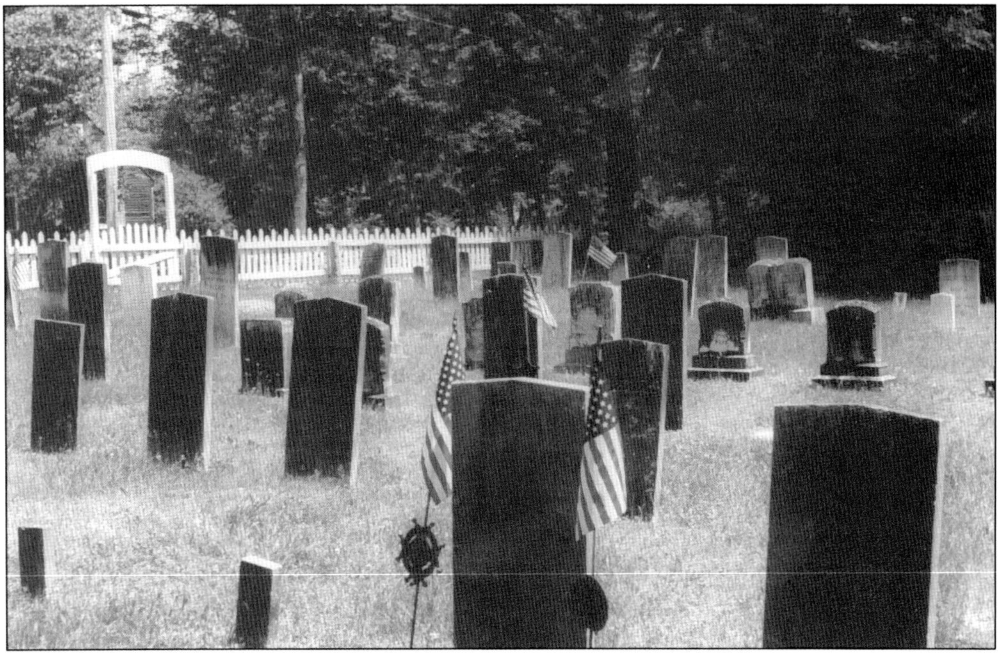

THOMAS CEMETERY, TUFTONBORO NECK. Located near the end of Tuftonboro Neck, this picturesque cemetery is one of the most charming and peaceful in town. It is named after the Thomas family, who possessed one of the finest farms on Tuftonboro Neck. The burials in this neighborhood cemetery date from around 1840 to the first decades of the 1900s. With its white picket fence and gateway, it is well maintained.

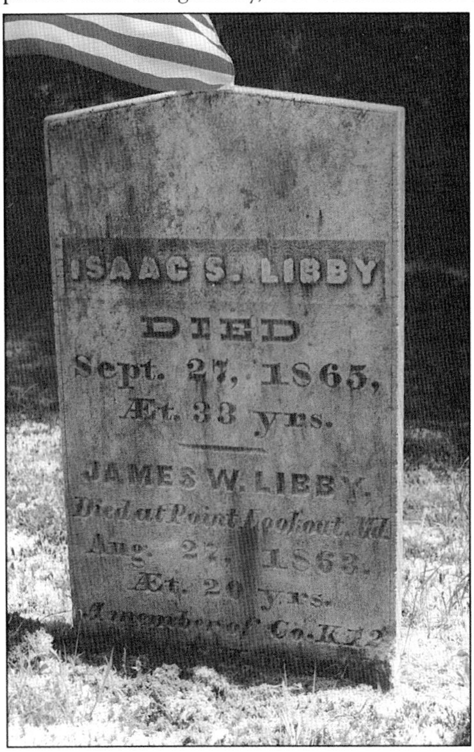

ISAAC (1865) AND JAMES (1863) LIBBY, THOMAS CEMETERY. While Isaac Libby stayed home, likely to maintain family affairs, his brother James went off to war. Serving in the 12th New Hampshire Regiment, James enlisted at Wolfeboro in July 1862 and fought in the bloody battles at Fredericksburg and Chancellorsville. Though posted missing during the carnage at Gettysburg, he was later found, only to succumb to disease in Maryland two months later.

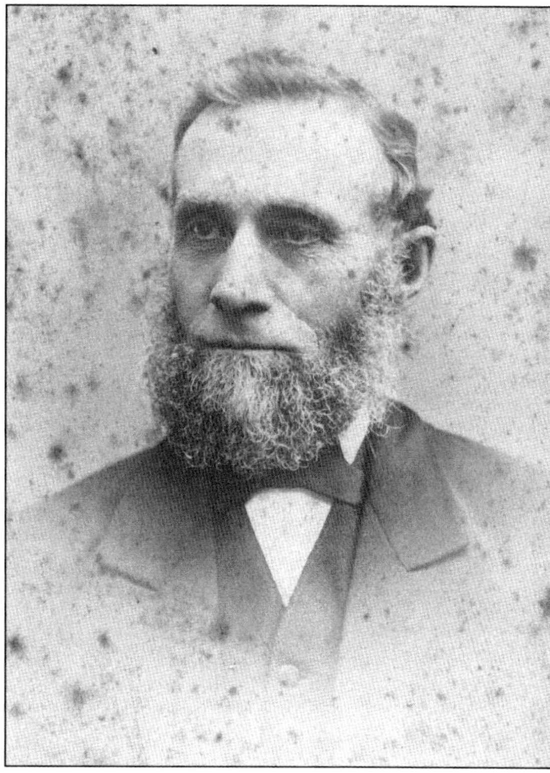

CAPT. AUGUSTUS WIGGIN AND THE *MOUNT WASHINGTON*. When it comes to the history of boating on Lake Winnipesaukee, few names are as famous as that of Capt. Augustus Wiggin. His grandfather was among the founding fathers of Tuftonboro, James Wiggin being an early surveyor and tavern keeper in 1796. Augustus was born in 1826 and was a farmer's son, working the land until he started working on lake boats in 1852. A genial man and a capable sailor, Wiggin (right) rose quickly through the ranks and soon gained his own command, the famed *Mount Washington* steamer (below). He commanded this large and most famous of lake vessels for many years and was renowned for his "sterling honor and morality" by passengers and crew alike. When not on the lake, Captain Wiggin lived on Tuftonboro Neck, not far from his final resting place in Thomas Cemetery. (Courtesy Wolfeboro Historical Society.)

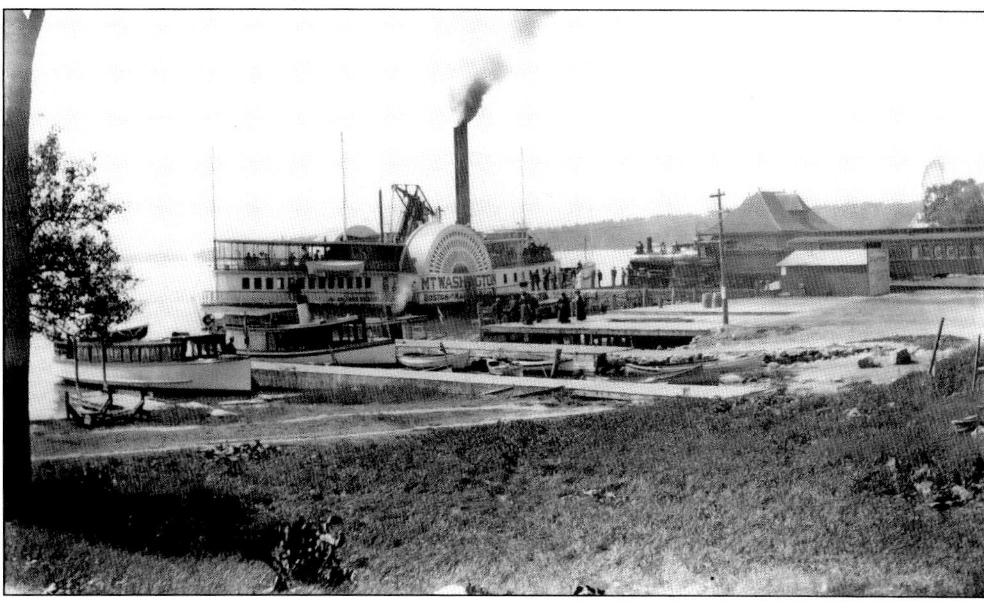

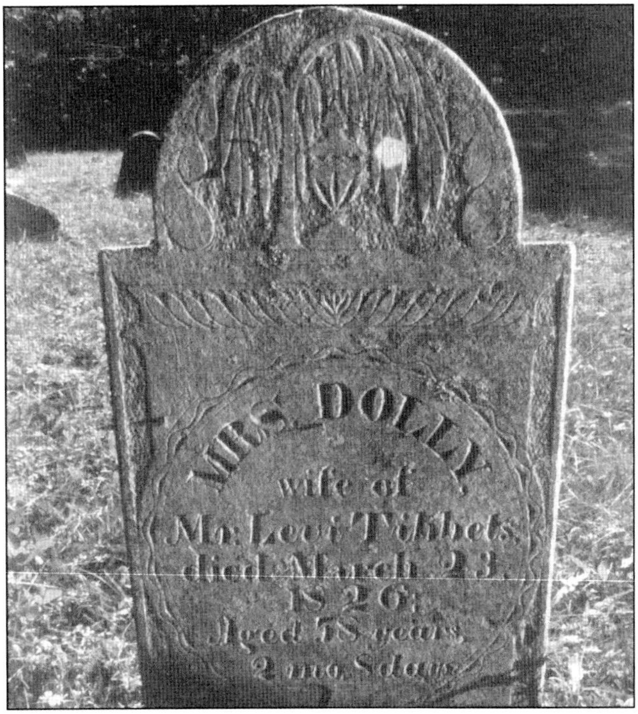

DOLLY TIBBETS (1826), TIBBETS-YOUNG CEMETERY. Dolly Tibbets was the wife of Levi, a founding member of the First Christian Church of Centre Tuftonborough in May 1820. Her attractive gravestone was carved by Matthias Weeks. A schoolteacher in North Wolfeboro in 1813, Dolly surely would have approved of the fine lettering etched on her gravestone.

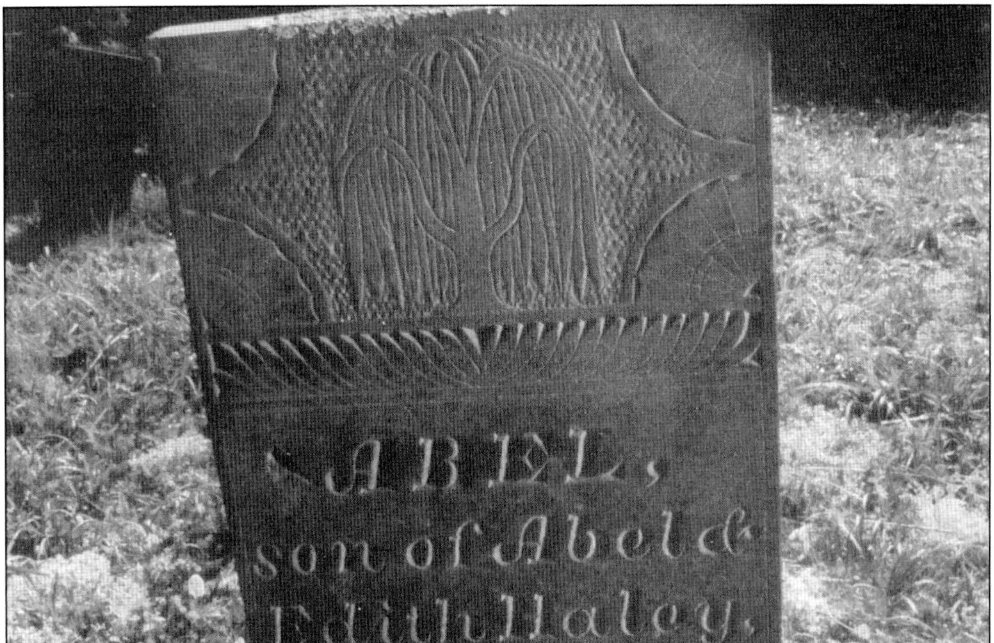

ABEL HALEY (1834), TIBBETS-YOUNG CEMETERY. Abel Haley was the first of the Haleys to make his name known in Tuftonboro affairs, serving as selectman for seven terms, from 1836 to 1847, before moving to Wolfeboro and serving as a trustee of the Wolfeborough and Tuftonborough Academy. The stone for his son, aged two, was carved by Matthias Weeks. Its square shape and lone willow tree are typical of Weeks's later work.

ELIZABETH (1897) AND JOHN (1927) HALEY, TOWN HOUSE CEMETERY. This brother and sister were natives of Tuftonboro and had quite interesting careers. Rev. John Haley (below) earned a divinity degree and was a schoolteacher in Tuftonboro, Moultonborough, Barrington, and Kittery, Maine. He was the author of a number of works, including several of a religious nature and his well-known work on Tuftonboro history. His gravestone notes one of his published works and has the epitaph "By grace are ye saved through faith." Elizabeth Haley was a trailblazer in her day, becoming an ordained minister at Stanfordville, New York, in 1877, when few women were active as preachers. Her epitaph, fitting for a minister, reads, "They that bring many to righteousness shall live as the stars forever and ever."

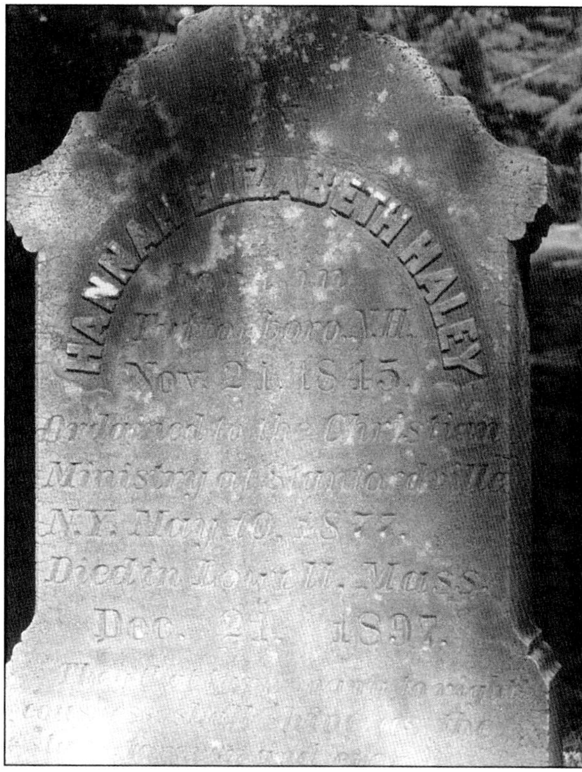

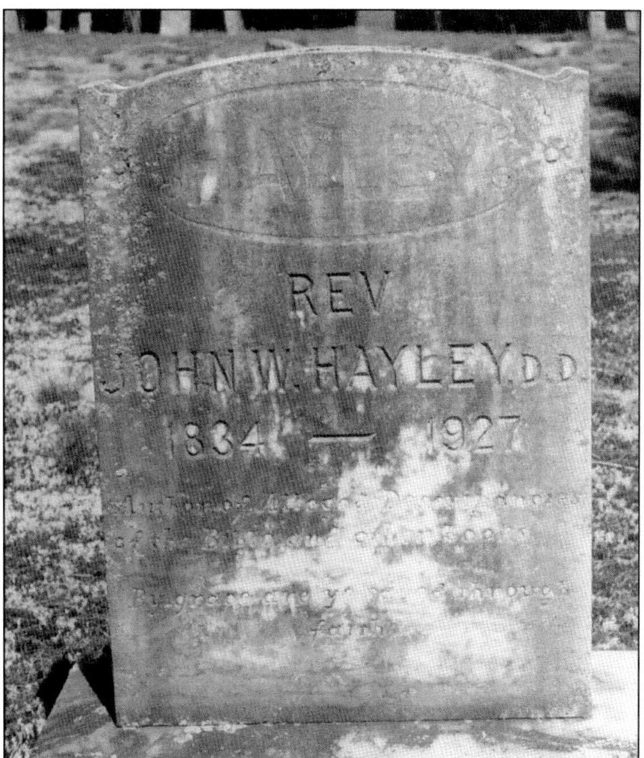

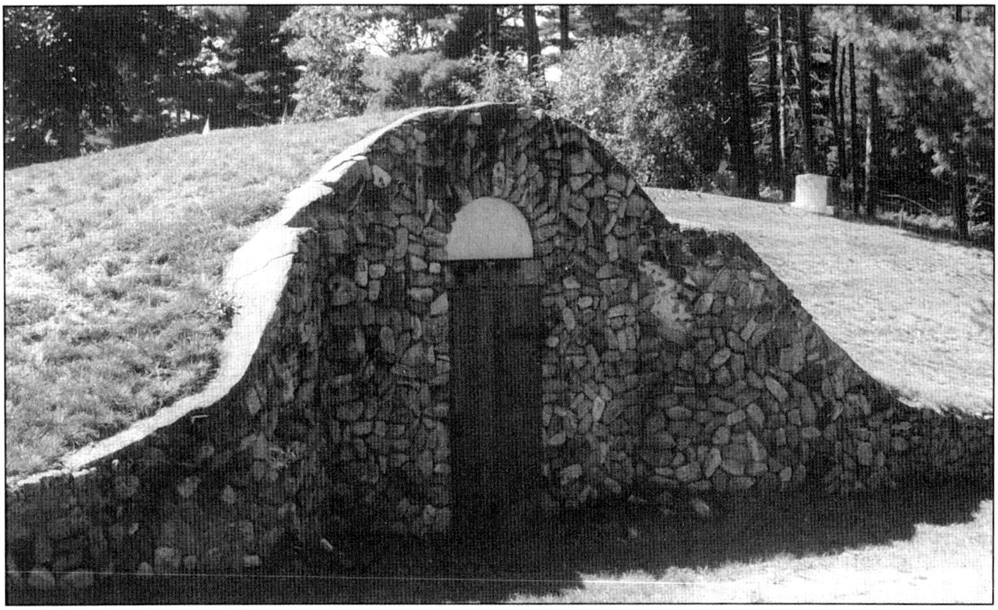

RECEIVING TOMB (1905), TOWN HOUSE CEMETERY. This hillside tomb, easily visible from the road nearby, is one of the most interesting features here. Receiving tombs, common in New England, were used to store bodies during winter months until the ground thawed and a final burial could be made. This one, with its granite facade covered with natural stone and a wooden plank door, has an attractive and rustic appearance.

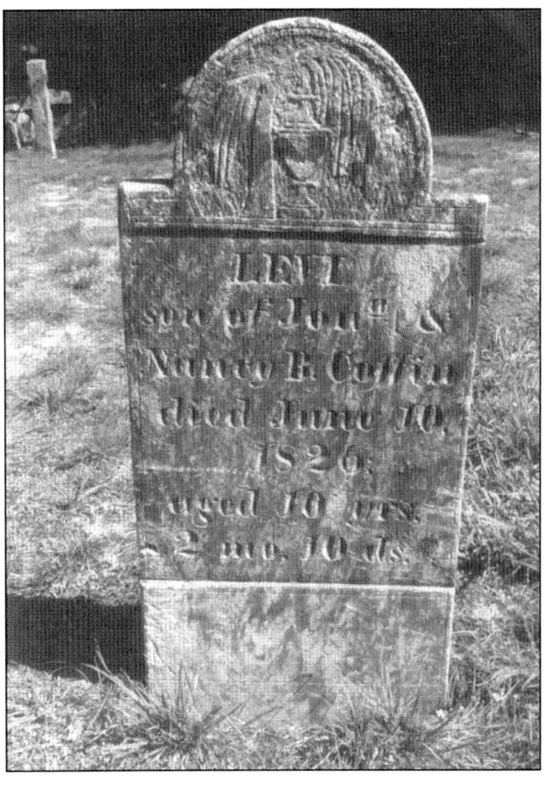

LEVI COFFIN (1826), TOWN HOUSE CEMETERY. This gravestone for young Levi Coffin, aged 10 at his death, is the oldest dated stone to be found in this cemetery. Levi's father, Jonathan, served as Tuftonboro town clerk in 1810 and from 1814 through 1820. Set apart by an iron chain, the Coffin family plot is the oldest identifiable plot in the oldest part of Town House Cemetery.

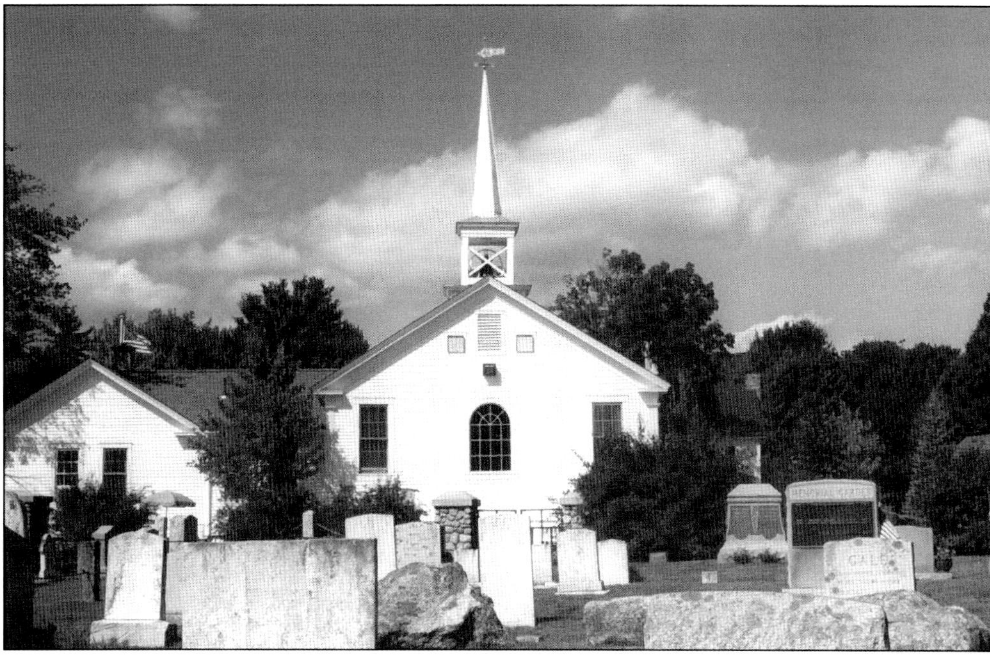

Melvin Village Community Church Cemetery. Located on a site overlooking the lake where the Melvin River empties into Moultonborough Bay, this cemetery is surely one of the most beautiful in the area. The Melvin Village Community Church was built in 1866, and the cemetery behind it was established about the same time.

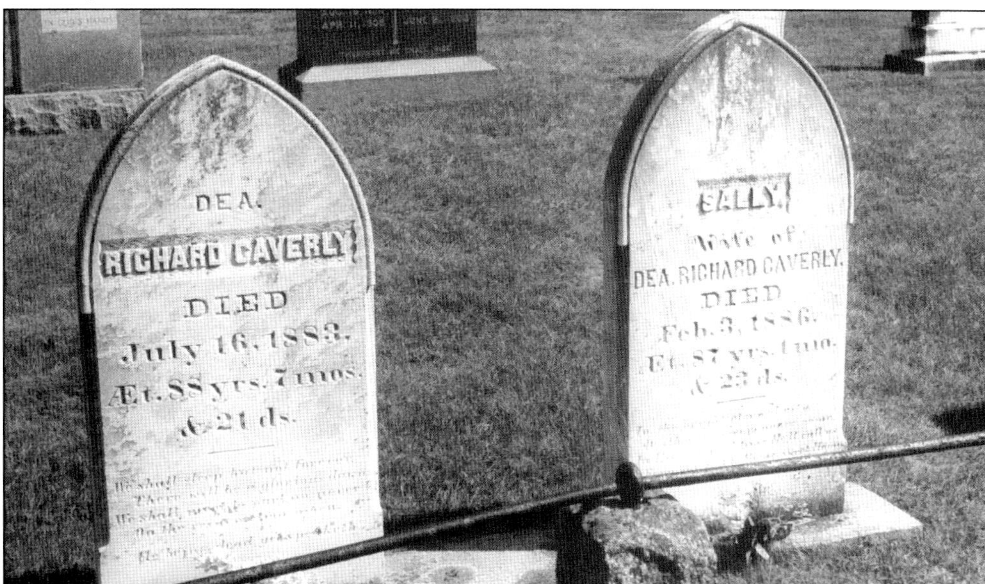

Richard (1883) and Sally (1886) Caverly, Melvin Village Community Church Cemetery. Deacon Richard Caverly was a founding member of this church when it was first formed in October 1837. The church suffered greatly when many of its members converted to Millerism in 1841, anticipating the coming of the Apocalypse in 1842–1843. When the church reorganized in 1852, Richard and Sally Caverly were amongst its few devoted followers who did not become ardent Adventists.

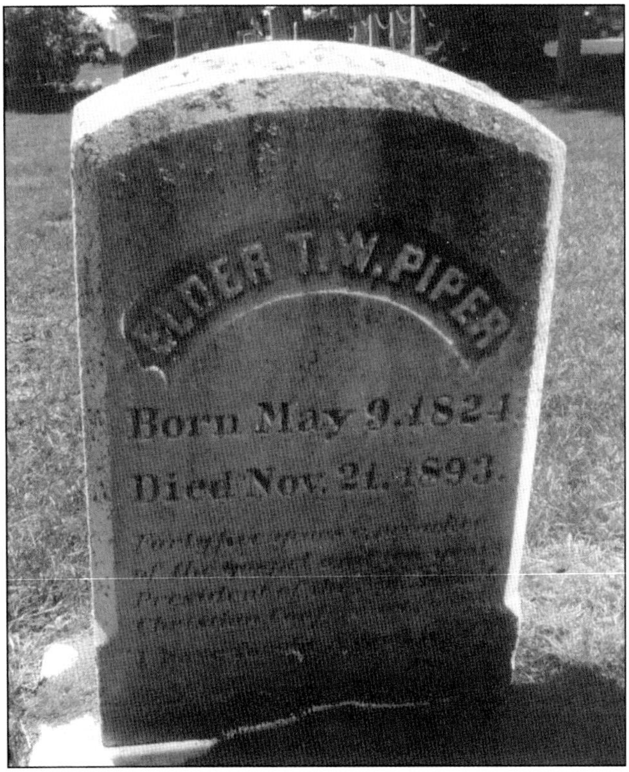

THATCHER PIPER (1893), MELVIN VILLAGE COMMUNITY CHURCH CEMETERY. An elder in the Second Advent Church in Melvin Village, Thatcher Piper began preaching in 1850, at age 26, and was ordained in 1858. Like many other ministers of his faith, established by William Miller in the 1840s, Piper preached throughout New England and led many local revivals. President for 11 years of the New Hampshire Conference of Adventists, he was highly regarded.

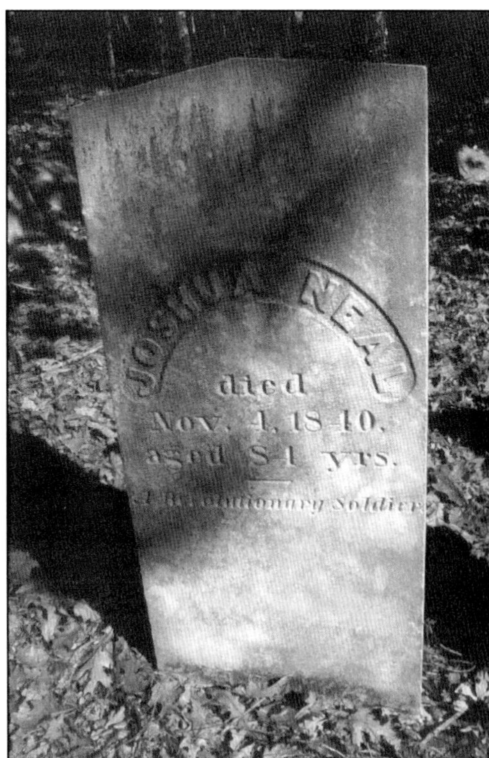

JOSHUA NEAL (1840), NEAL CEMETERY. A founding member of the First Christian Church of Centre Tuftonborough in 1820, this Revolutionary War soldier "fought several times in the retreat from Ticonderoga." A fifer in the militia company of Capt. Thomas Berry, Joshua Neal later served under Capt. John Calfe in Col. Pierce Long's regiment. Serving for one year from August 1776, Neal experienced heavy battle action at Fort Anne and Saratoga.

Four

MOULTONBOROUGH

The land that would later become the town of Moultonborough was granted to a group of Hampton men headed by Col. Jonathan Moulton in 1763. Prior to negotiating the grant, they had surveyed the area to see for themselves how suitable the land might be. Their findings were not encouraging and, referring to the "badness" of the land, they negotiated another "gore" of land, called Moultonborough Addition, that would later become New Hampton and parts of the future towns of Meredith and Center Harbor. While the first landing by white men on the lake's northern shore occurred at Clark's Landing in 1742, it was not until 1765 that the first official citizens, Stephen Sanborn and family, arrived. By 1770, the settlement was well established, and in 1777, it was incorporated.

Perhaps more than any other town in study, Moultonborough followed in the footsteps of older New Hampshire towns when it came to church matters. A meetinghouse was built in 1773, in East Moultonborough, and was used by visiting clergy. In 1779, Rev. Jeremiah Shaw was hired as minister. He would remain for the next 46 years until his retirement in 1825. Moultonborough was indeed the exception in the Lakes Region; its residents were ardent Congregationalists during a time when that faith's once predominant influence was generally waning elsewhere and Baptist faiths, especially Free Will Baptists, were gaining an increasing number of adherents. When Shaw died in 1834, he was buried in Shaw Cemetery, close to the site of the old meetinghouse. It was truly the end of an era. Thus it is that Shaw Cemetery is a must-see in Moultonborough, both because of the interesting persons buried there and also for the fine examples of some of the oldest gravestones found in the area.

Many other historical cemeteries, too numerous to mention in full, abound in Moultonborough: the Richardson Cemetery at Clark's Landing, possibly the oldest cemetery in town where members of the Clark family are buried, as well as original settler Col. Bradbury Richardson; Lower Neck Cemetery, pleasantly situated on a narrow, sloping piece of land, the final resting place of members of the Moulton family that died of disease on the same day in 1834; Red Hill Cemetery, the final resting place of famed silent film star Claude Rains and his wife; and the Rollins Cemetery, which has a particularly interesting wrought-iron cemetery gate with an hourglass design.

Finally, Moultonborough is also of interest because of the resident gravestone carver, Matthias Weeks. He moved here from Gilmanton in 1829 and practiced his trade for over 20 years. His work is found in many of the town's cemeteries and mark the resting places of some of its most noteworthy citizens. A typical pair of his gravestones, such as those for Duncan McNaughton, buried in Shaw Cemetery in 1831 at the age of 115, cost about $14. Dying was good business for Weeks; by 1850, he had an estate valued at $2,000, respectable for the time.

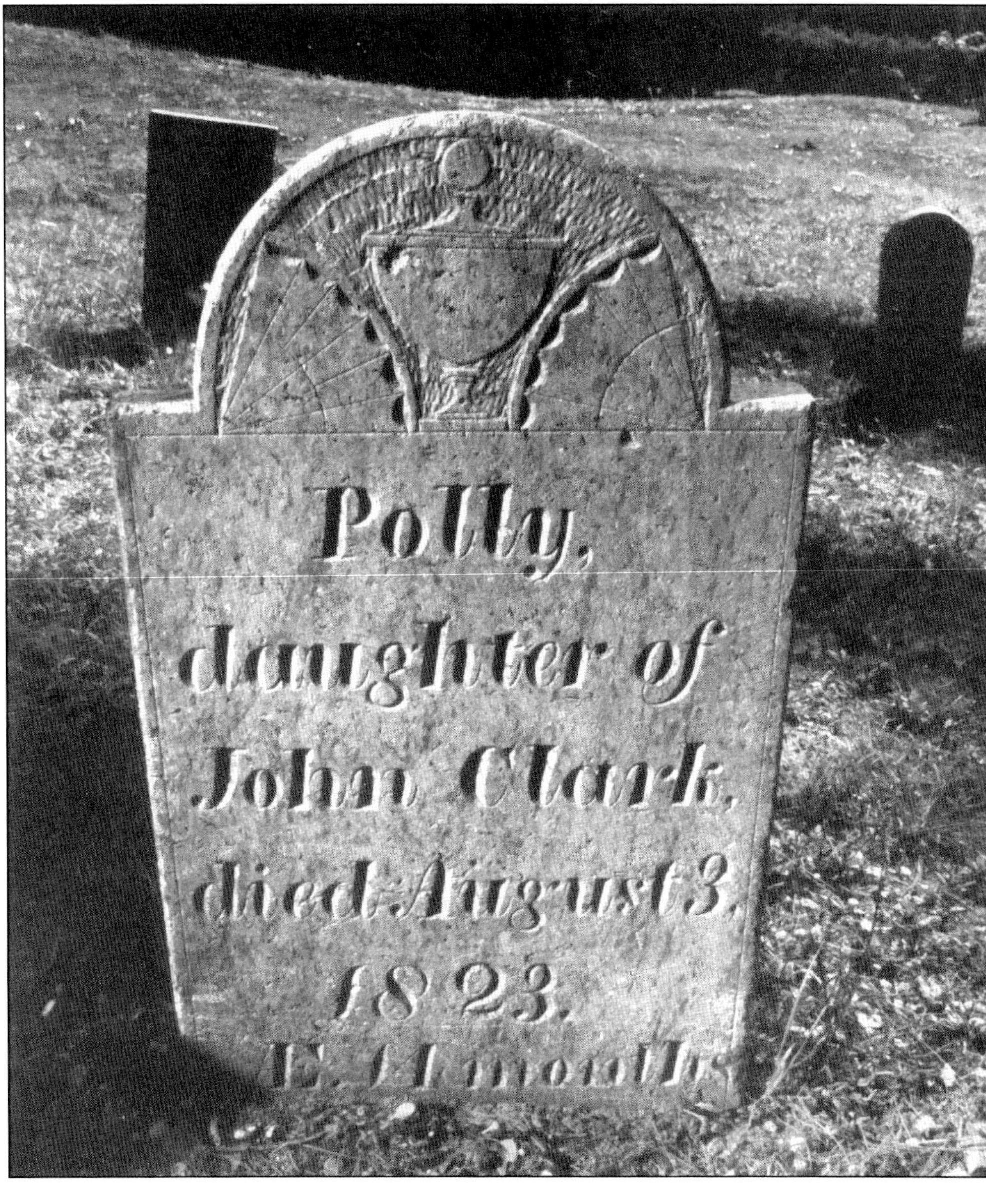

Polly Clark (1823), Richardson Cemetery. Appropriately enough, many members of the Clark family are buried in this cemetery at Clark's Landing. This stone for Polly, the 14-month-old daughter of John and Judith Clark, is one of the oldest dated stones here and was carved by Matthias Weeks. It is interesting that Polly's mother is not named on the stone, perhaps indicating that she had died previously.

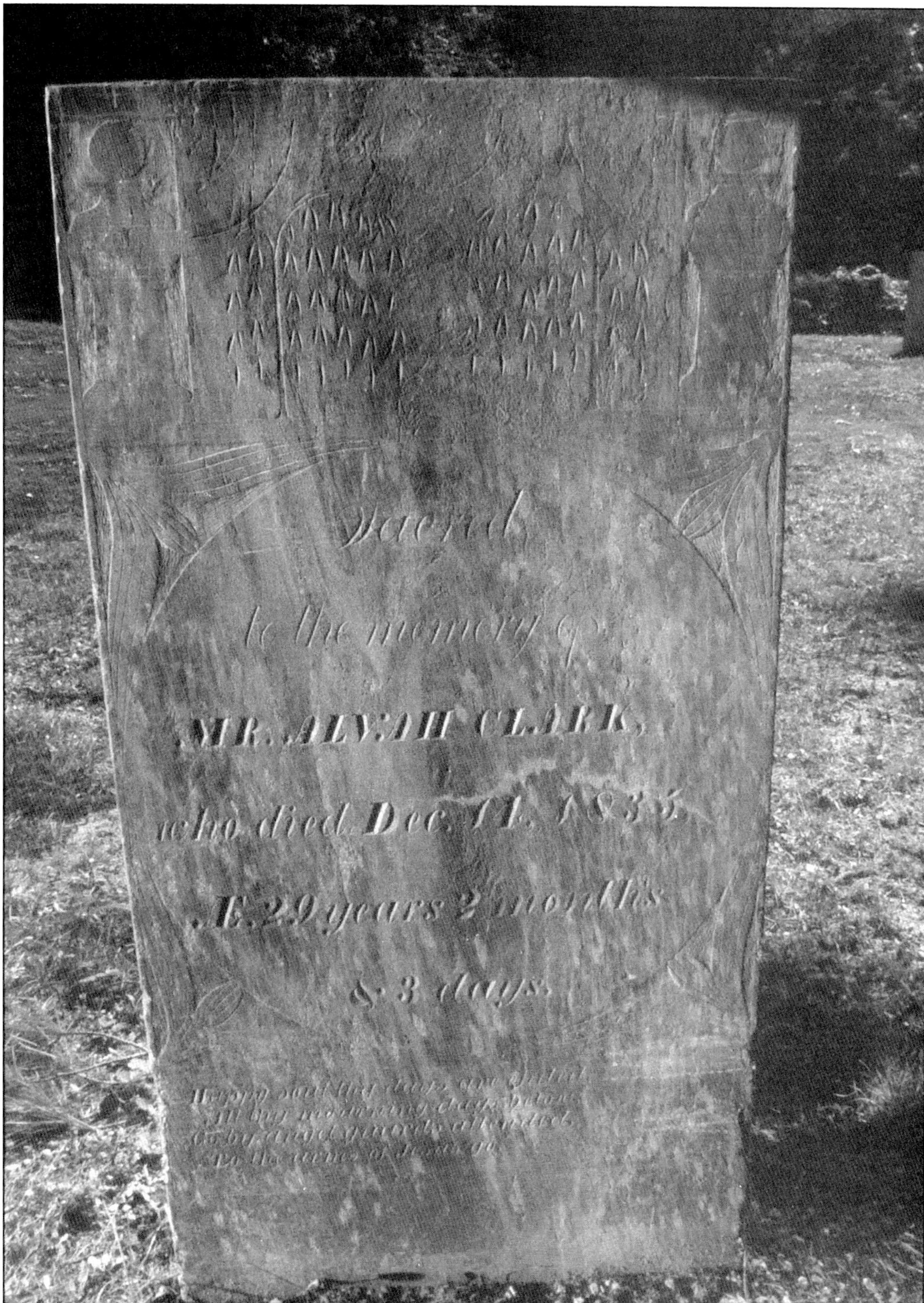

ALVAH CLARK (1833), RICHARDSON CEMETERY. This young man was likely the son of John and Judith Clark. Alvah's death in the prime of life may have been due to a contagious illness that hit others in Moultonborough several winters in a row during this time period. His stone was likely carved by Matthias Weeks in one of his later styles.

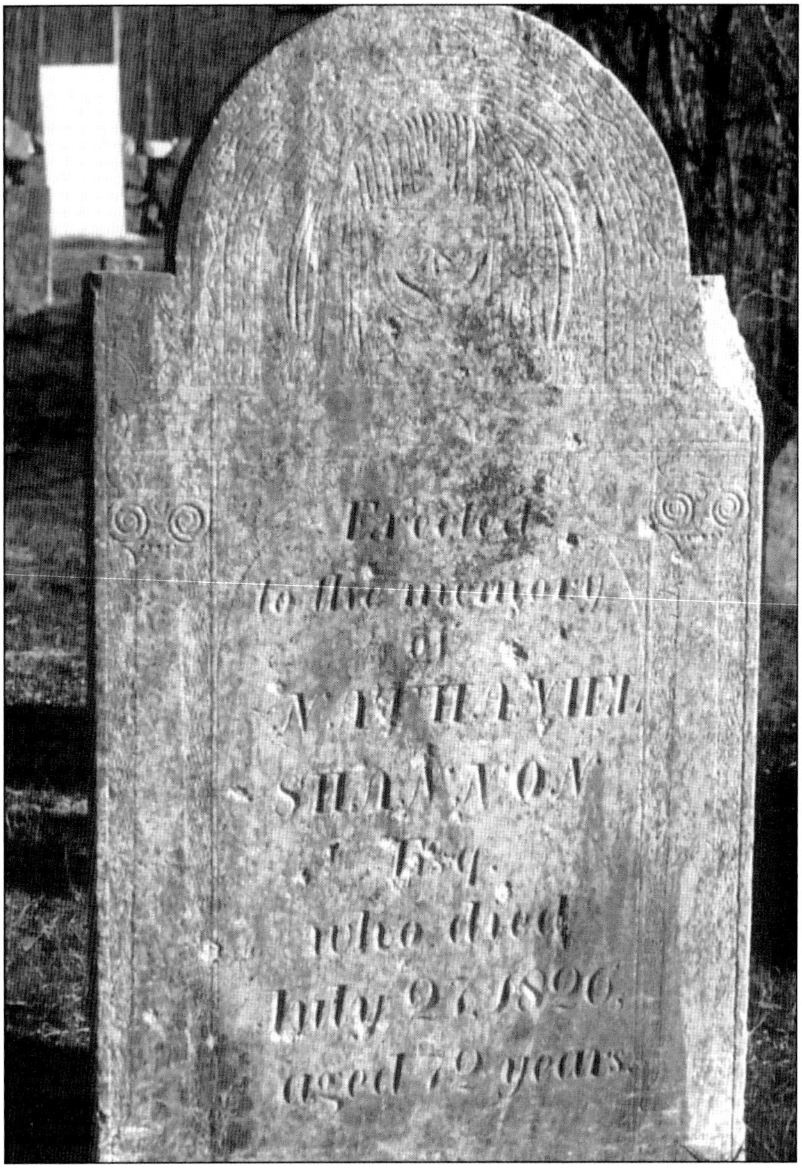

NATHANIEL SHANNON (1826), SHANNON CEMETERY. This stone, carved by Matthias Weeks, marks the final resting place of one of Moultonborough's original proprietors. Active as both a prominent businessman and involved in political affairs at a local and state level, Nathaniel Shannon, along with Rev. Jeremiah Shaw, was one of the most respected men of his day. While it was said of him that he "bore rather hard on his workmen," Shannon "was very much looked up to," and people "always went to Squire Shannon to settle their disputes." A small man, Shannon "was very prompt in his decisions" and independent minded; as delegate to the Constitutional Convention, he had been instructed by his constituency, the towns of Moultonborough, Wolfeboro, Tuftonboro, and Ossipee, to reject the Constitution. Shannon instead voted for its ratification, a fellow townsman commenting years later that "I guess the people liked him all the better for it afterwards." Among the children of Nathaniel and his wife Mary was Dr. Thomas Shannon. All quoted material was taken from George Hodgdon's *Shannon Genealogy*. (Courtesy Sandra Barnes.)

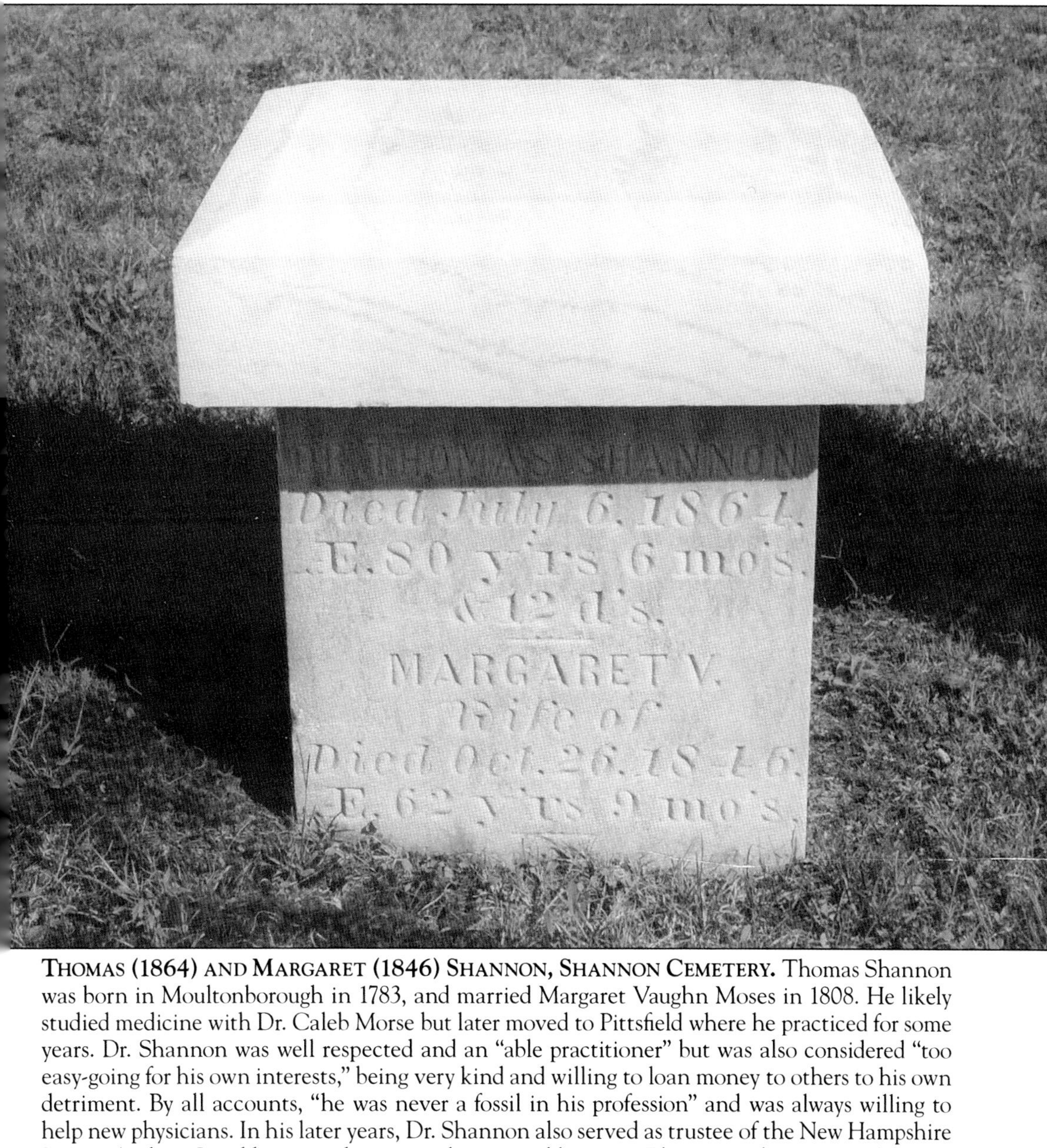

THOMAS (1864) AND MARGARET (1846) SHANNON, SHANNON CEMETERY. Thomas Shannon was born in Moultonborough in 1783, and married Margaret Vaughn Moses in 1808. He likely studied medicine with Dr. Caleb Morse but later moved to Pittsfield where he practiced for some years. Dr. Shannon was well respected and an "able practitioner" but was also considered "too easy-going for his own interests," being very kind and willing to loan money to others to his own detriment. By all accounts, "he was never a fossil in his profession" and was always willing to help new physicians. In his later years, Dr. Shannon also served as trustee of the New Hampshire Insane Asylum. In addition to this unusual square table-stone, Thomas and Margaret also each have their own individual gravestone nearby, her epitaph reading, in part, "God's glorious image freed from clay in Heaven's eternal sphere shall shine a star of day."

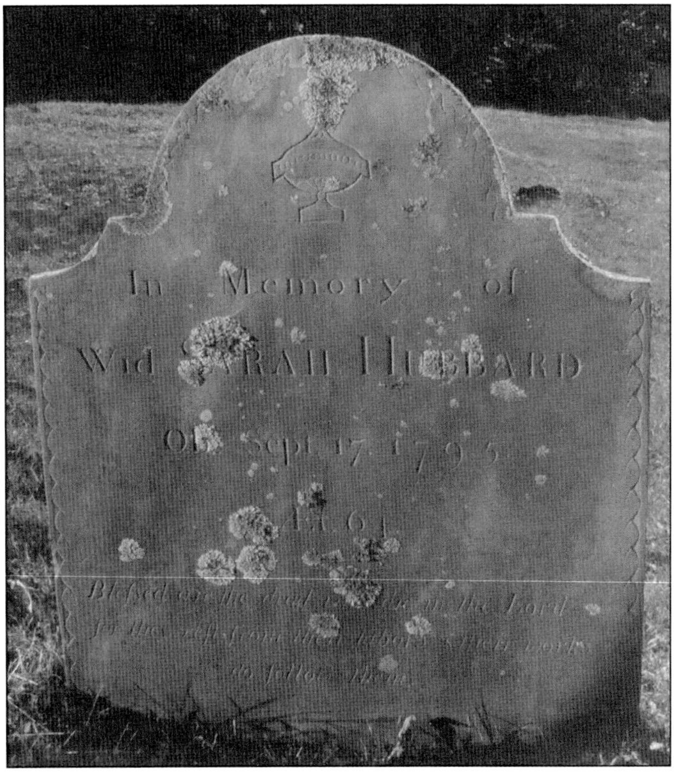

SARAH HUBBARD (1795), SHAW CEMETERY. The Shaw Cemetery is notable for its many fine gravestone carvings, including those crafted locally by Matthias Weeks and several from distant Portsmouth. However, none have come from so far away as this stone for "Widow" Sarah Hubbard, carved by Attleboro, Massachusetts, native Levi Maxcy. Sarah's husband was John Hubbard, who paid $11.50 for their pew in the meetinghouse in East Moultonborough in 1788.

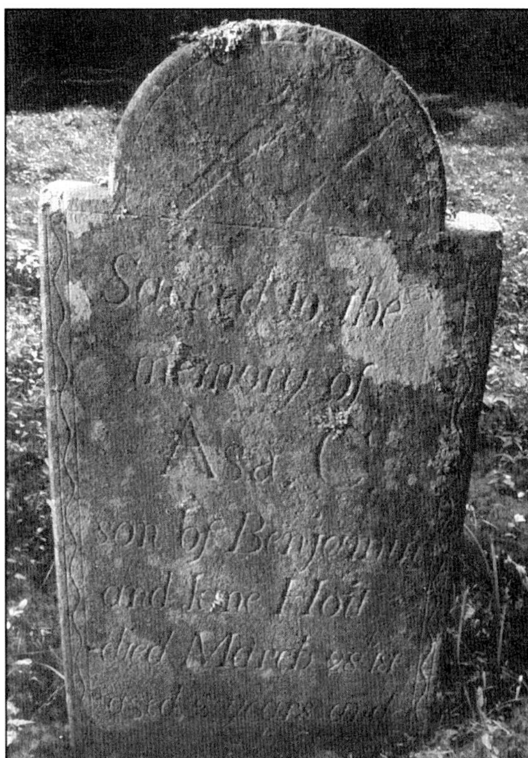

ASA HOIT (1815), SHAW CEMETERY. This interesting stone was carved by Matthias Weeks. The stone is unusual because of its Masonic motif, the compass and set-square, rarely seen on a child's gravestone. However, its presence is easily accounted for; the family arrived early in town, Nathan Hoit settling here in 1776. Asa's father, Benjamin, was the son of Col. Nathan Hoit, master of the first Masonic lodge in Carroll County.

EPHRAIM BRADBURY (1819), SHAW CEMETERY. Ephraim Bradbury was an early settler in Moultonborough, arriving in town by 1777. In March of that year, he was one of many town citizens who signed the Congregational church covenant. His gravestone is one of the easiest to spot in Shaw Cemetery due to its tall and narrow shape and shining white color and is thought to be the work of carver Matthias Weeks.

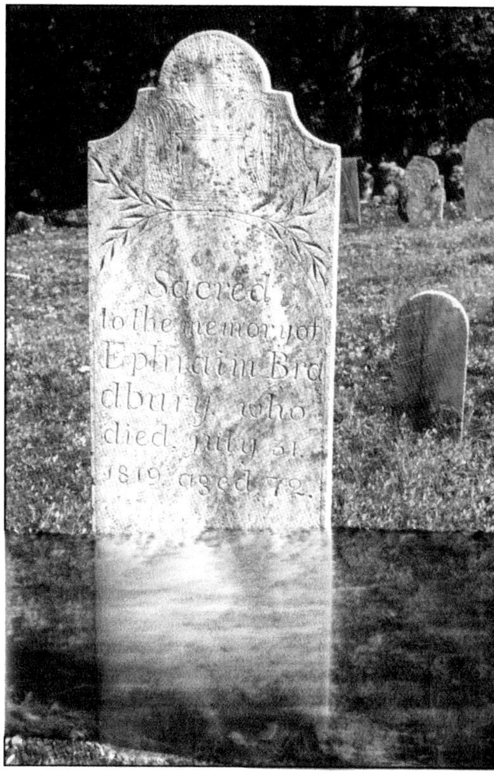

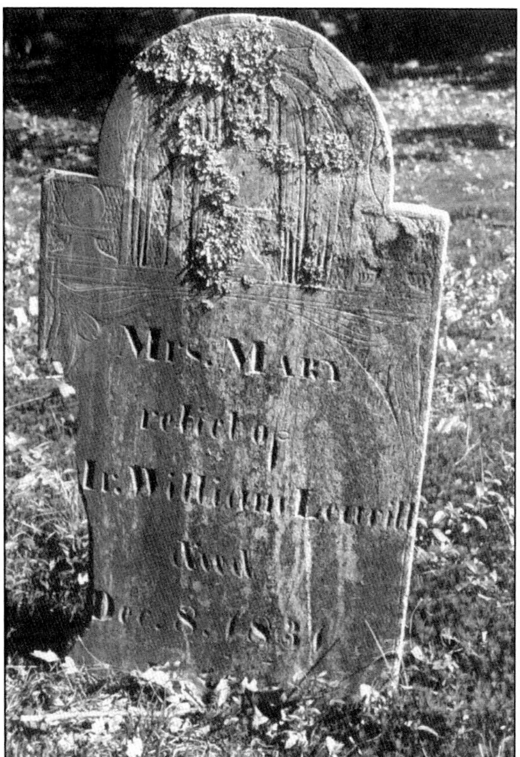

MARY LEAVITT (1831), SHAW CEMETERY. Little is known about Mary Leavitt or her husband William, who died in 1818 at the age of 67 and is buried nearby. They were members of the Congregational church by 1788, when William Leavitt purchased a pew for $14. Located near the west end door of the church, not far from the pulpit, their pew price was greater than that paid by Nathaniel Shannon.

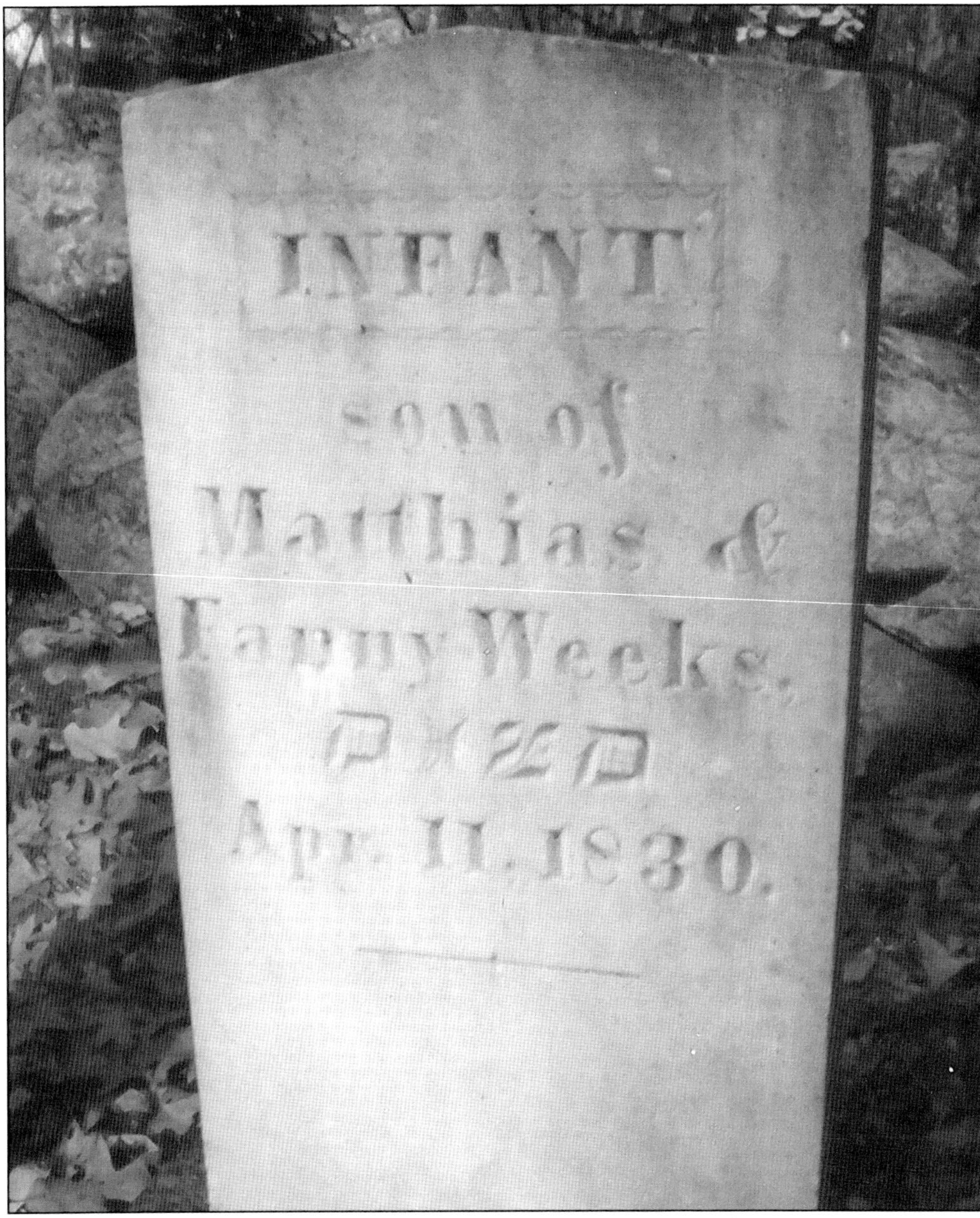

INFANT SON (1830) OF MATTHIAS WEEKS, SHAW CEMETERY. Matthias Weeks was born in Gilmanton in 1797, one of seven children of Matthias and Mary Weeks. He seems to have become a stonecutter by 1815, and in 1821, he married Fanny Morgan. In December 1829, Matthias Weeks bought land in Moultonborough "on the westerly side of the road leading to the meeting-house" from Jotham Lawrence. By this time, Fanny and Matthias had at least one son, Franklin, and the move in wintertime to a new residence across the lake could not have been easy. Things were made even more difficult by the fact that Fanny Weeks was pregnant. Whether due to the rigors of the move, severe weather, or the normal difficulties of early childhood so common at the time, the baby died in April 1830. Though Matthias was a gravestone carver, he did not carve this stone for his son, perhaps too grief-stricken to do so. Instead this stone was likely set some 10 or even 20 years after the infant's death, possibly carved or erected by Franklin Weeks.

ALBERT SHAW (1864), SHAW CEMETERY. Albert Shaw enlisted for Civil War service in 1861, in the 5th New Hampshire Regiment. Serving under Col. Edward Cross, Shaw survived bloody battle at such places as Fair Oaks, Antietam, Fredericksburg, Gettysburg, and Cold Harbor, only to die of disease at Point Lookout, Maryland. He is buried near his son Lonnie, aged four, born after his dad went off to war and died in 1866.

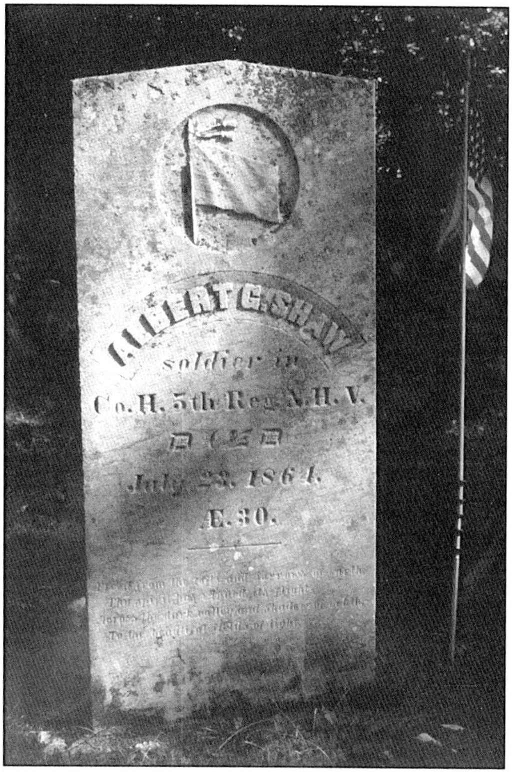

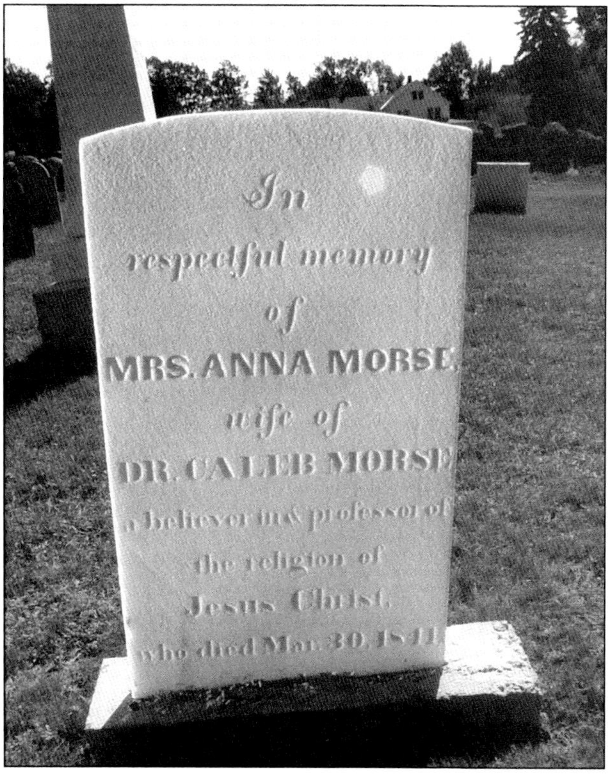

ANNA MORSE (1841), FREESE-HOLLAND HILL CEMETERY. Anna Ambrose Morse was the daughter of one of the earliest settlers in East Moultonborough and wife of one of its most outstanding citizens, Dr. Caleb Morse. Caleb came from Maine in 1780 and married Anna in 1783. Together they had 12 children. Dr. Morse practiced for 62 years in town before his death in 1843. Both were active in the Congregational church.

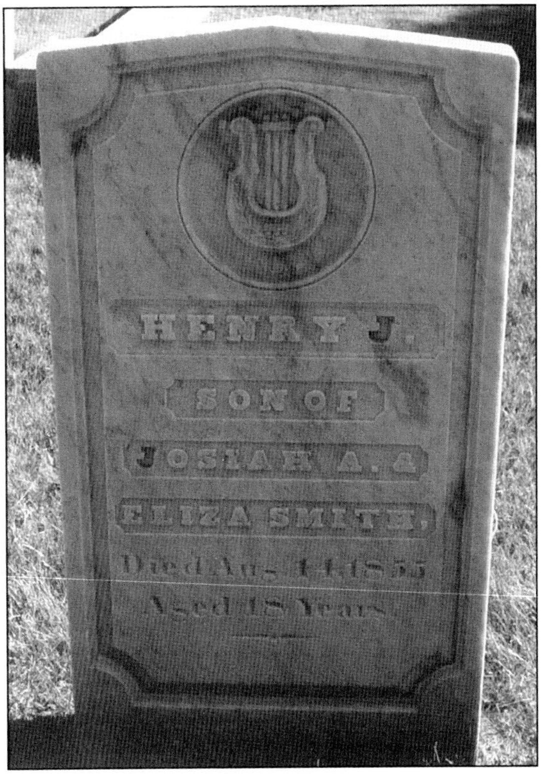

HENRY SMITH (1855), MIDDLE NECK CEMETERY. Most of the stones in this attractive cemetery date from the Victorian era. Carved out of marble, many have interesting motifs symbolic of love, salvation, and redemption. The harp shown on the gravestone for this young man is often indicative of Irish heritage but also, like the anchor, is a symbol of hope.

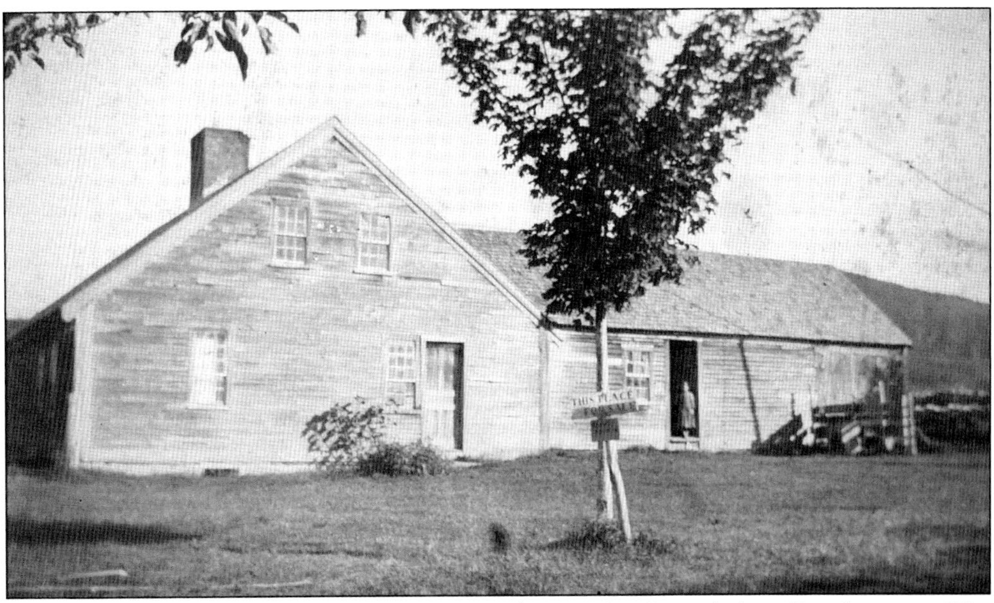

THE LEE FAMILY HOMESTEAD, BUILT 1792. The Lee family, including Revolutionary War soldier Ebenezer Lee, was prominent in the early settlement of Moultonborough. They lived in the settlement on Ossipee Mountain, 700 feet above the lake, and built this house that stayed in the family for 121 years. The land they once lived on and farmed is now the location of the Castle in the Clouds. (Courtesy Mary Dunn.)

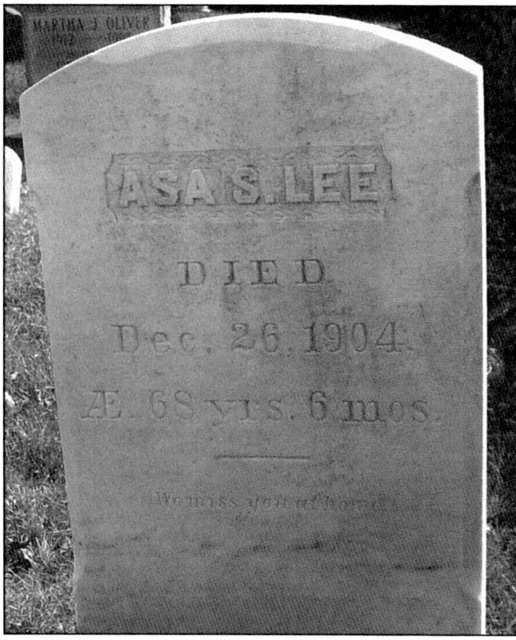

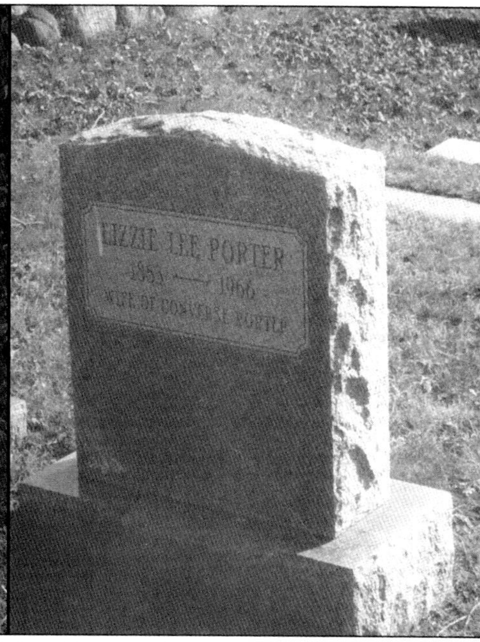

Asa Lee (1904) and Lizzie Lee Porter (1966), Lee Family Cemetery. Asa Lee's family, like generations before, worked the land. Indeed, farming was a way of life that involved the whole family, as is evidenced by the photograph below showing Asa and his daughter, young Lizzie, tending to their oxen. Nine years after Asa's death, millionaire Thomas Plante, the builder of the Castle in the Clouds, would ruthlessly pursue ownership of Lee's 150-acre homestead by erecting a "spite" fence, a horrible thing 20 feet high designed to block the view of Lake Winnipesaukee and painted an ugly color. The Lees fought Plante but, in the end, relented by selling their land to him at the price they wanted. The unneighborly Plante added insult to injury when he desecrated the family cemetery, but town folk would not tolerate this and forced Plante to restore the cemetery in full. (Bottom photograph courtesy Mary Dunn.)

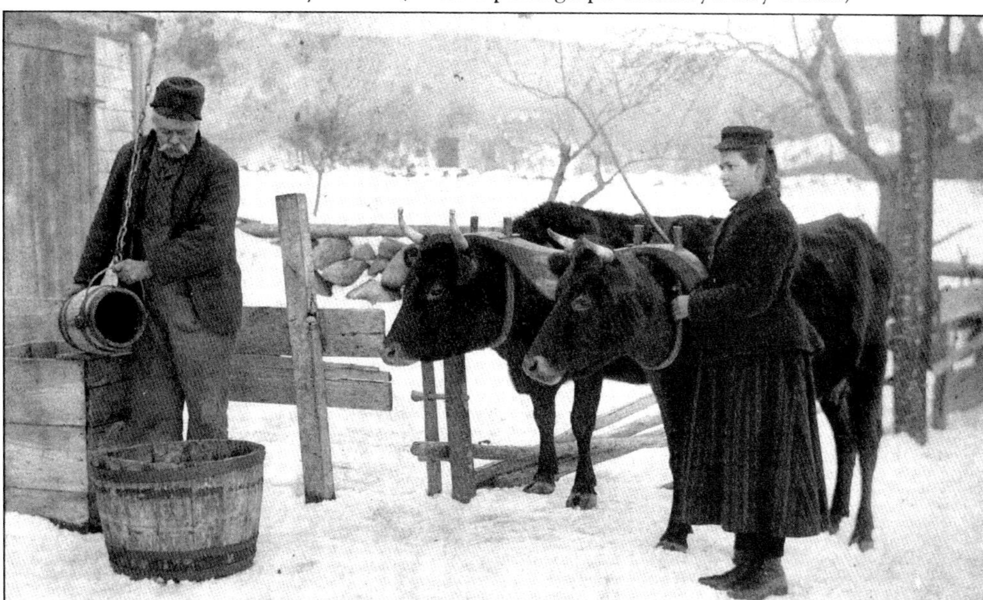

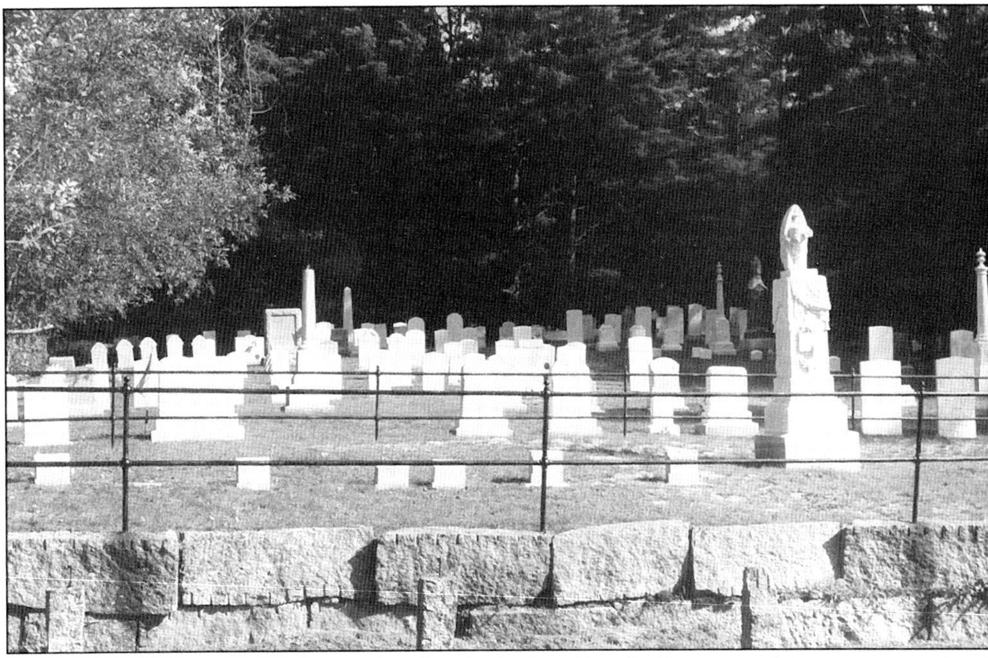

THE LEE CEMETERY. Not to be confused with the Lee Family Cemetery, this cemetery on Lee's Mill Road is one of the largest in Moultonborough and is notable for its many marble gravestones and monuments from the Victorian era. Prominent among those buried here are members of the Lee family that first settled in this part of Moultonborough.

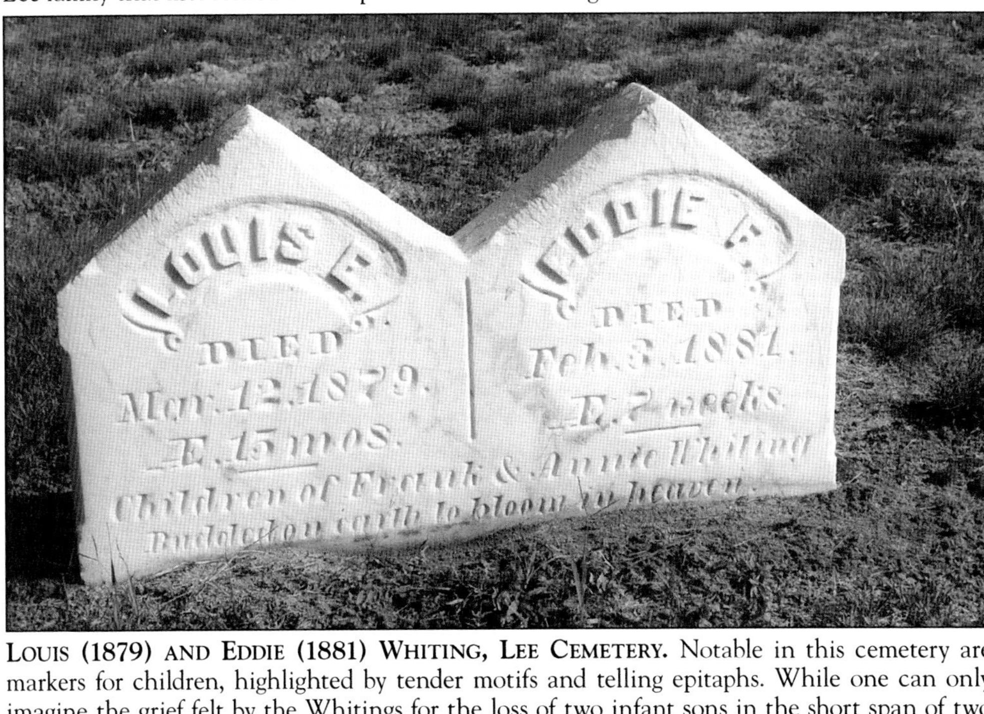

LOUIS (1879) AND EDDIE (1881) WHITING, LEE CEMETERY. Notable in this cemetery are markers for children, highlighted by tender motifs and telling epitaphs. While one can only imagine the grief felt by the Whitings for the loss of two infant sons in the short span of two years, their faith and hope in life after death is also clear, the babes' epitaph reading "Budded on earth to bloom in heaven."

Five

SANDWICH

Located on the shores of Squam Lake, Lake Winnipesaukee's smaller sister, Sandwich is the most northerly of the towns in this study. The land that now comprises the town was granted to a group of Exeter men in 1763–1764. The settling of Sandwich proceeded rapidly, and by November 1767, the town's first seven houses were built in the area of Little Pond. The first citizen, Orlando Weed, formerly of Gilmanton, received for his efforts 700 acres of land, seven cows, and £70 "lawful" money. Seven, indeed, was a lucky number in the early days of Sandwich.

The advance of religion in Sandwich during its early years is quite interesting. The first established church was that of the Baptist faith, with Rev. Jacob Jewell as its shepherd by 1776. A formal meetinghouse, replacing an earlier "primitive" church building, was built around 1793. Historic Rural Cemetery is located adjacent to this meetinghouse, still standing today though much altered, in true churchyard fashion, and the dates of its earlier markers, mostly of the fieldstone variety, leave no doubt that this cemetery was established about the same time as the first church building built on this spot.

Equally interesting are the Little Pond and the Quaker Cemeteries. Because the area of Little Pond was the first to be settled, the Little Pond Cemetery may be the oldest public cemetery in Sandwich. Not only are some of the town's earliest inhabitants buried here, but the gravestones themselves are fascinating. Many of the oldest were carved by Matthias Weeks of neighboring Moultonborough, but others came from carvers in more distant locales, such as Asa Risley Jr. of Hanover, Rowe and Hodge of Plymouth, Lorenzo Day of Rochester, and others not yet identified. Such "imported" stones are indicative of Sandwich's early prominence and the corresponding wealth of its citizens.

No less compelling is the Quaker Cemetery established around 1776. Members of this society came to Sandwich early and were numerous enough by 1802 to warrant the establishment of their own Sandwich Monthly Meeting. It is estimated that from 1802 to 1833, there were in excess of some 700 Quakers in Sandwich. Among the prominent family names mentioned are the Varneys, Hoags, and Beedes. Like most Quaker cemeteries, that in Sandwich is simple, with many stones within only crudely lettered, or just plain fieldstones, and is in stark contrast to other local cemeteries. This alone, and the historical "feel" that this important site exudes, makes it well worth visiting.

Sandwich's varying topography, from mountains in the north and Squam Lake to the south, meant that the town's early inhabitants were scattered over a wide area in such communities as Center Sandwich, North Sandwich, East Sandwich, Sandwich Lower Corner, and an "embryo city" at Squam Lake, which died out soon after a road to nearby Thornton through Sandwich Notch was opened in 1801. Because of this, Sandwich has more cemeteries, over 90 in number and some now vanished, than any town in the area.

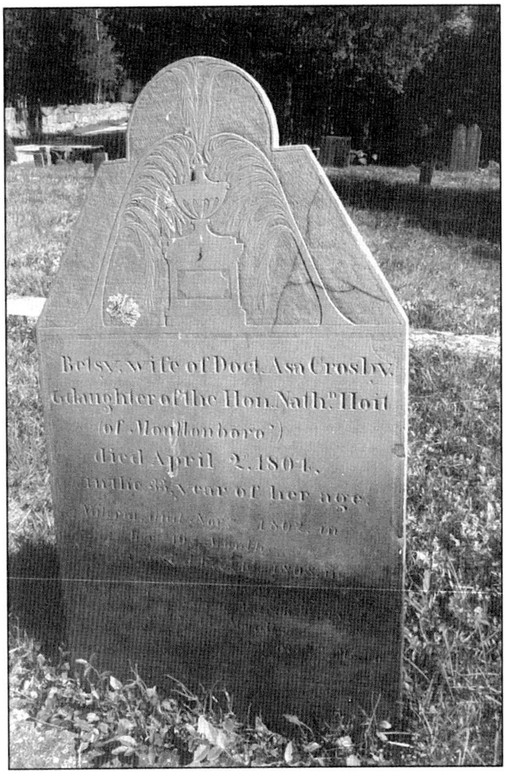

BETSY CROSBY (1804), LITTLE POND CEMETERY. Betsy Crosby's husband was one of the most prominent men in Sandwich, while her father was equally prominent in nearby Moultonborough, serving as an officer in the Revolutionary War. This stone for Betsy was erected at least nine years after her death, as the epitaph below her own records the deaths of her children Valeria (1802), Priscilla (1808), and Charles and Robert (1813).

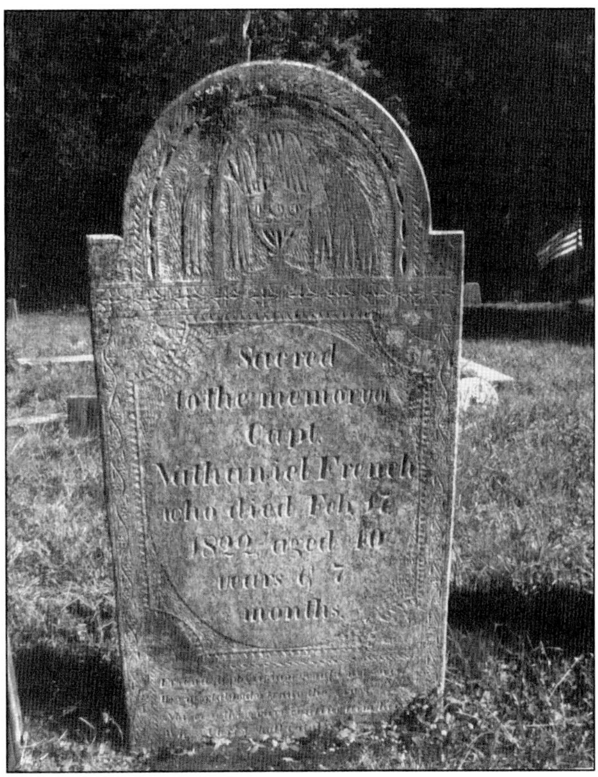

NATHANIEL FRENCH (1822), LITTLE POND CEMETERY. Nathaniel French was the son of one of Sandwich's most influential early citizens, Ezekiel French. Born July 9, 1781, he married Grace Crosby, and together they had two sons. French earned the title of captain from his militia service. His gravestone was carved by Matthias Weeks and is one of his most impressive stones.

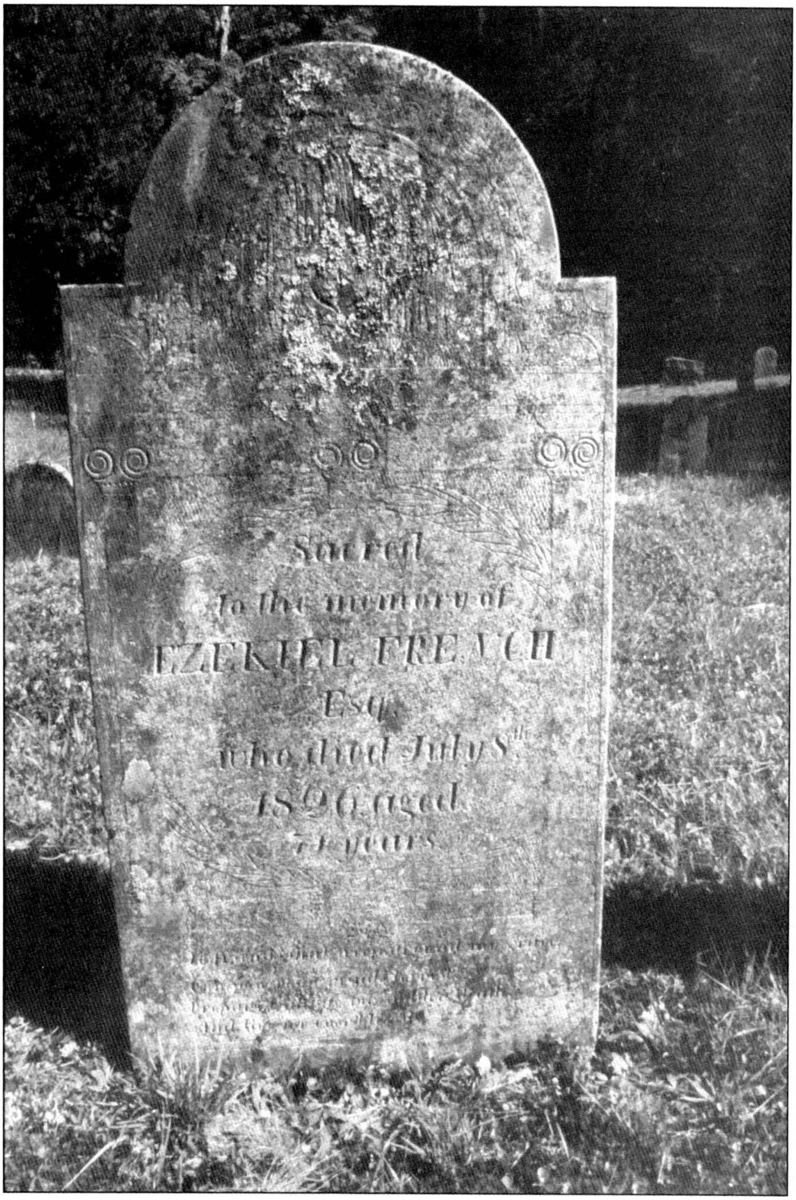

EZEKIEL FRENCH (1826), LITTLE POND CEMETERY. This gravestone marks the final resting place of early Sandwich settler Ezekiel French. Born in Deerfield, New Hampshire, in 1754, French learned the trade of a carpenter, practicing in Epping, and served in the Revolution. By the end of the war, French moved to Sandwich and married Phoebe Weed in 1778. Living the remainder of his life at his farm on Wentworth Hill, Ezekiel and Phoebe had nine children. An influential citizen, Ezekiel served for many years as a selectman and also served as a surveyor and town representative. However, he is best remembered as the architect and builder of the First Congregational Church in Sandwich, erected on land the Congregational Society purchased from him in 1825. The church, now gone, was completed in the summer of 1825, with 70-year-old Ezekiel supervising the building. On the day the frame was raised, he was there with the words "Are you all ready" and with his workers' affirmative reply commanded, "Then take it up," staying perched on the frame until it was set in position.

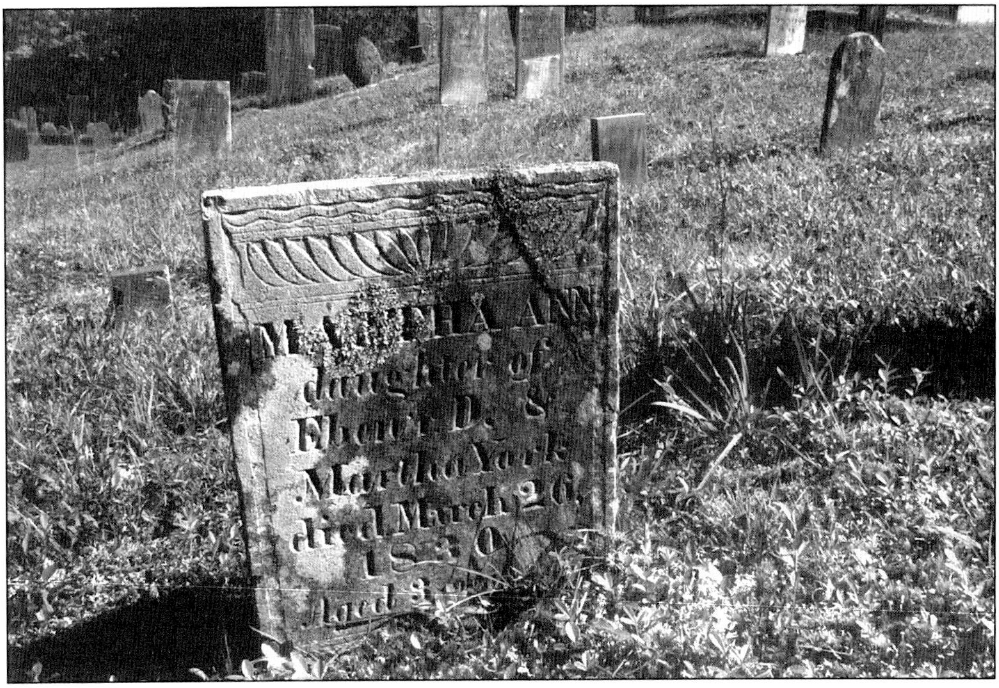

MARTHA ANN YORK (1830), LITTLE POND CEMETERY. The little girl buried here, the daughter of Ebenezer and Martha York, was just three years old at her death. Her simple stone, decorated with a flower petal border, was carved by Matthias Weeks of nearby Moultonborough. This was not the last tragedy the Yorks suffered; another child of theirs died just a year and a half later.

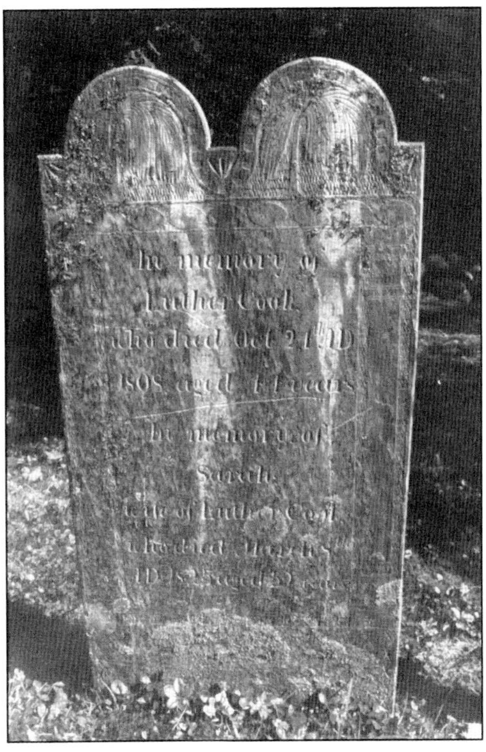

LUTHER (1808) AND SARAH (1825) COOK, LITTLE POND CEMETERY. This unusual double gravestone was carved by Matthias Weeks. Luther Cook's more well-known extended family members and descendants included Sandwich's second doctor, Lot Cook, who came here from Temple, New Hampshire, in 1805 and died in 1819, longtime Sandwich resident Joel Cook, and War of 1812 veteran and early abolitionist John Cook, who died in 1887.

GEORGE YORK (1831), LITTLE POND CEMETERY. Likely carved by Matthias Weeks of Moultonborough, this gravestone for young George York, only seven years old, is quite unusual. Not only does it have a traditional motif at the top, in this case a funeral urn, it also has a weeping willow tree beneath the epitaph.

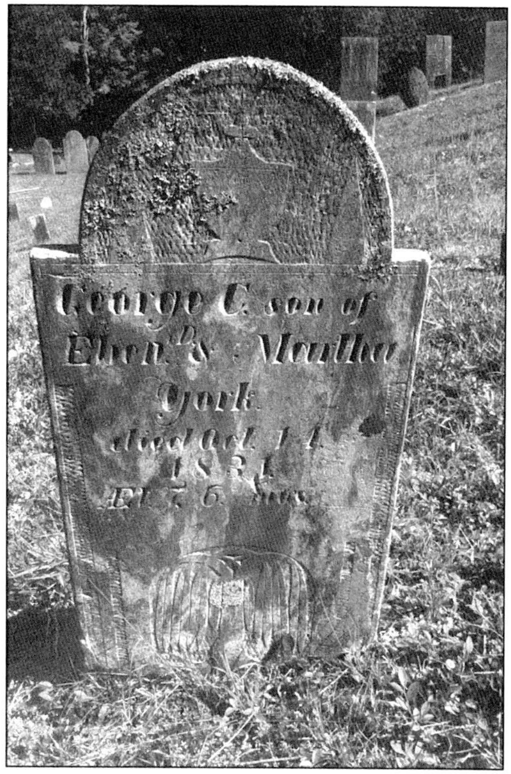

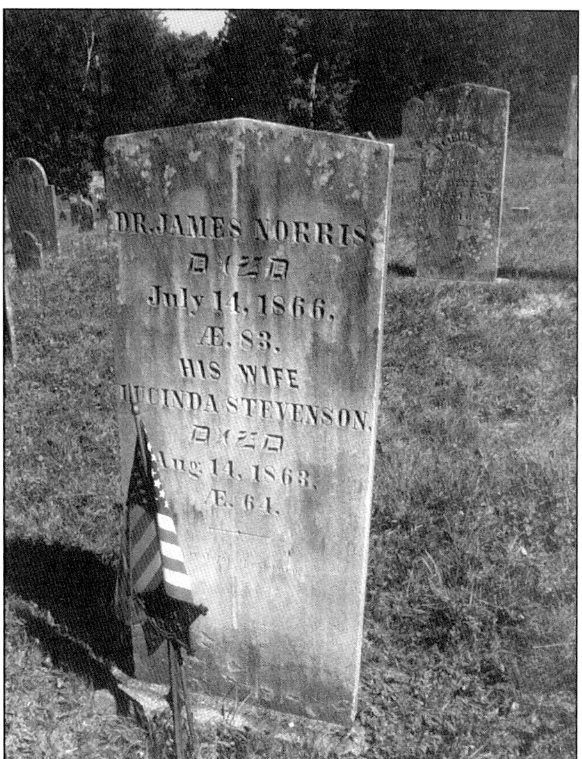

JAMES NORRIS (1866) AND LUCINDA STEVENSON (1863), LITTLE POND CEMETERY. James Norris was "a physician of thorough learning." His first years as a doctor were spent in the U.S. Navy, receiving his baptism under fire as a surgeon in the War of 1812 during the battle between the USS *Enterprise* and HMS *Boxer* off Portland Light. After his military service, Norris moved to Sandwich to practice medicine more peacefully.

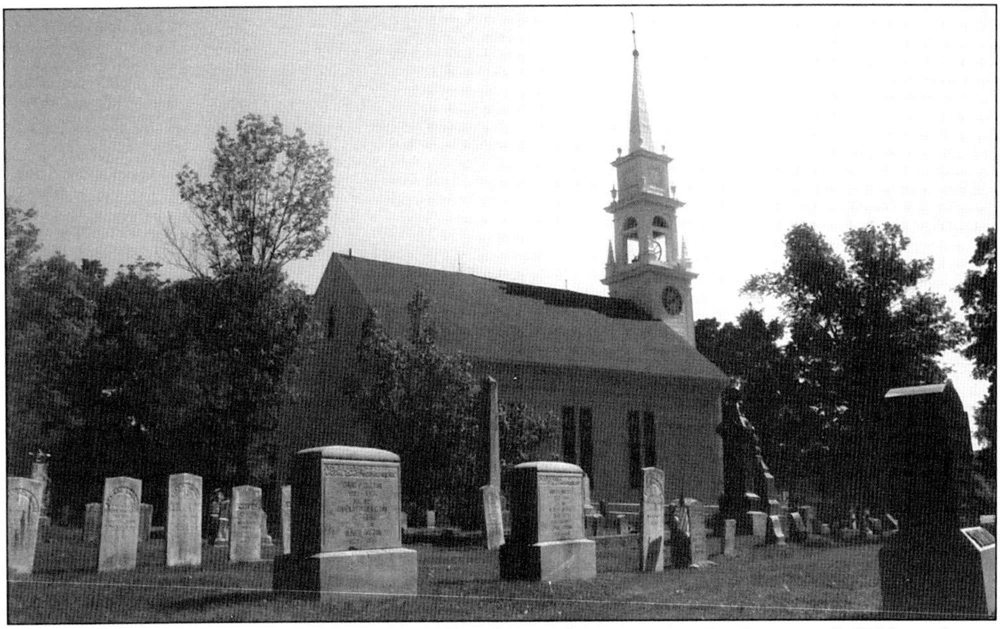

SANDWICH OLD MEETINGHOUSE. The church on this site was built around 1793 and was extensively remodeled in 1847. In the early years, it was used by both Free Will Baptists and Methodists on an alternating basis until the Methodists built their own church in 1825. Through all these years, the adjoining churchyard, Rural Cemetery, has continued in use, and the gravestones found within help to document the changing times.

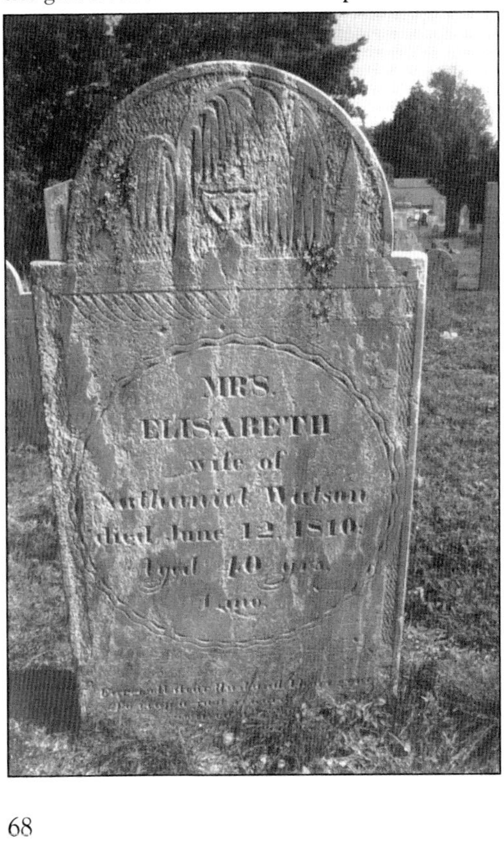

ELISABETH WATSON (1810), RURAL CEMETERY. While little is known about Elizabeth Watson, her final resting place is one of the oldest dated burials within Rural Cemetery. However, despite its early 1810 date, this gravestone by Matthias Weeks is backdated. It was not carved until a later date, maybe as many as 10 or 20 years, perhaps to replace an original marker that was either broken or more plain in appearance.

WILLIAM HAM (1864), RURAL CEMETERY. Born in Farmington, William Ham enlisted as sergeant in the 12th New Hampshire Regiment for Center Harbor in August 1862. Among the Civil War's older recruits, he fought at Gettysburg and Chancellorsville and was promoted to second lieutenant in January 1864. Ham's luck ran out when he was one his regiment's numerous wounded at Cold Harbor on June 3, 1864, and subsequently died on June 15.

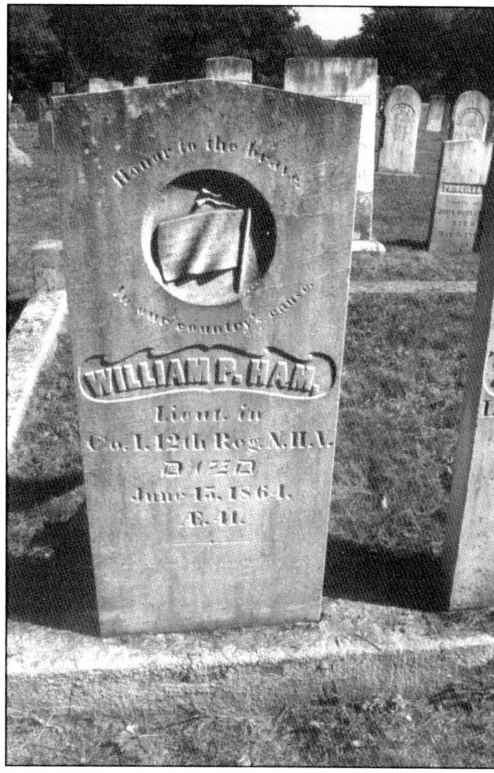

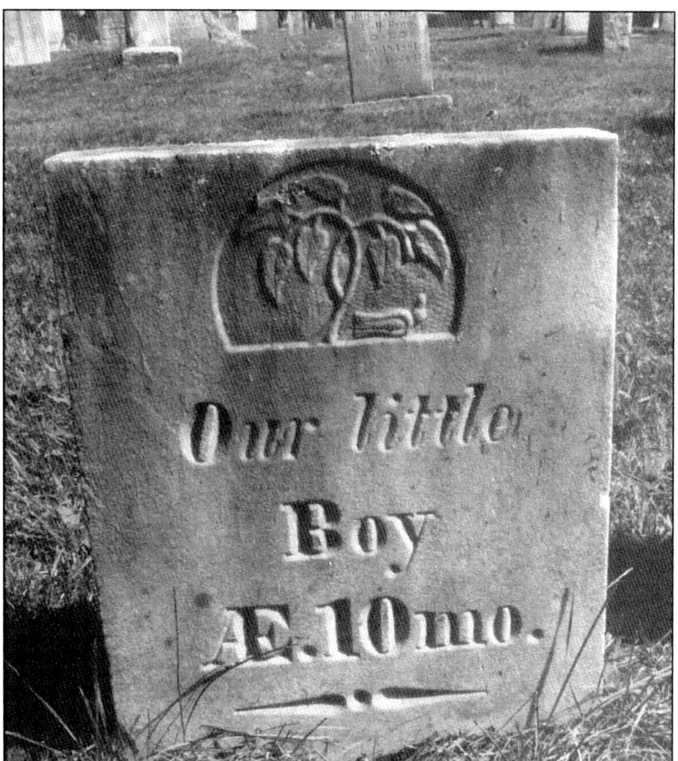

"OUR LITTLE BOY," RURAL CEMETERY. This unusual and attractive little gravestone marks the burial site of an infant son of William Ham and his wife. It is located close to the marker for his father, and is notable for the small peacock sitting under a group of what appears to be morning glories. Both are symbols of hope, salvation, and resurrection in Christian tradition.

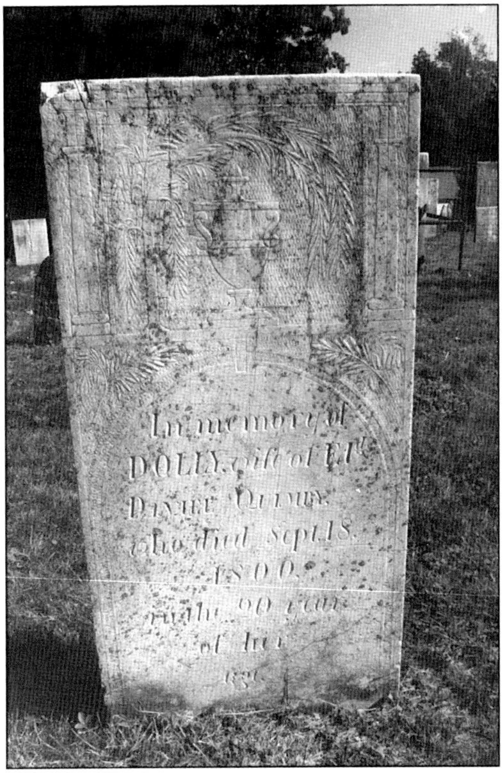

DOLLY QUIMBY (1800), RURAL CEMETERY. Dolly Quimby was the wife of Free Will Baptist elder Daniel Quimby. Elder Quimby resided in Sandwich from 1781 to 1816 and was called "an industrious and successful minister." He worked very closely with evangelist John Colby and likely traveled with him to many of his trips "in every part of the United States and Provinces," perhaps an indicator that his wife died while he was away from home.

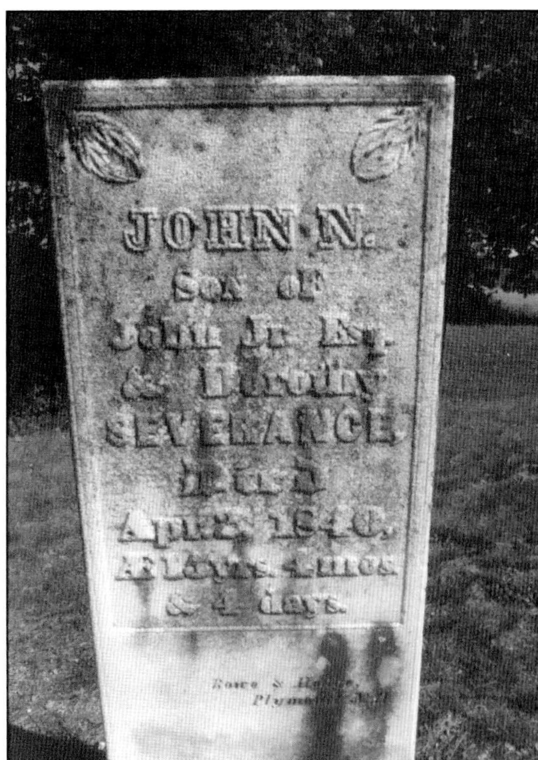

JOHN SEVERANCE (1840), RURAL CEMETERY. Young John Severance, passing away while on the verge of manhood, was the son of John Severance Jr., a onetime town selectman, and the grandson of Capt. John Severance, who arrived in town by 1780 and married one of the daughters of Sandwich's first minister, Elder Jacob Jewell. Note on this stone the name of its maker, Rowe and Hodge of Plymouth, at lower right.

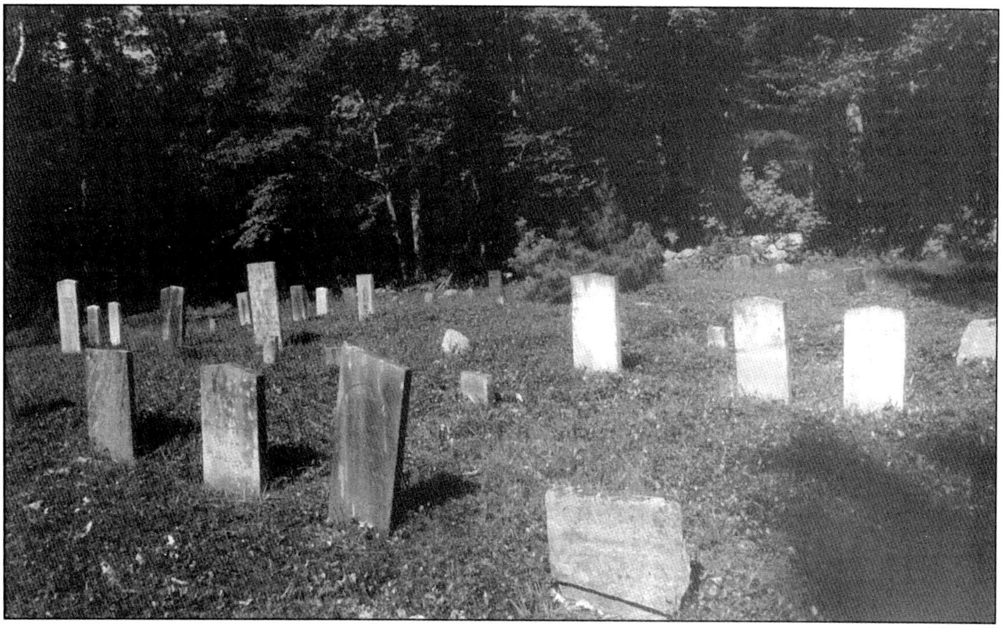

QUAKER CEMETERY. The Quakers came early to Sandwich from places such as Dover, Rochester, Weare, and Gilmanton and, by 1777, had about 40 members. With such families as the Hoags, Varneys, Beedes, and Hoits predominating, the Quakers were a vibrant part of Sandwich for over 80 years. Their numbers declined with the nation's westward movement beginning in the 1850s, though their presence in North Sandwich remained strong for another generation.

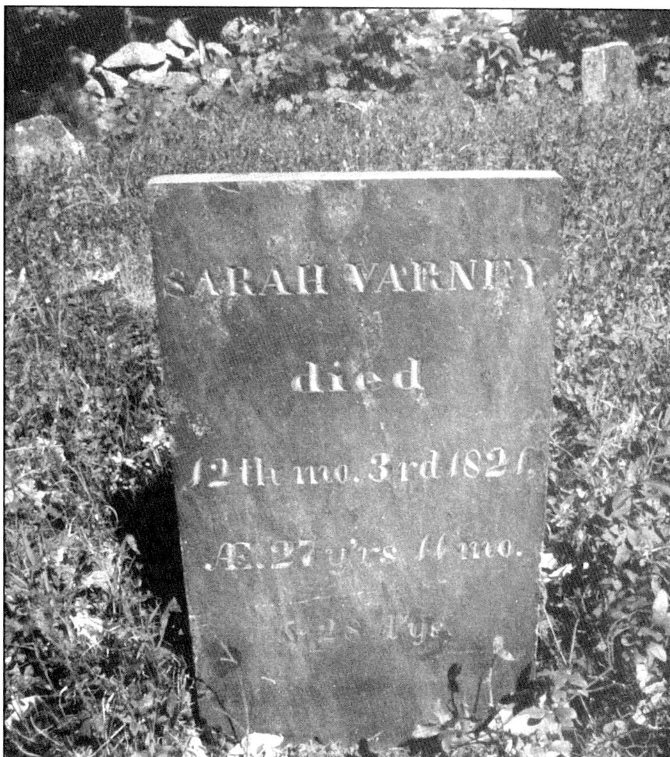

SARAH VARNEY (1821), QUAKER CEMETERY. Many Varney family members are to be found here, an indicator of their prominence in Sandwich. In their early years in America, Quakers followed the older custom of not marking their burial places with gravestones of any kind. Thus, many Quaker cemeteries like this one are devoid of gravestones marking early burials. Note how Sarah Varney's death on December 3, 1821, is noted on her gravestone.

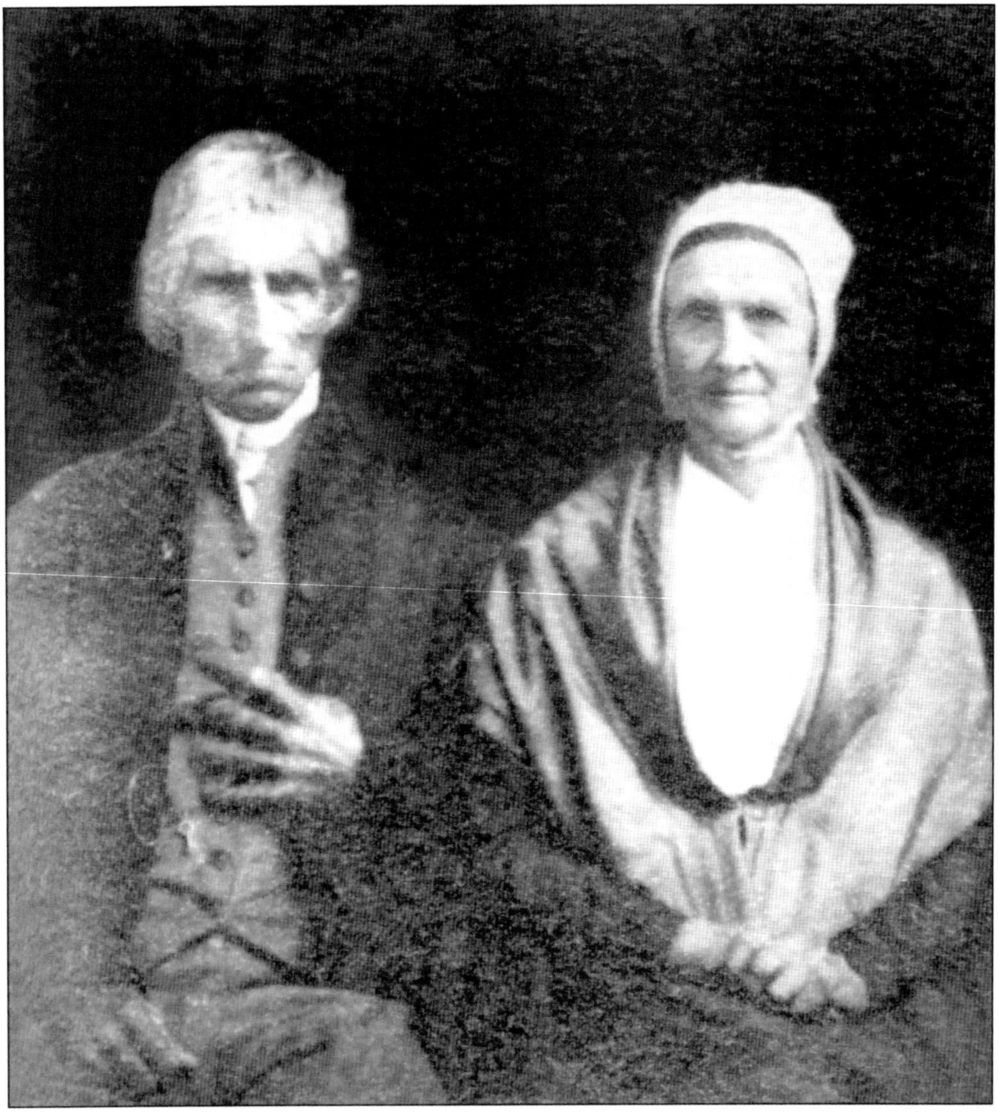

JOSHUA AND HANNAH HOAG PORTRAIT, C. 1855. The Hoags were one of the most prominent Quaker families in Sandwich. Joshua was the son of Enoch Hoag, who arrived here from Dover in 1786 and was a goldsmith. Hannah, born 1776, came from an equally distinguished Quaker family, the daughter of Benjamin Scribner. Benjamin arrived in town early and was one who refused to sign the 1776 Association Test, due to his unwillingness, based on his religious principles, to "with arms oppose the hostile proceedings of the British Fleets and Armies." Hannah grew up on the family farm on Scribner Hill, married Joshua Hoag, and lived with him on their place known as the Goodwin farm. That Joshua was a farmer is evidenced by his hands, large and arthritic looking. Notable, too, are the Quaker garments of Hannah. Joshua died in September 1859, while Hannah Hoag died in October 1861. It is believed they are buried in the Quaker Cemetery. (Photograph from Anna Scattergood Hoag's *The Record of My Ancestry; the Hoag-Ewing Family*, 1938, courtesy Sarah Blanchet.)

Six

New Hampton and Center Harbor

The early history of both of these towns is intimately tied to that of Moultonborough. Both were part of a parcel of land called Moultonborough Addition, granted to Hampton's Col. Jonathan Moulton in 1765 and settled about that same time.

Colonel Moulton petitioned for separate incorporation as a town for both Moultonborough and Moultonborough Addition in 1773, but it was not granted. In late 1777, yet another petition was made, and this time it succeeded. In honor of Moulton's hometown, the new town on this "small gore of land" was called New Hampton. The reason for the separation of the two townships only made sense and followed in the tradition of second-generation New Hampshire towns. It was simply too much of a hardship for settlers in Moultonborough Addition to travel to attend church at East Moultonborough or to attend to town and business affairs at Center Moultonborough or Moultonborough Falls. The 20-odd miles from the southern border of what is now New Hampton to Moultonborough today seems like an easy ride, but back in the days of horse and wagon travel, it was a long and arduous journey over hilly terrain and involved several stream and river crossings.

New Hampton is divided into several distinct areas today. The town center is located about seven miles south of the lake, close to the Pemigewasset River. It is here that the town's first church was built and the Village Cemetery, with burials dating back to at least 1815, is found. The area closest to Lake Winnipesaukee is known as the Winona District. Here are found many family and neighborhood cemeteries, the most interesting of those being the Robert Smith Cemetery, the sadly neglected Robinson Cemetery, and the unusual Boynton Cemetery, which sits on a boundary line and lies partly in New Hampton and part in Meredith.

The town of Center Harbor, occupying the strip of land between Squam Lake and Lake Winnipesaukee, was set off from New Hampton in 1797. Its first petition for township in 1788 was denied. Now a popular tourist town, Center Harbor was once "somewhat celebrated as a watering-place," according to one early historian. Relatively small in land area compared to the other towns in this study, Center Harbor has correspondingly fewer cemeteries, and many persons prominent in early town affairs are buried in cemeteries in neighboring Moultonborough and Meredith. While family cemeteries predominate in Center Harbor, one of the most interesting being the Hawkins Cemetery on College Road, the town's oldest public cemetery is located across from the old Congregational church, built in 1837, and pleasantly located on a spot with a fine view of the waters of Center Harbor. Established nearly 200 years ago when one its first "occupants," selectman Charles Little, was buried here, this cemetery has witnessed the coming and going of steamships on the lake from its beginnings down to the present day.

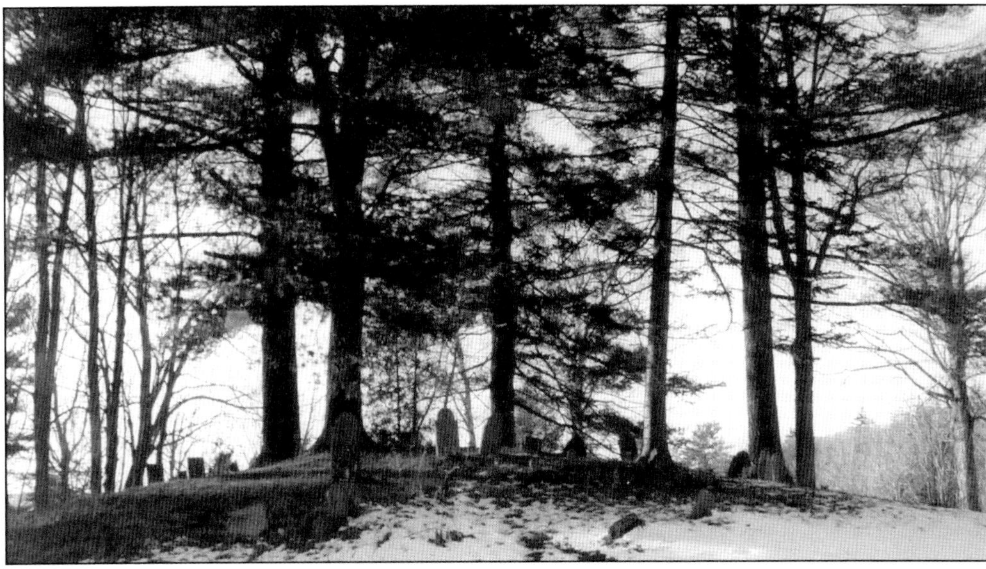

NEW HAMPTON VILLAGE CEMETERY. The establishment of this cemetery was provided for in 1800 when Salmon Hibbard was ordained as the town's first Congregational minister. Hibbard was granted 150 acres of land, "exclusive of six acres to be round the meeting house for the convenience and accommodation of the town as a common burying ground." This view shows the oldest part of Village Cemetery, now much expanded into three sections.

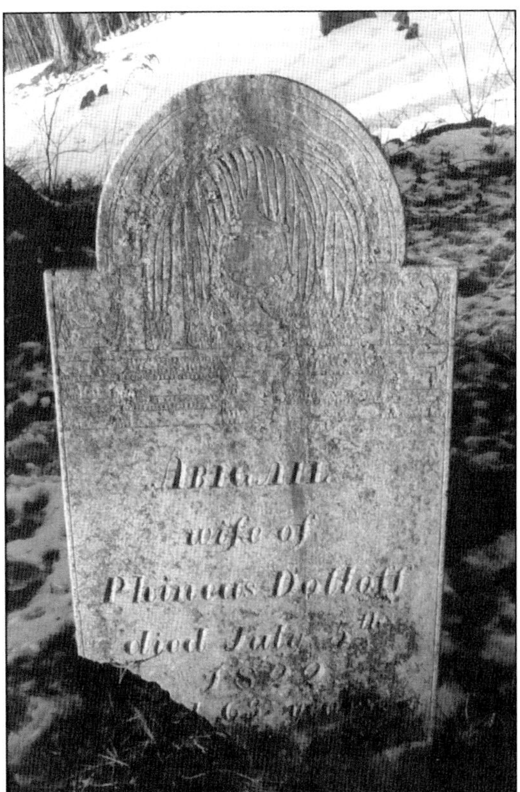

ABIGAIL DOLLOFF (1822), VILLAGE CEMETERY. Phineas Dolloff was one of the early settlers in New Hampton, and the road built from his homestead was an important route to the southwest part of town. Dolloff Hill is named after his family. This stone for Abigail Dolloff, located on a knoll in the oldest part of the cemetery, is one of the oldest to be found here and was carved by Matthias Weeks.

JOHN CALVIN GORDON (1871), VILLAGE CEMETERY. John Calvin Gordon, born in New Hampton, was a farmer and wool manufacturer, making stockings and gloves. He is remembered as deacon of the Calvinistic Baptist Church, town clerk, and "a man of sterling and inflexible character, highly respected and universally trusted." His epitaph, carved by the Day brothers, reads, "And after he had served his own generation, by the will of God fell on sleep."

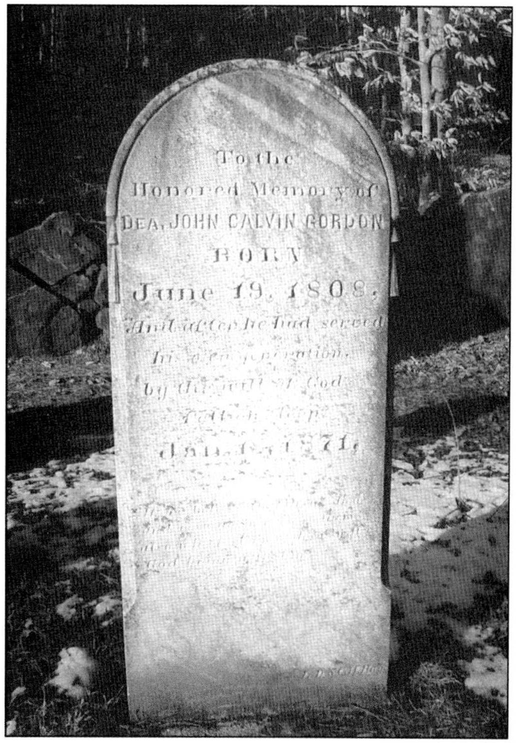

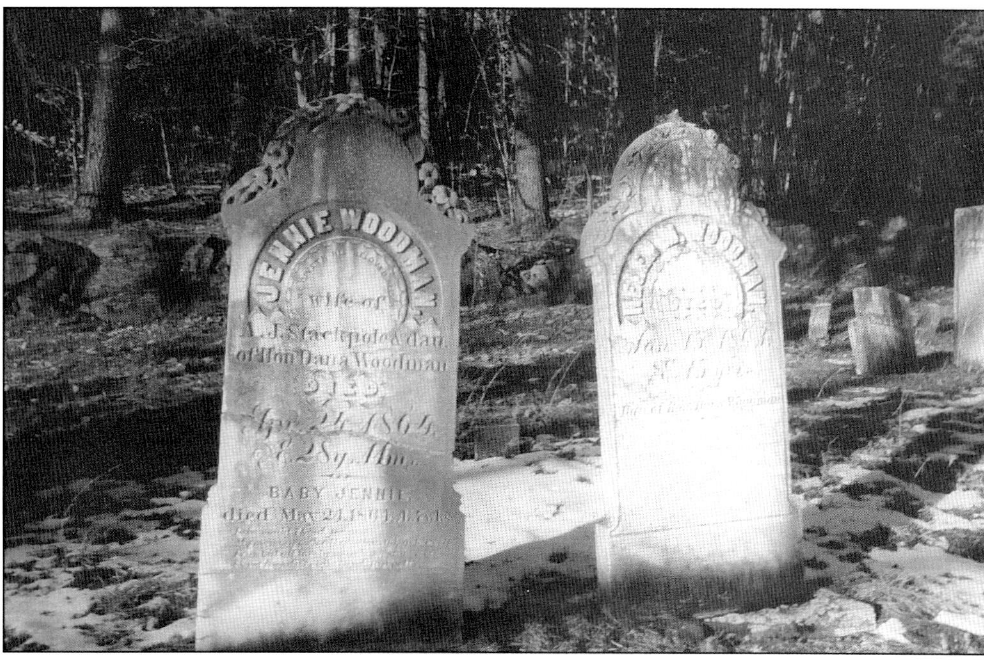

JENNIE STACKPOLE AND DAUGHTER (1864) AND HELEN WOODMAN (1863), VILLAGE CEMETERY. Dana Woodman, a graduate of the New Hampton Literary Institute, was one of the most prominent local and state officials of his day. Sadly, two of his children died young. Helen (right) died at age 15, while Jennie Woodman Stackpole probably died from the effects of childbirth, her namesake daughter following her to the grave a month later.

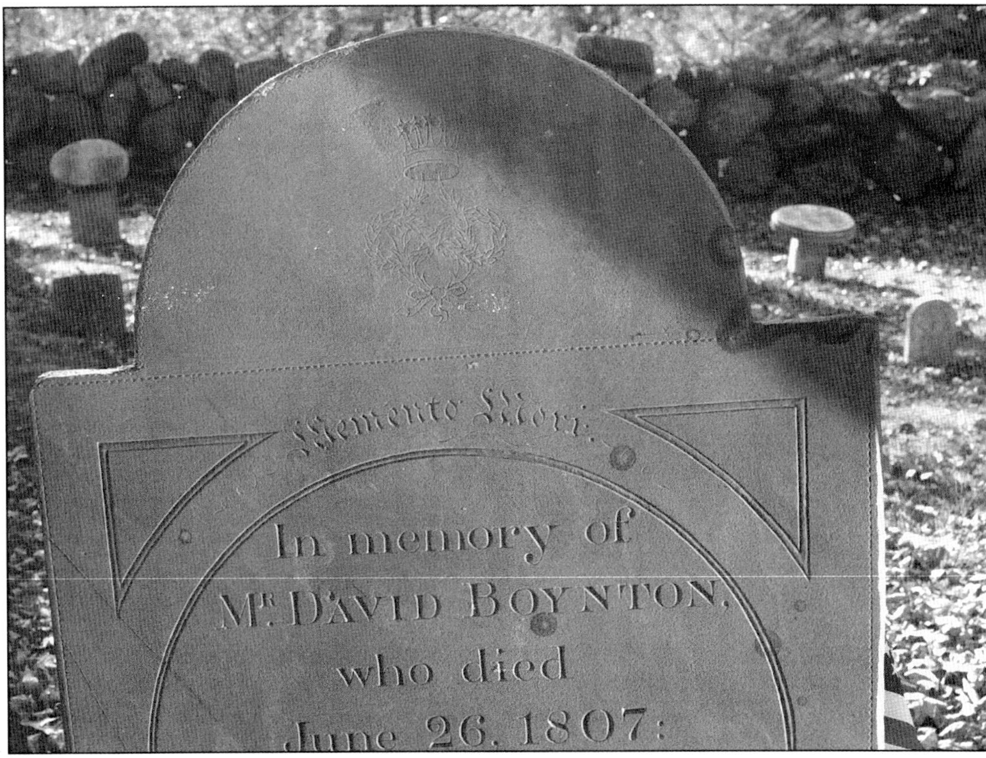

DAVID BOYNTON (1807), BOYNTON CEMETERY. This stone is one of the most unusual gravestones in the area, and one of the oldest. It was carved by Alpheus Cary and is the only known gravestone by this carver found in the area. In fact, Cary was noted for his fine carving style (see detail at left), and his works were even imported to such far-off places as Hawaii. Despite the state's close proximity to his Boston-area workshop, relatively few of Cary's stones are found in New Hampshire. Boynton and his brother Richard, a prominent General Court representative, arrived here from Massachusetts around 1790. David Boynton was a tavern keeper and is buried on land owned by his brother. That the Boyntons were a family of wealth and maintained their Massachusetts ties is evidenced by this costly gravestone.

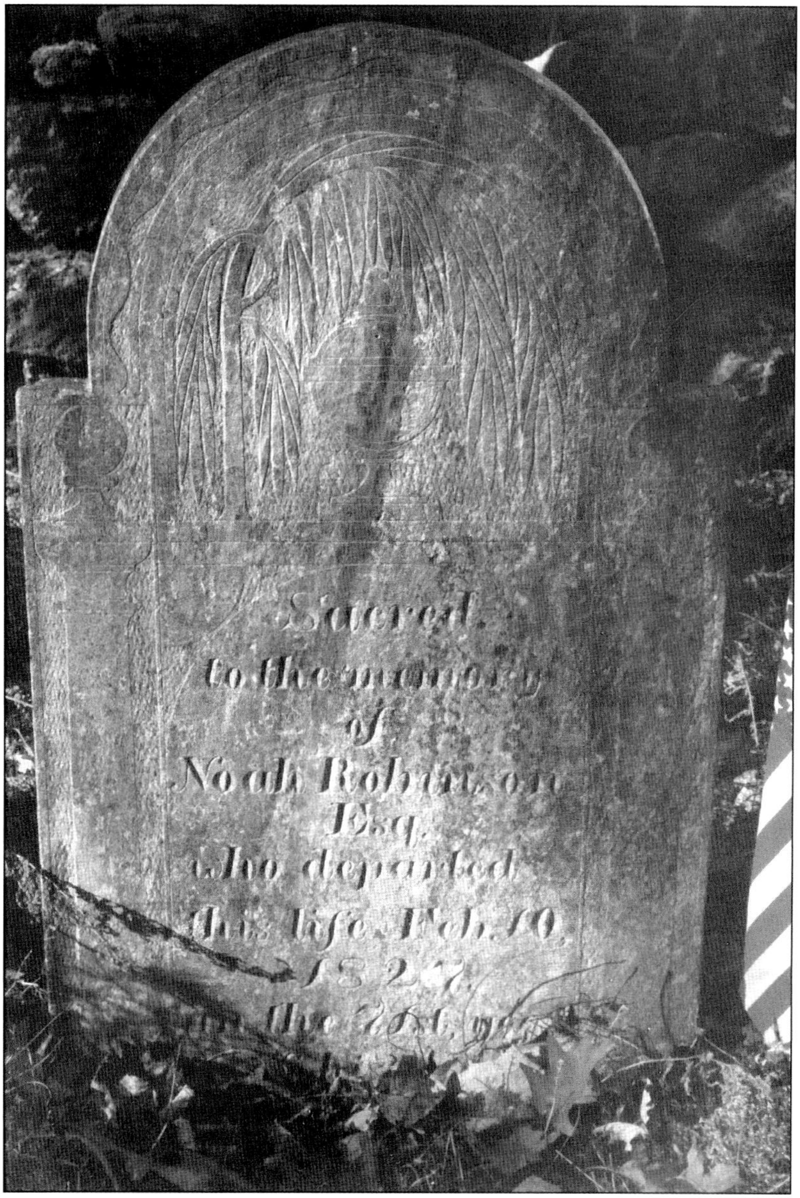

NOAH ROBINSON (1827), ROBINSON CEMETERY. This cemetery is one of the most interesting in New Hampton and also the most endangered. Noah Robinson was prominent as an early town settler and moderator of town meetings for over 20 years but also saw incredible service in the Revolutionary War. He enlisted early in 1775 and served until 1781, being promoted from private to captain by 1779. He was at the winter battles of Trenton and Princeton in 1776–1777, partaking in General Washington's famed crossing of the icy Delaware River. Now a sergeant, Robinson continued serving in the 2nd New Hampshire Regiment. In September 1777, he fought at the Battle of Bemis Heights in Saratoga under Lt. Col. Winborn Adams and saw bloody action. Though his regiment helped turn the tide and save the day, Robinson's commander, Winborn Adams, was killed in action. After this battle, Robinson was promoted to officer's rank as an ensign and went on to fight in such battles as Monmouth and Newtown. Described as "aggressive" and "dignified," Robinson was a highly respected and powerful man.

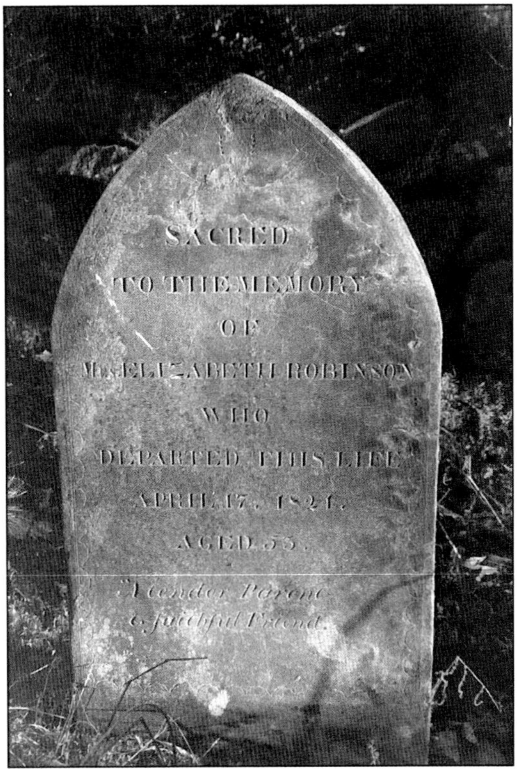

ELIZABETH ROBINSON (1824), ROBINSON CEMETERY. Noah Robinson owned a large farm in New Hampton and, with his three wives, had a large family. Elizabeth, probably his last wife, was younger than Noah by 14 years. Her Gothic arch–style stone, with its scalloped border and small funeral urn at top, is most unusual for the area. Its carver is unknown.

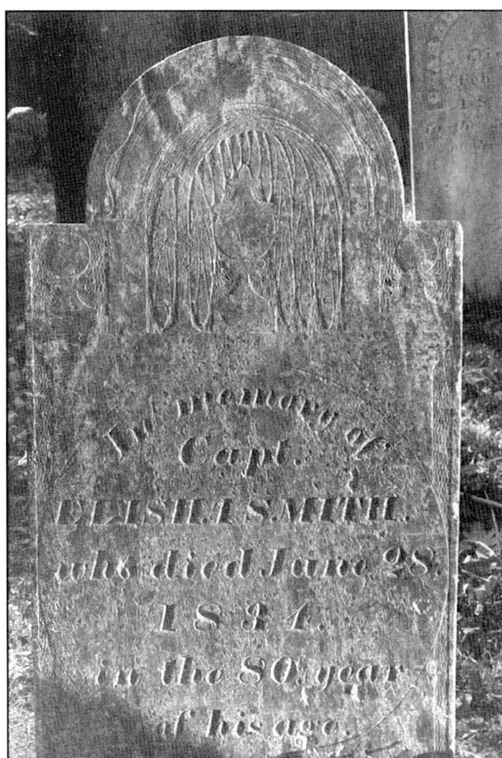

ELISHA SMITH (1834), ELISHA SMITH CEMETERY. The Smith family was large in New Hampton and had several branches. Elisha Smith may have gained his military title through service in the Revolutionary War or, more likely, as a local militia officer. His gravestone was carved by Moultonborough's Matthias Weeks and is a typical example of his later work.

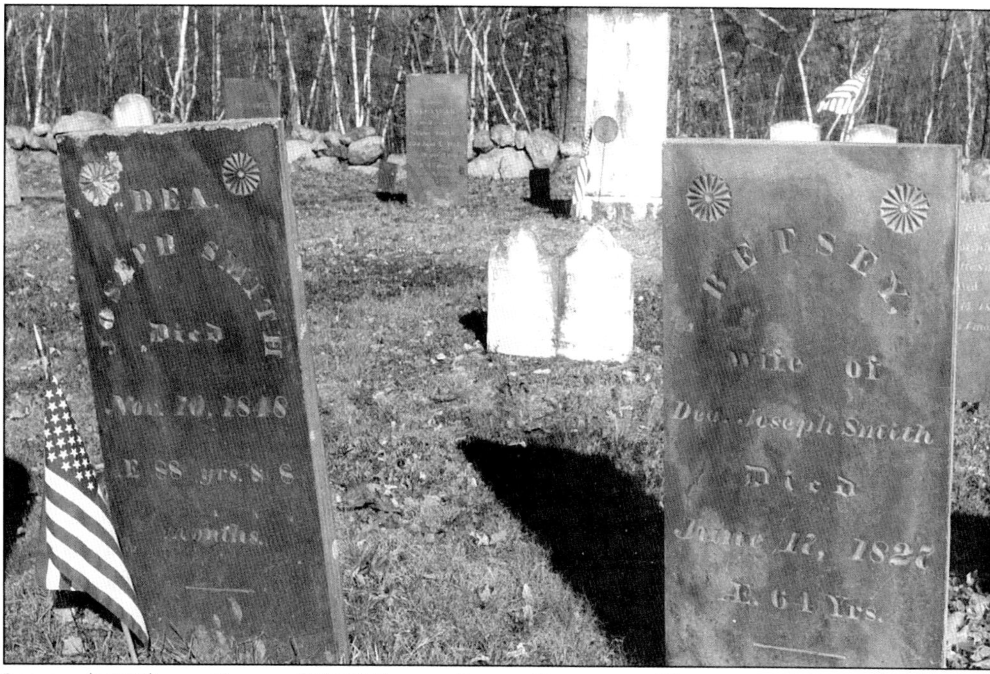

JOSEPH (1848) AND BETSEY (1827) SMITH, SMITH CEMETERY. This cemetery lies in the Winona District of New Hampton, close to Meredith. Joseph Smith may be the man who enlisted from New Hampton during the Revolution as a ranger in defense of the state's northern frontier. His deaconship was possibly held in the First Congregational Society of Center Harbor and Meredith or in the Free Will Baptist church in Oak Hill, Meredith.

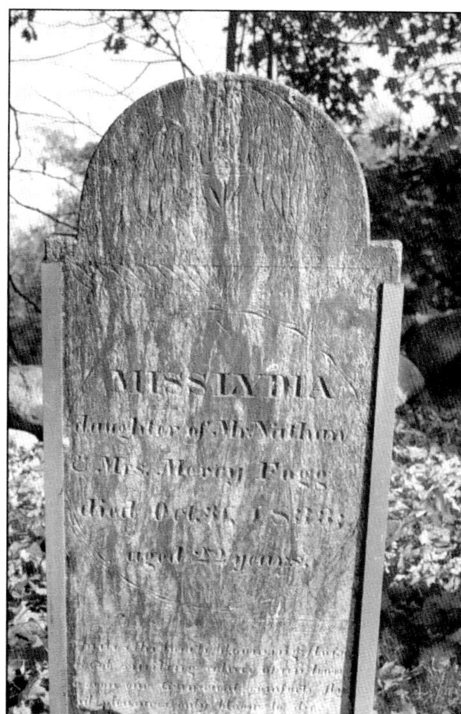

LYDIA FOGG (1833), COLLEGE ROAD CEMETERY. This attractive cemetery has among those buried here descendants of the town's earliest inhabitants. The Fogg family came to what is now Center Harbor before 1790. Simon Fogg had a homestead at the point of Lake Waukewan, while there was a Fogg Tavern in the nearby Winona District. This stone by Matthias Weeks was repaired with the addition of aluminum braces on each side.

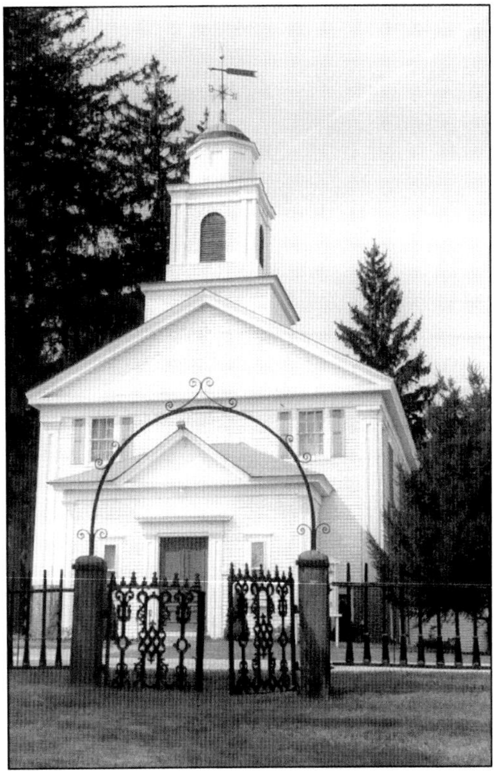

ALMON BENSON (1884), CONGREGATIONAL CHURCH CEMETERY. Rev. Almon Benson came to Center Harbor in October 1840 and "commenced his labors among this people." Though the church had no settled minister at the time, the Congregational Society asked him to settle in Center Harbor after hearing him preach on two successive Sabbaths. Benson accepted the call and was ordained on December 23, 1840. His salary was to be $350 yearly and his firewood supplied, as was the long-standing custom. The church Benson preached in (to the left) was "a neat and commodious house" built in 1837 at a cost of $1,700 and was located next to a small cemetery that had previously been established around 1808. Benson remained the settled minister for 23 years before his dismissal in 1863, due to a lack of funds.

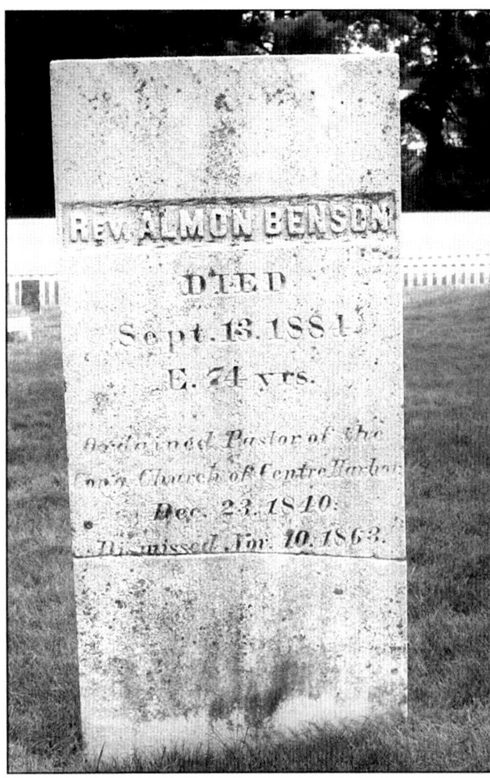

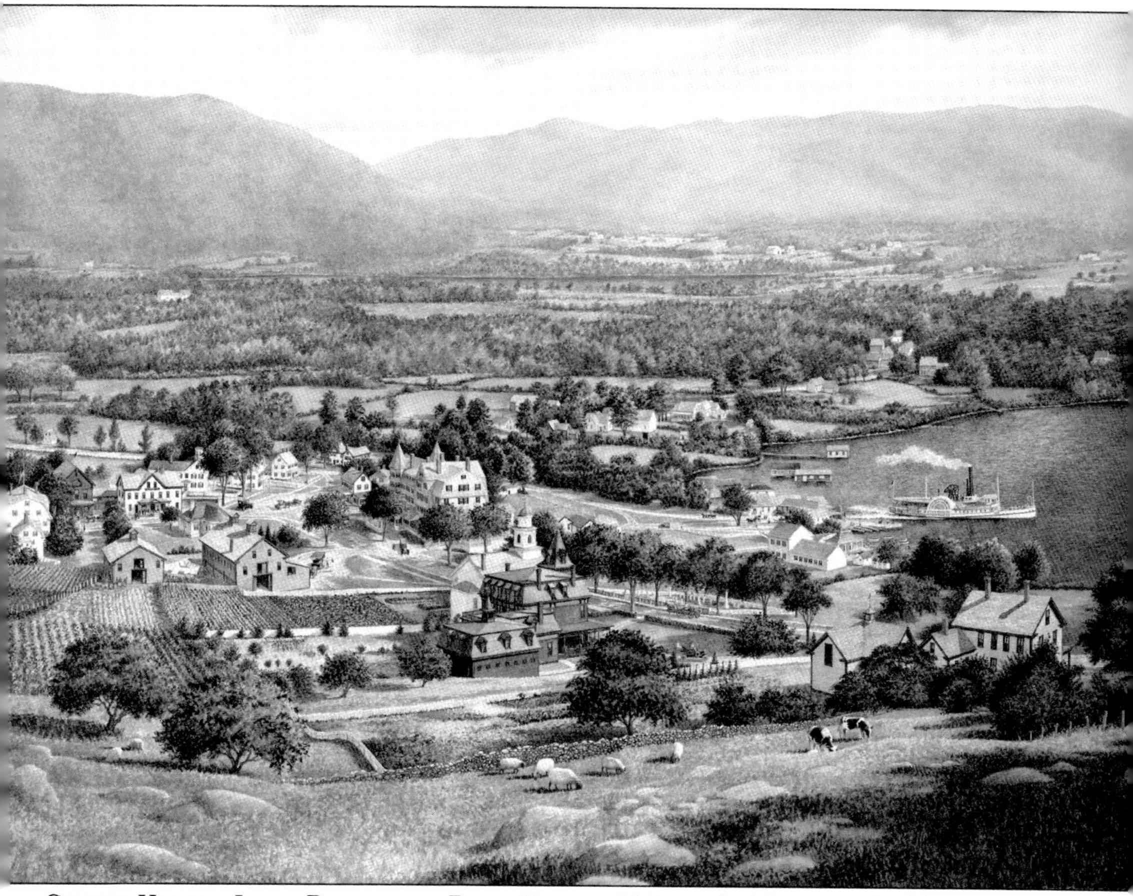

CENTER HARBOR *IDYLL*, PAINTING BY PETER FERBER. This wonderful painting by Alton artist Peter Ferber shows how the town of Center Harbor appeared around 1915. This historic view was created with the help and documentation of old town records, maps, and vintage photographs. While Center Harbor today, especially in the summertime, is a bustling town, it still retains much of the rural appeal that is depicted here. Note the Congregational church at center and the old cemetery to its right (see opposite page). The stately trees that once surrounded this attractive little cemetery as shown here are now long gone. Now Route 25 runs directly on the cemetery's lake side, where once there was an open field. Still, some things never change. Just as the *Mount Washington* steamer frequently ported here in days of old, it still calls Center Harbor home today. (Courtesy Peter Ferber.)

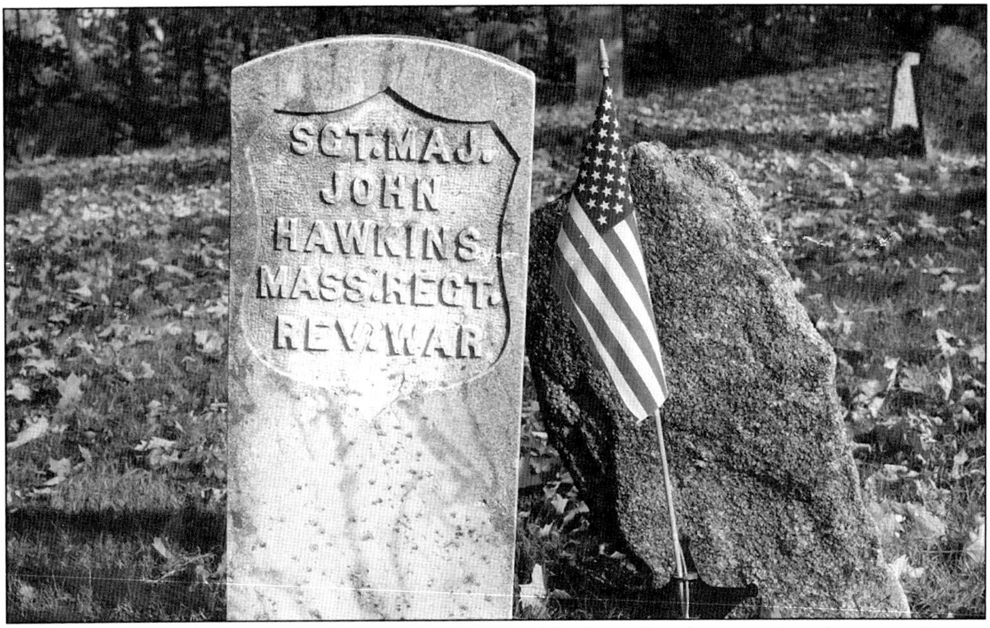

JOHN HAWKINS, COLLEGE ROAD CEMETERY. The Hawkins family arrived early on in Center Harbor, and today's Hawkins Pond is named after them. Sgt. Maj. John Hawkins served in the Revolution from Massachusetts, serving under Capt. Isaac Martin in Col. Ezra Wood's regiment, and later under Lt. Col. Nathan Tyler, both militia units. During 1776–1777, Hawkins, possibly from Beverly, Massachusetts, served in Rhode Island and may have served again in 1781.

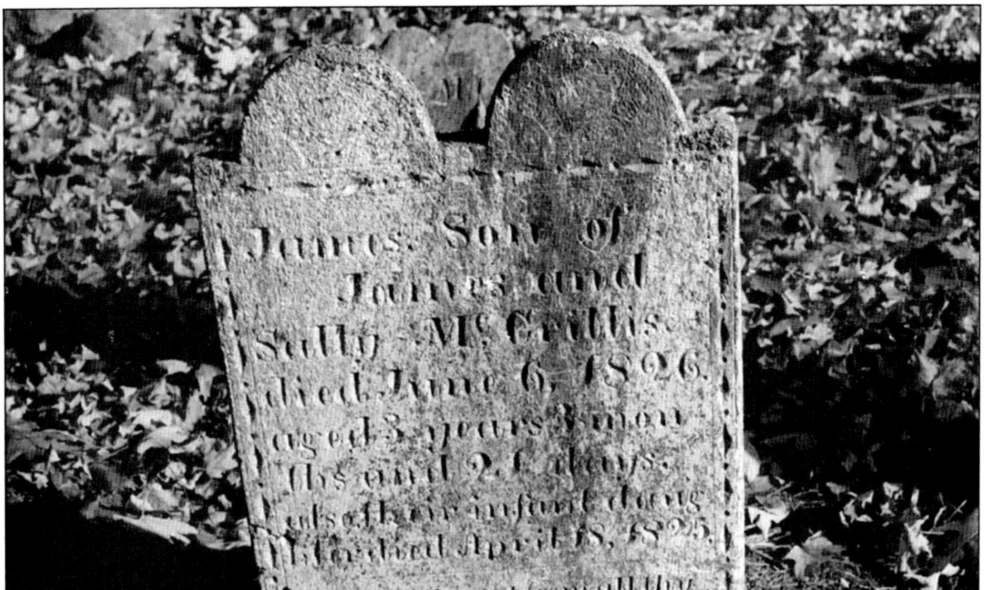

INFANT (1825) AND JAMES (1826) MCCRILLIS, COLLEGE ROAD CEMETERY. This diminutive double gravestone marks the resting place of children of James and Sally McCrillis. James McCrillis Sr. was born in Sandwich in 1790, the son of Henry and Margaret McCrillis who came from Epping in 1780, carrying their belongings on a sled. The McCrillis name is remembered in Center Harbor today with the tallest peak in town, McCrillis Hill.

Seven

Meredith and Holderness

The land that now comprises Meredith was granted as the township of Salem in 1748. With no settlers by 1754 and an additional grant of land on what is now Meredith Neck, the town was renamed New Salem. It was first permanently settled in 1765. Among these settlers were James Quimby and George Bean, while one proprietor, William Mead, cleared six acres of land and built his house. In 1768, the town was incorporated, changing its name to Meredith. The town was settled in three divisions; the part north of Winnisquam Lake to Lake Winnipesaukee was known as Meredith Bridge until set off as the town of Laconia in 1855. It was here where the area's first settlers lived and operated a sawmill. The other divisions include Meredith Center, at the head of Winnisquam Lake, and the village of Meredith, located on the northern shore between Lake Waukewan and Meredith Bay on Lake Winnipesaukee. A number of cemeteries that are the final resting places of some of Meredith's earliest settlers are now located in the boundaries of Laconia. However, there are many other historic cemeteries within Meredith's current borders. The most extensive is Meredith Cemetery, the public cemetery located on what was once called the Plymouth Road (Routes 3 and 25). Here are some of the oldest burials to be found, including veterans from both the Revolutionary and Civil Wars. Family and neighborhood cemeteries, too, are numerous in Meredith. Among the most interesting are those in the Oak Hill area and on Meredith Neck.

The town of Holderness was granted in 1751. While the area was surveyed by Samuel Lane, no settlement was made due to the fear evoked by the French and Indian War, and the charter lapsed. The charter was regranted in 1761 and included among its proprietors such prominent Portsmouth men as Rev. Arthur Browne, rector of Queen's Chapel, and Samuel Livermore, judge advocate of the Admiralty Court and son-in-law of Reverend Browne. The first settlers in town were William Piper and his wife Susanna, who built a cabin in 1763 between Whiteoak Pond and Squam Lake.

Holderness is unique in the Lakes Region because the town, influenced no doubt by the Livermore family, adopted the Episcopal form of worship and, in 1797, built Trinity Church. It was only the second Anglican church built in New Hampshire and the first to serve as a town meetinghouse. This church still stands today, and beside it is Trinity Church yard, laid out in similar fashion to Anglican churches in Boston and Portsmouth, with table-stone grave markers for members of the Livermore family right under its eaves. A number of other historic cemeteries are found in Holderness, including the ancient-looking Bridge Cemetery on a hill overlooking Squam Lake, and several Cox family cemeteries in East Holderness. A number of other cemeteries that relate to the history of Holderness can also be found in the town of Ashland, set off from Holderness in 1869.

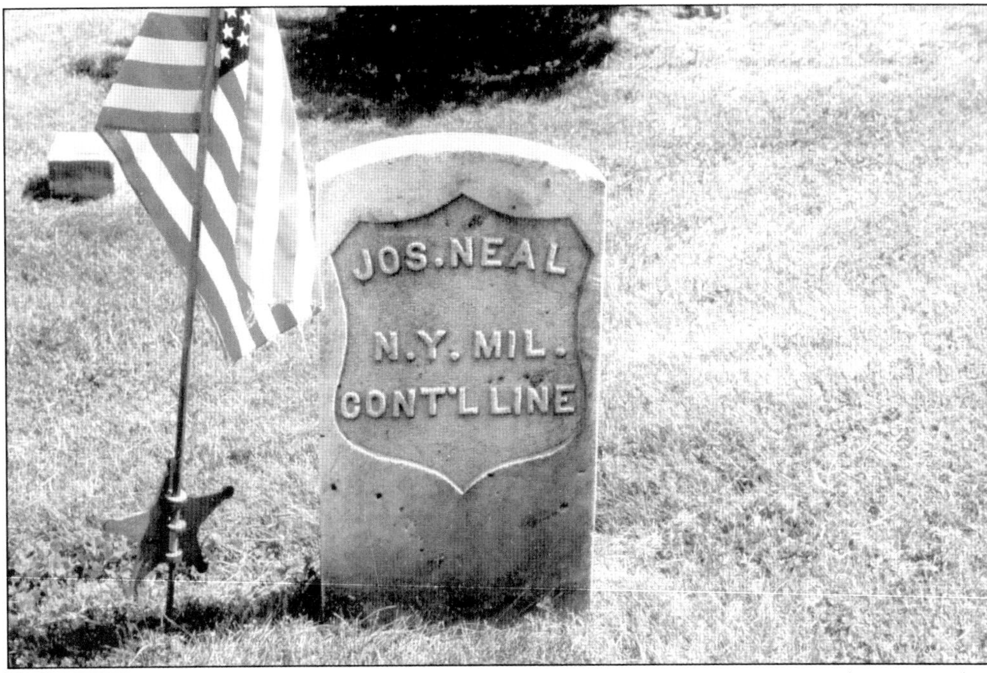

JOSEPH NEAL (1836), MEREDITH CEMETERY. Joseph Neal, a native of Newmarket, arrived in Meredith after his service in the Revolutionary War, following his cousin by the same name. This Joseph Neal served seven months during the war, including a term of militia duty in 1775 and a short term in the Continental Army in New York late in the war. Neal was originally buried on his own land, and this marker was erected at a much later date. Unfortunately, the marker's designation of his service is incorrect; Neal did not serve in a New York militia unit, but for New Hampshire. Interestingly, Neal was called "Red Oak Joe" to distinguish him from his cousin, "White Oak Joseph," both of whom were named after the types of trees that grew on their property. The Meredith Cemetery gate (below) was erected in 1916.

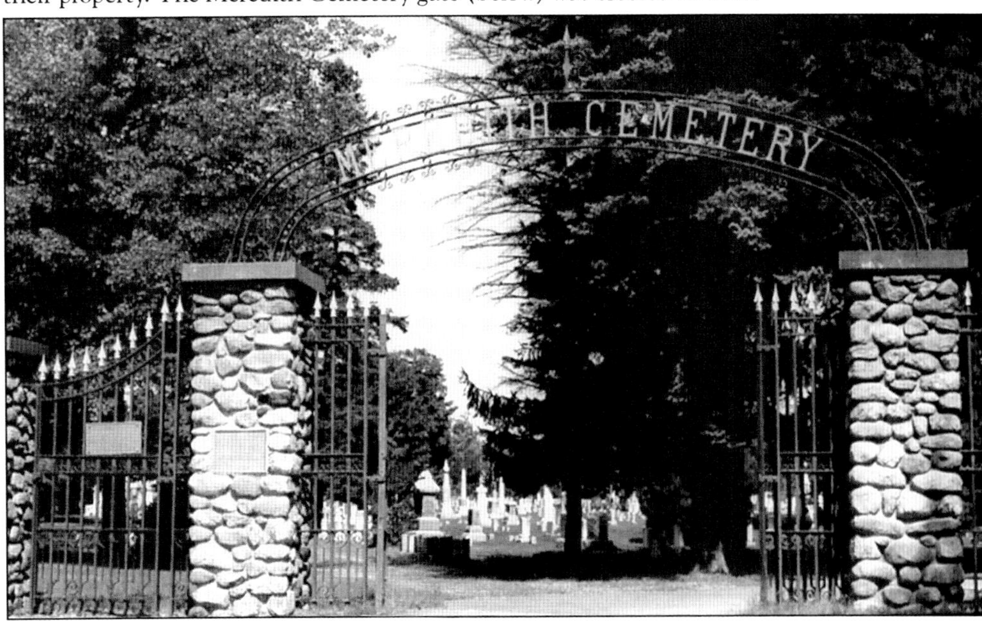

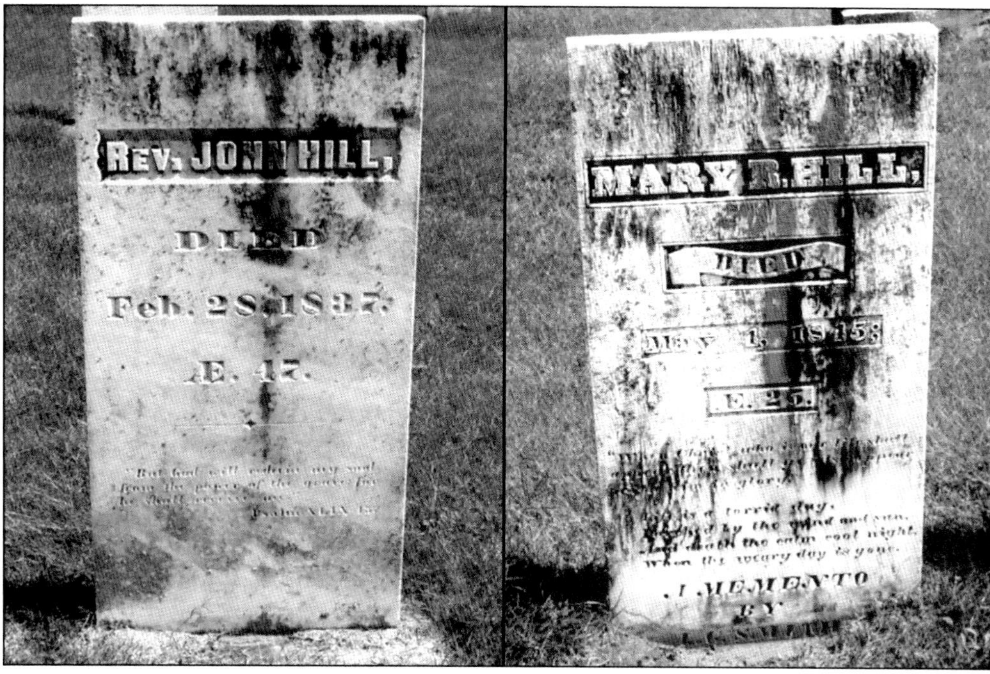

JOHN (1837) AND MARY (1845) HILL, MEREDITH CEMETERY. John Hill was a Free Will Baptist minister of Meredith, born in 1790. He likely preached at the Pottle Meetinghouse on Oak Hill but may have also been a traveling minister who preached wherever his services were needed, perhaps at branch churches in Meredith Village or on Meredith Neck. His wife's stone has its maker noted at the bottom in unusual fashion.

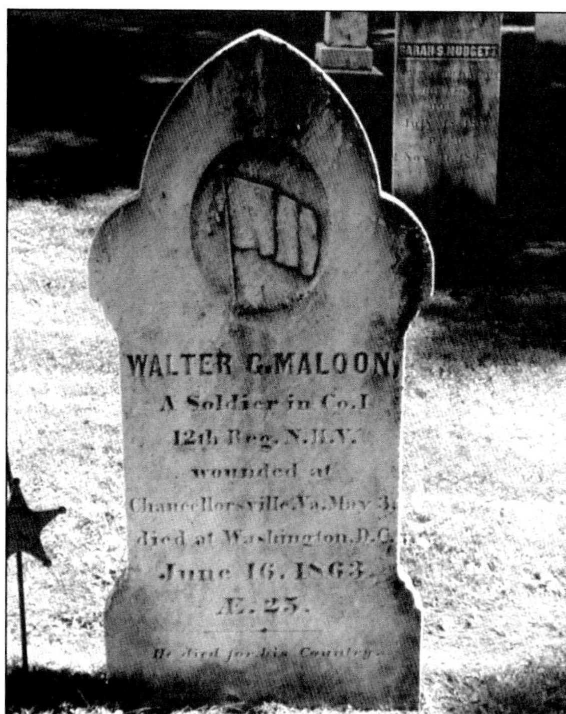

WALTER MALOON (1863), MEREDITH CEMETERY. The Maloon family is notable in Meredith and Center Harbor for the hotels they built. Walter enlisted from Meredith in the 12th New Hampshire Regiment during the Civil War. He joined his unit in August 1862 as a private and was wounded during the Battle of Chancellorsville on May 3, 1863. He died of his wounds in a Washington hospital less than two months later.

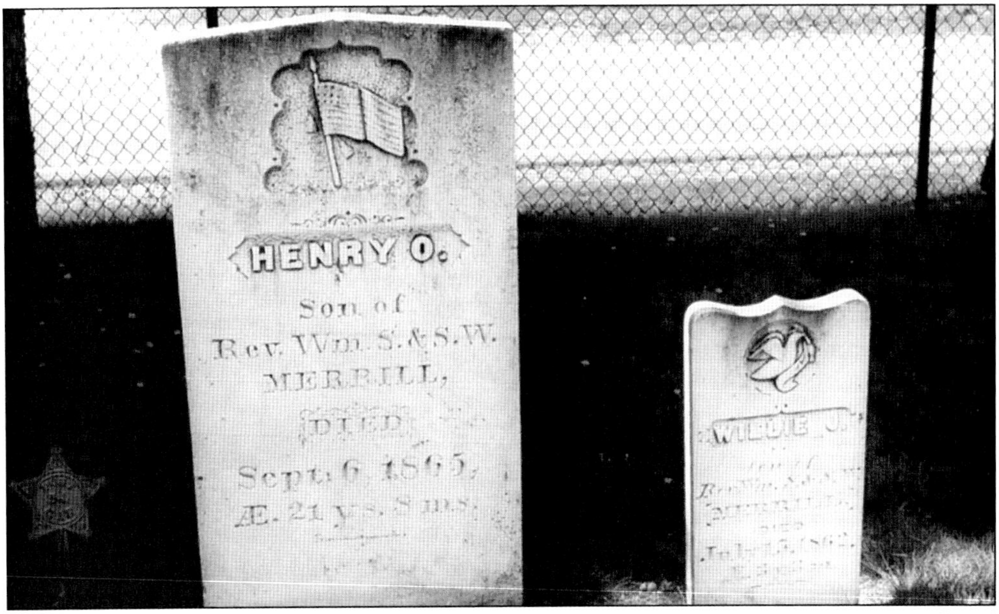

HENRY (1865) AND WILLIE (1862) MERRILL, MEREDITH CEMETERY. Rev. William Merrill and his wife lost two sons during the Civil War. Young Willie (right) probably died due to childhood illness. Henry Merrill was a volunteer in the 12th New Hampshire Regiment. Wounded at Chancellorsville in May 1863, he continued to serve until June 1865. He died less than three months after leaving the army, possibly due to camp fever.

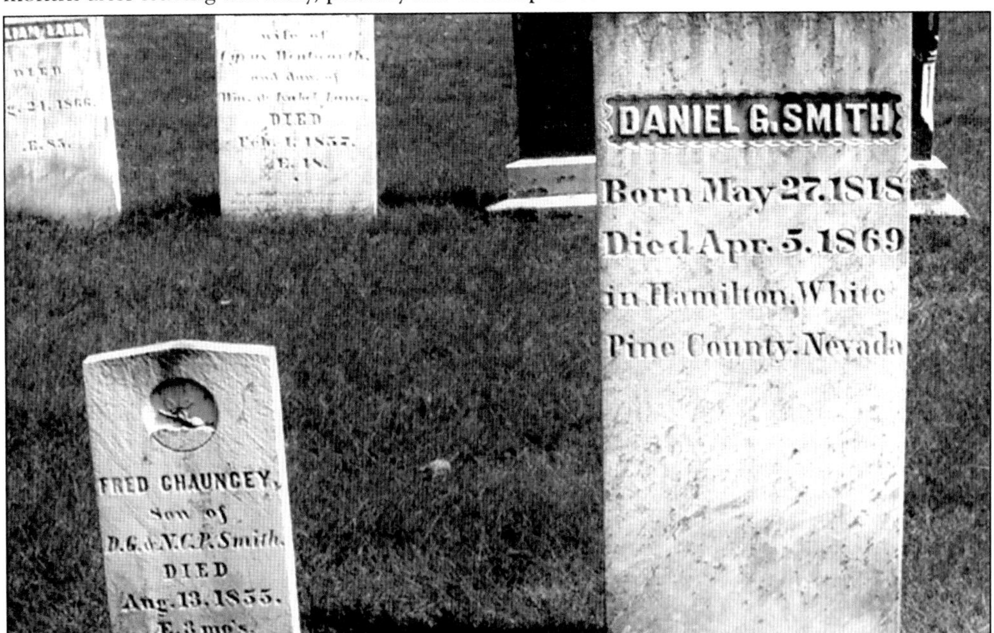

FRED (1855) AND DANIEL (1869) SMITH, MEREDITH CEMETERY. The gravestones for this father and son, and the intervening years between their deaths, surely tell an interesting and sad story. Young Fred Smith died in 1855 at the age of three months. Fourteen years later, his father, Daniel, likely descended from the first white child ever born in Meredith, died in far-off Nevada, perhaps while on a search for land or gold.

JOHN SANBORN (1870), MEREDITH CEMETERY. This "principle physician" of Meredith is described in D. Hamilton Hurd's *History of Merrimack and Belknap Counties, New Hampshire*, 1885, as "a man of great value . . . who is remembered as one who did more to inculcate a desire for knowledge in the minds of the youth than . . . any other person who ever lived here."

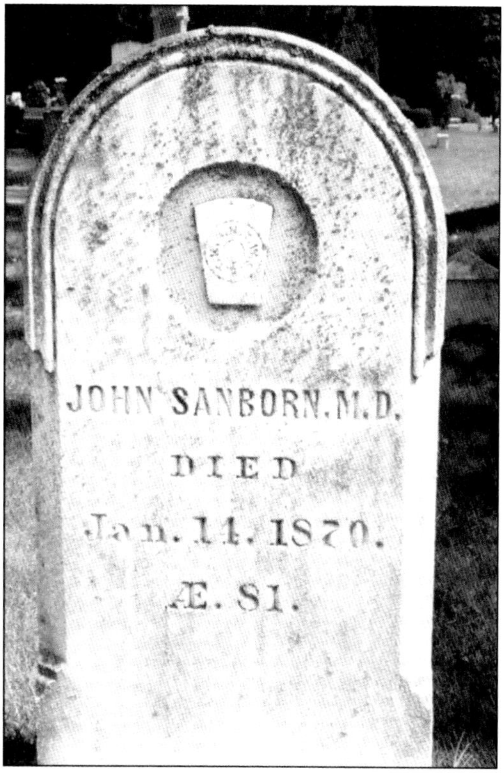

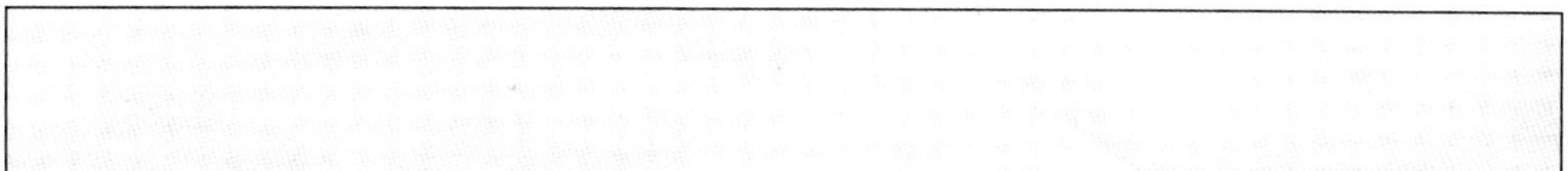

HORSE BOAT ON LAKE WINNIPESAUKEE. With a horsepower of exactly one, craft such as this made their appearance on the lake in 1837 and at Bear Island off Meredith in 1839. Though crude, and soon eclipsed by steam power, their wide beam made these horse-powered paddle boats ideal for carrying all manner of heavy loads, including bricks, as shown here, and possibly even gravestones. (Courtesy Wolfeboro Historical Society.)

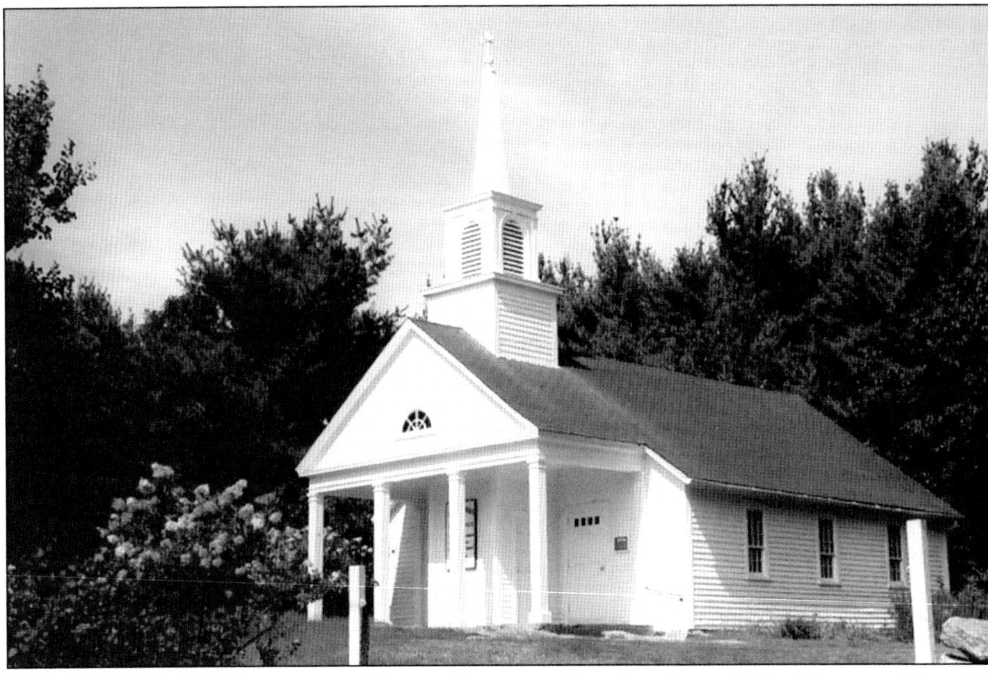

MEETING HOUSE CEMETERY AND UNION CHURCH. The church established here on Meredith Neck around 1839 was originally of the Free Will Baptist denomination. Union Church, rebuilt in 1951, has no "settled" minister today and, as in the days of old, offers summer services from a variety of visiting pastors. Given the rugged and independent nature of its inhabitants, those who lived on Meredith Neck and Bear Island were always considered a distinctly different part of Meredith. Among those buried in this quiet cemetery, established at the same time the first meetinghouse was built, are Revolutionary War veteran Chase Wiggin, who lived to the age of 99, and War of 1812 veteran Theophilus Dockham, who was a British prisoner of war and Bear Island's first permanent settler.

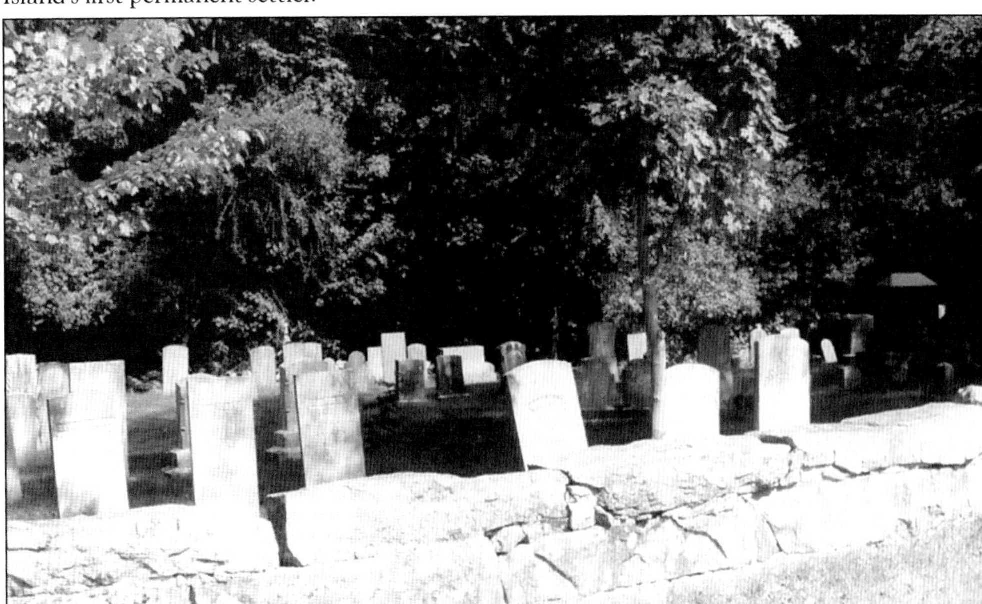

FIDO (1880), MEETING HOUSE CEMETERY. Fido the dog is probably the most unusual inhabitant of this cemetery, or any other in Meredith for that matter. His owner was David Maloon, who died in December 1879 at the age of 41. Fido followed soon after and was buried close by his master. His gravestone reads, "He mourneth the loss of his master."

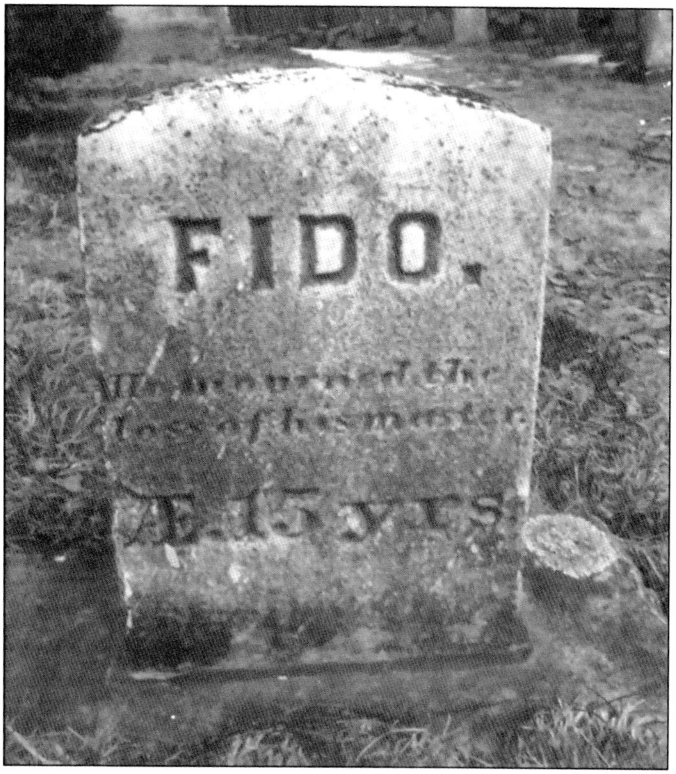

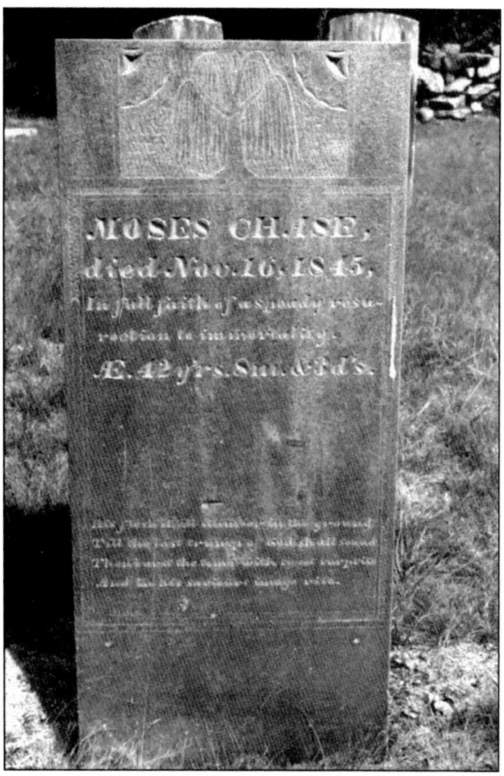

MOSES CHASE (1845), MEETING HOUSE CEMETERY. That Moses Chase was a devout member of the Free Will Baptist church on Meredith Neck is evident in his epitaph, which reads, "In full faith of a speedy resurrection to immortality." Unlike the old-time Calvinistic Baptists, who believed that the fate of one's soul was preordained and could not be changed, the Free Will Baptist faith offered its believers the path to redemption.

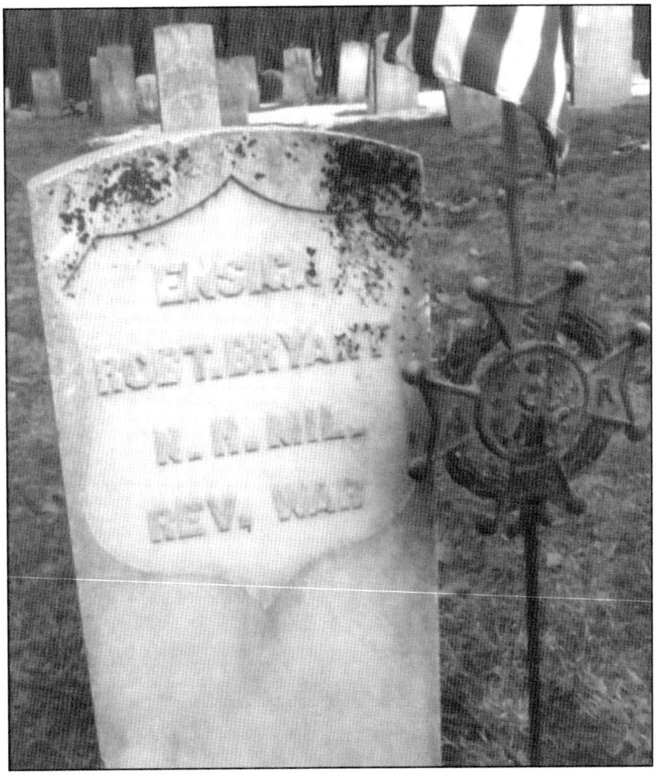

ROBERT BRYANT (1830), MEETING HOUSE CEMETERY. Robert Bryant was an early settler on Bear Island, arriving after the Revolutionary War from Newmarket after living a short time in Meredith Village. Married to Johanna Stevens in 1765, he had a large family. An orderly sergeant in Capt. John Moodey's militia company in 1776, Bryant later served as ensign in Col. Thomas Stickney's militia regiment and fought at the Battle of Bennington in 1777.

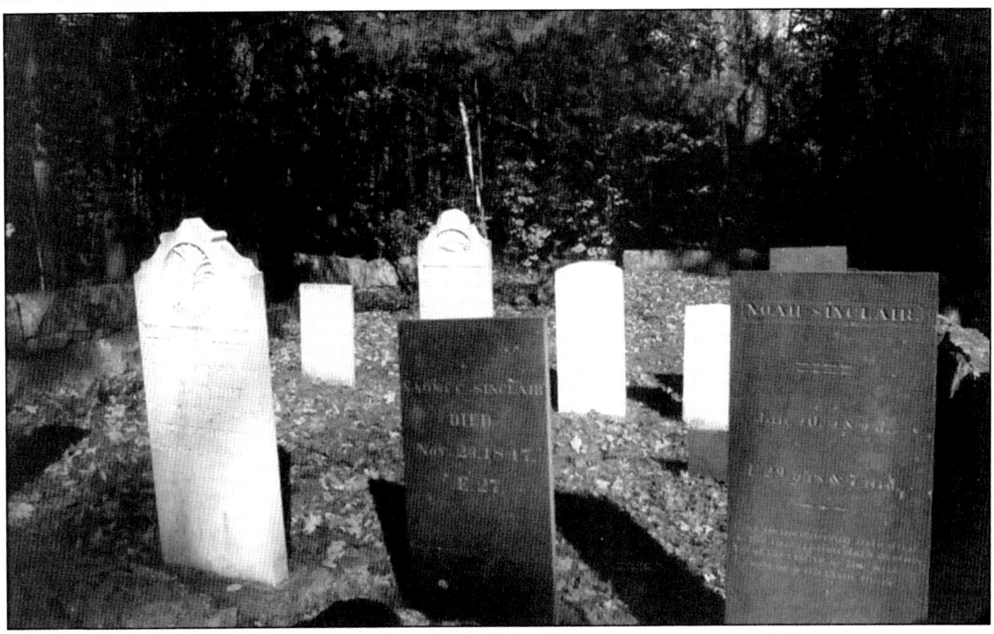

SINCLAIR CEMETERY, MEREDITH. This shaded family cemetery is one of the most interesting in Meredith. It is located on Oak Hill Road, not far from where the Pottle Meetinghouse once stood, in the aptly named Oak Hill District. Among those buried here are Revolutionary War soldier Thomas Sinclair and John Sinclair, a Free Will Baptist pastor who preached at the Pottle Meetinghouse.

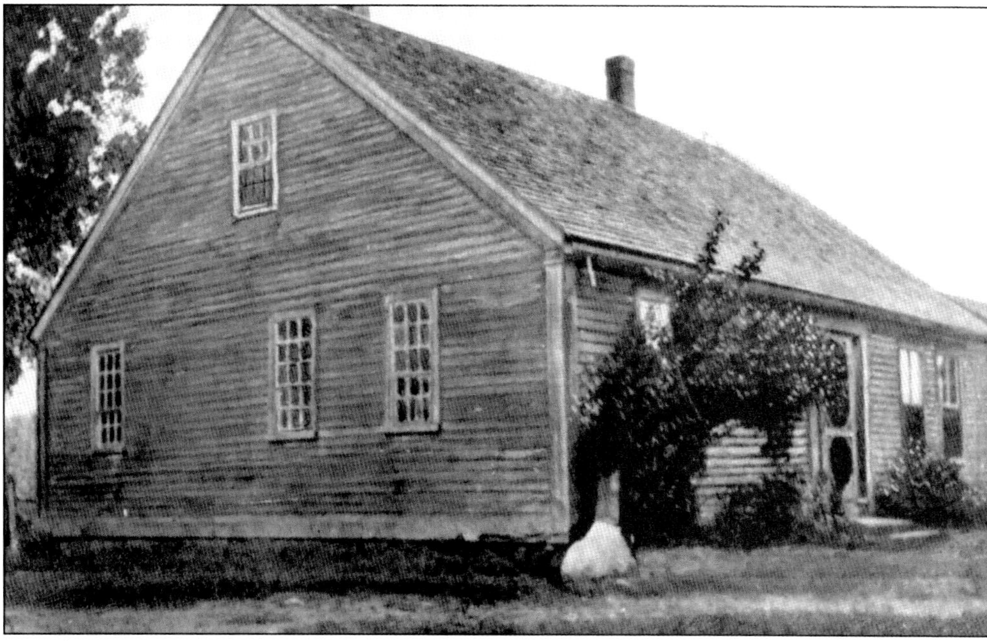

The Samuel Shepard House, Holderness. Though against the American Revolution, Samuel Shepard was one of Holderness's most influential men in its early days. First a clerk of the proprietors and then town clerk from 1776 until his death in 1817, town meetings were held at his inn, still standing, near Owl Brook. (Photograph from George Hodges's *Holderness; An Account of the Beginnings of a New Hampshire Town*, 1907.)

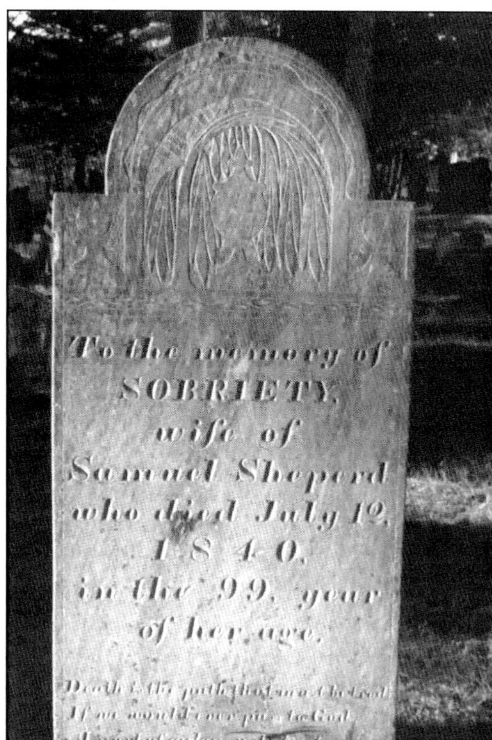

Sobriety Shepard (1840), Bridge Cemetery. Sobriety Shepard was the wife of town elder Samuel Shepard and lived 23 years his widow. At her death in 1840, at the age of 99, this grand dame was surely one of the last links to the early beginnings of Holderness. Her epitaph at bottom reads, in part, "Death is the path that must be trod, If we would ever pass to God."

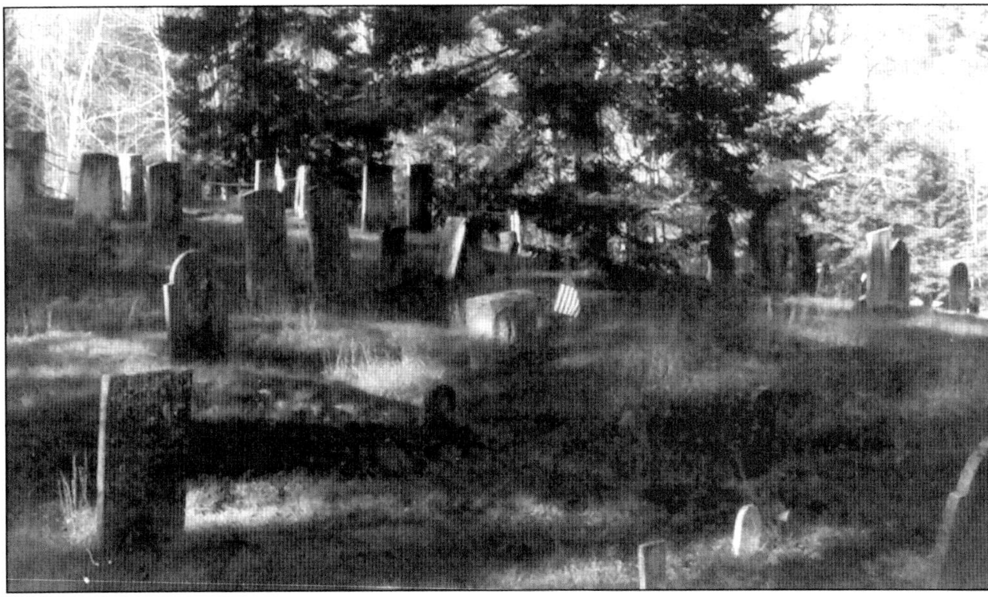

BRIDGE CEMETERY, HOLDERNESS. Located on a knoll overlooking Squam Lake, this cemetery has an old-time air about it underscoring the fact that it is the oldest public cemetery in Holderness. Here are found buried many of the town's earliest settlers and their descendants. This cemetery site was determined in 1772 by town vote but likely not fully established until a church was built here in 1803, which later burned down.

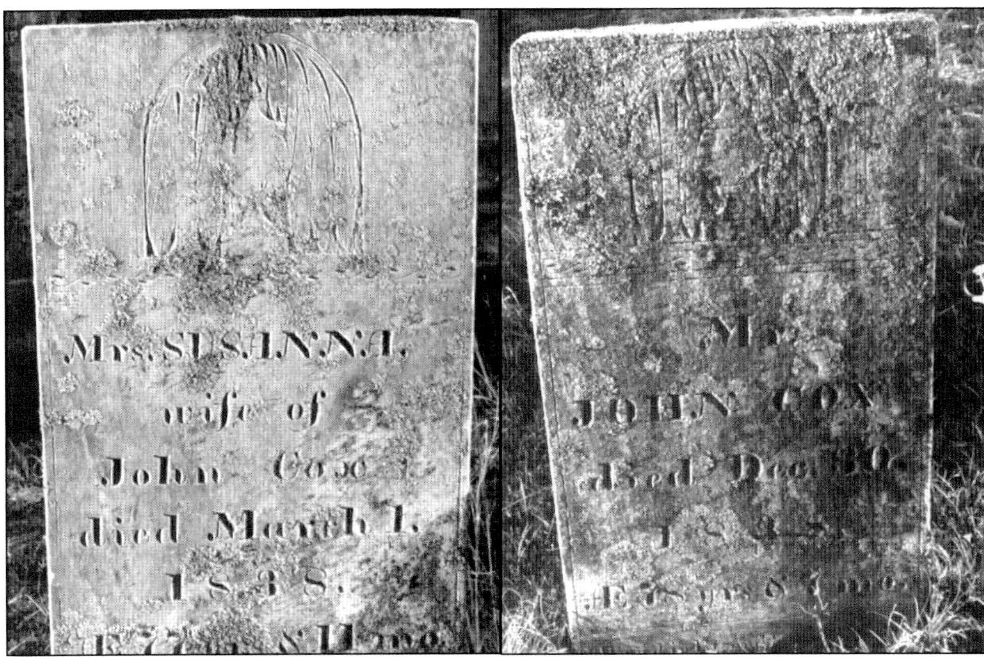

JOHN AND SUSANNA COX (1838), BRIDGE CEMETERY. The Cox family was prominent in the early settling of Holderness, with seven Coxes among its original grantees. John was likely the son of original settler John Cox, who settled in Lot 3 of the first division. This couple died within 10 months of each other in 1838, not an uncommon occurrence even today. Both gravestones were likely carved by Moultonborough's Matthias Weeks.

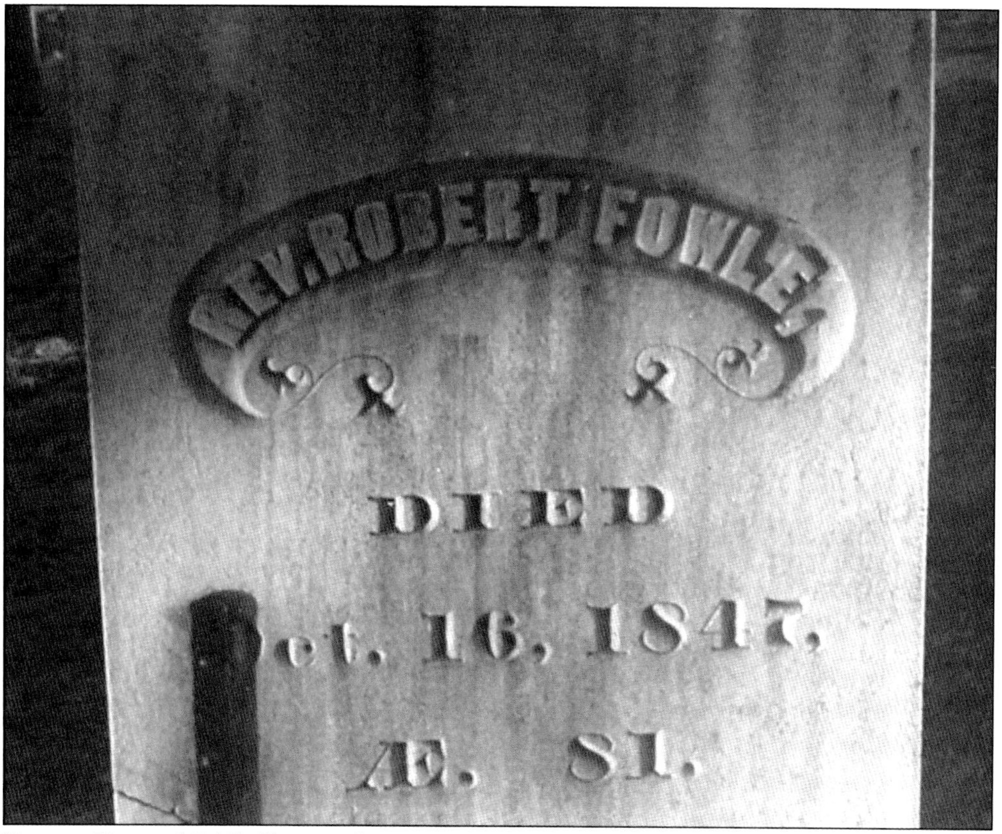

ROBERT FOWLE (1847), BRIDGE CEMETERY. Parson Robert Fowle, an interesting character, originally came from Newburyport, Massachusetts, acting as a tutor for the son of Samuel Livermore. He was subsequently a lay reader for the Church of England services held at Livermore's house. Fowle was ordained a priest in Boston in 1791 and would preach in Holderness for the rest of his life. Local lore records that a ferrywoman, Mrs. Cockran, was instrumental in getting Fowle, by then aged 25 and still living with the Livermores, to marry schoolmistress Martha Smythe. Described as "a grave and rather silent man," Fowle (right) often wore a black coat and white cravat. At the end of his life, while he "quietly failed," the "emotional presentation of religion" in Holderness "prevailed." (Right photograph from George Hodges's *Holderness; An Account of the Beginnings of a New Hampshire Town*, 1907.)

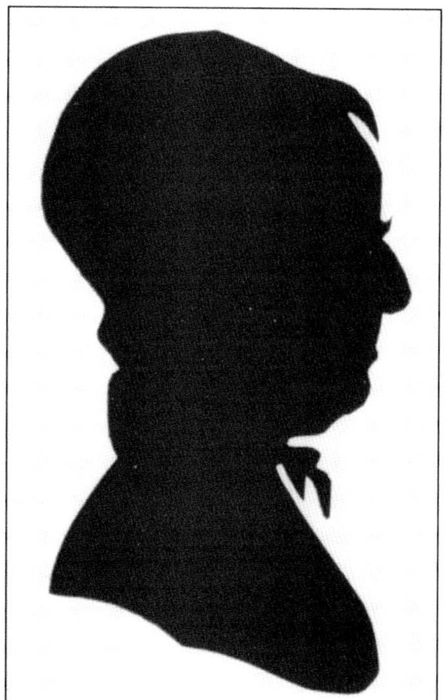

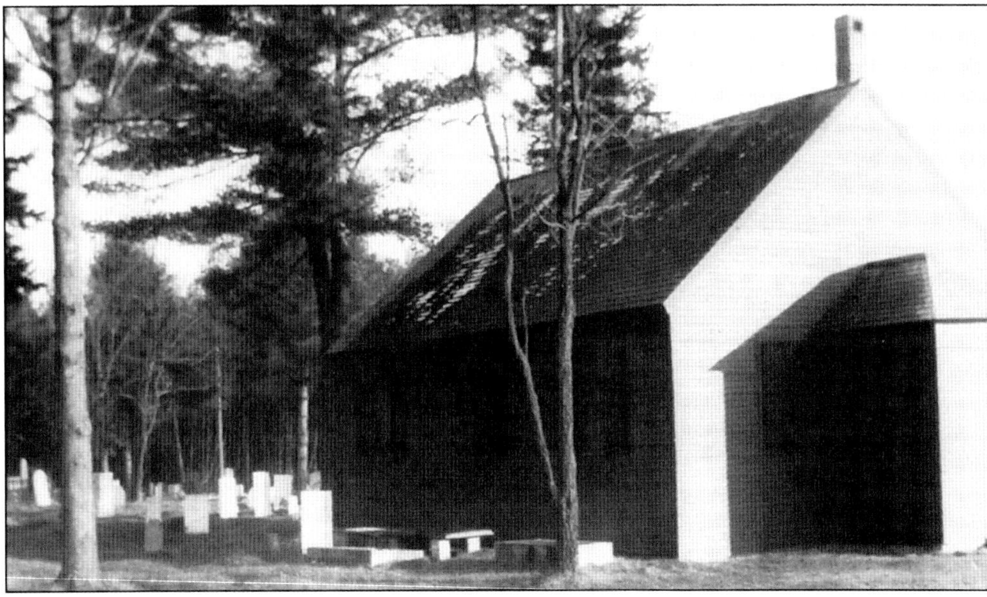

TRINITY CHURCH AND CHURCHYARD, HOLDERNESS. This modest Episcopal church (above), still standing, was built as a private chapel by Samuel Livermore in 1797 on his own land. A proprietor of Holderness, Livermore and his wife, Jane (below), the lively daughter of Rev. Arthur Browne of Portsmouth's Queen's Chapel, moved to their country home in 1774. Despite his Church of England ties and position as king's attorney, Livermore took no part in the American Revolution and emerged with his reputation and fortune intact. Despite their social standing, the Livermores were beloved by the people of Holderness and always lent a hand to those in need. Samuel and Jane Livermore lie buried under the table stones beneath the eaves of Trinity Church. (Top photograph from Eva Speare's *Colonial Meeting-Houses of New Hampshire,* 1938; bottom photograph from George Hodges's *Holderness; An Account of the Beginnings of a New Hampshire Town*, 1907.)

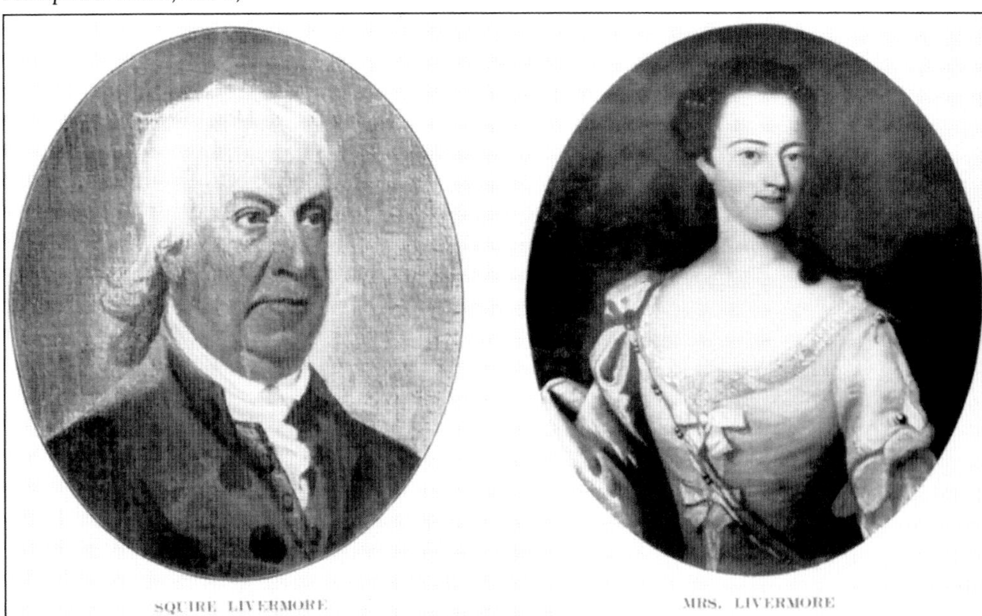

WILLIAM SHEPARD (1814), TRINITY CHURCHYARD. The Shepards were another prominent family in the early affairs of Holderness, with five of that family being among its original grantees. The locale of Shepard Hill is named after this family. This stone for young William, only 11 years old at the time of his death in 1814, was likely erected some 10 or 20 years after his death.

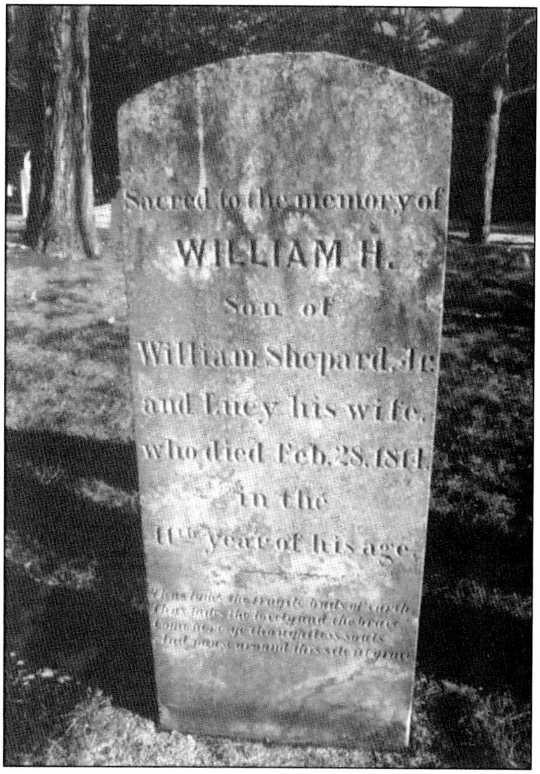

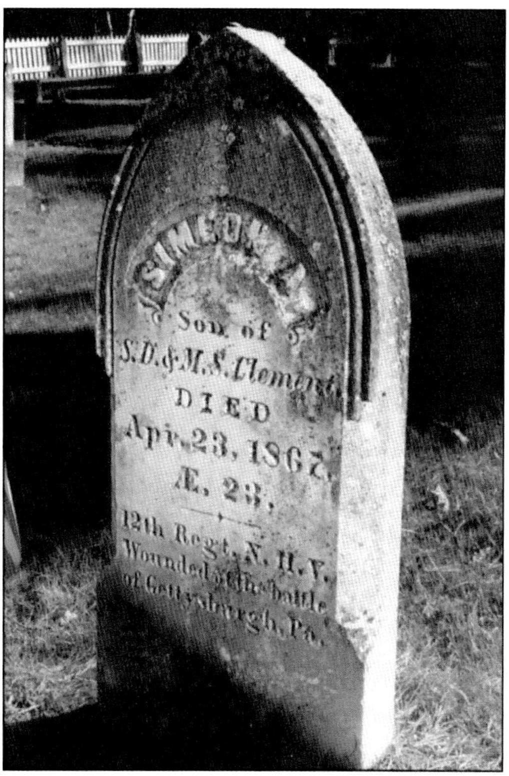

SIMEON CLEMENT (1867), EAST HOLDERNESS CEMETERY. While his gravestone states otherwise, New Hampshire records indicate that Simeon Clement served in the 9th New Hampshire Regiment, was captured in September 1864 at Poplar Springs Church in Virginia, paroled soon after, and died in Center Harbor on April 14, 1866. Whatever the case may be, it is certain that Clement's early death was brought on by the rigors of his war service.

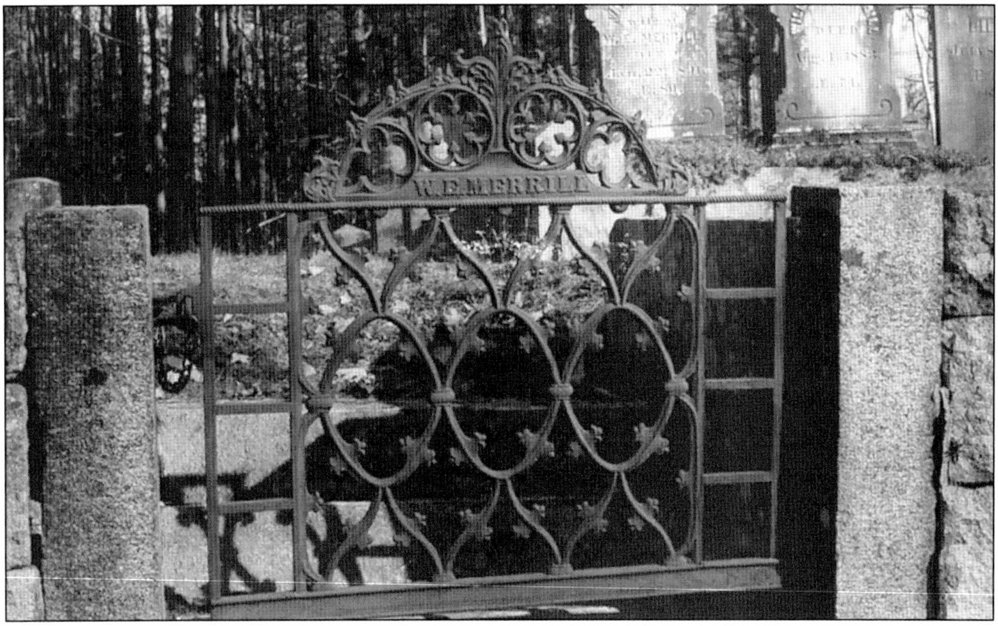

MERRILL-SMITH CEMETERY, EAST HOLDERNESS. This elaborate family cemetery lies very close to the boundary line with Center Harbor on Winona Road. The elaborate wrought-iron gate inscribed with William Merrill's name was likely erected near the time of his death in 1883. Merrill was one of the most prosperous farmers in the area, with property and personal belongings valued at over $3,000 in 1860, a large sum for the time.

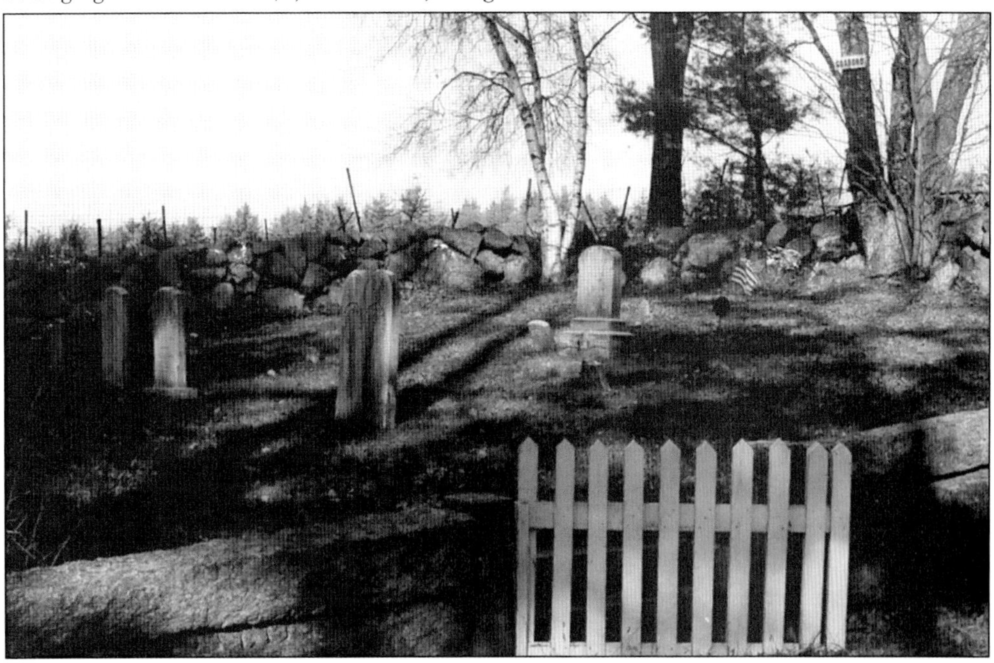

COXBORO CEMETERY, EAST HOLDERNESS. As is evidenced by this well cared for rural family cemetery, the Cox family was predominant in East Holderness. The most prominent burial here is for Capt. Thomas Cox (born 1782, died 1830), and his wife Miriam Dearborn. She was born in 1787, remarried after the death of Thomas Cox, and died in 1873 at an advanced age.

Eight

LACONIA

Formerly known as Meredith Bridge and set off from Meredith as a town in 1855, Laconia is officially one of the younger towns in this survey. However, the land that now comprises the city has an extensive history that makes it the oldest settled area around Lake Winnipesaukee. At the outlet of the lake is a spot known as the Weirs. Here was where Native Americans had lived seasonally for thousands of years before the coming of the white man, in a village called Aquadoctan, and caught fish during their seasonal runs in W-shaped traps, called weirs, made of rock, brush, and nets. The area became more familiar to white men when, beginning in 1638, surveying parties from the Massachusetts Bay Colony set out up the Merrimack River to determine its source. Because Massachusetts's northern boundary was claimed to be at a line determined by the source of the Merrimack River, this was important information. In 1652, Gov. John Endicott organized an expedition, led by Capt. Simon Willard with the guidance of several Native Americans. They journeyed up the Merrimack River and made it all the way to the Weirs, and it was here that they carved the name of Governor Endicott on a large rock, a historic site lost and rediscovered in 1854 that can still be seen today.

With the granting of Salem, later Meredith, in 1748, the settlement of what is now Laconia eventually commenced. The first settlers lived at the head of Round Bay on land purchased by Ebenezer Smith, and the town's first sawmill was established by William Mead and Smith at the Weirs in 1766. The most important man in the growth of the town was undoubtedly Ebenezer Smith. He moved to the area in 1766 and is described by one historian as one who was "autocratic and controlled the infant town as a Czar, but his rule was for the public good." Smith was buried in Round Bay Cemetery, one of the most important and interesting of all of Laconia's historic cemeteries. Here also is buried Washington Smith, one of four men to die as a result of "the Great Catastrophe," which occurred in 1855 when the unfinished town meeting hall collapsed. Interesting family cemeteries in Laconia are the Blaisdell, Page, and Lawrence cemeteries, in which a number of the area's Revolutionary War soldiers are buried. Probably the best-known cemetery in Laconia is Union Cemetery, established during the Victorian era. For those who have an interest in older and more varied gravestone carvings, the Meredith Bridge and Hillside Cemeteries are even more fascinating. The Meredith Bridge Cemetery, in particular, is one of the oldest in Laconia, and is one of only several cemeteries in this study to be established in a waterfront location, in this case along the Winnipesaukee River.

Lastly, Laconia is also interesting for its resident gravestone carvers. The first known stonecutter in Meredith Bridge was Albert Hull, who later worked with several partners, including John Seaver and Jonathan Merrill. Hull's work, often signed, is found throughout the Lakes Region.

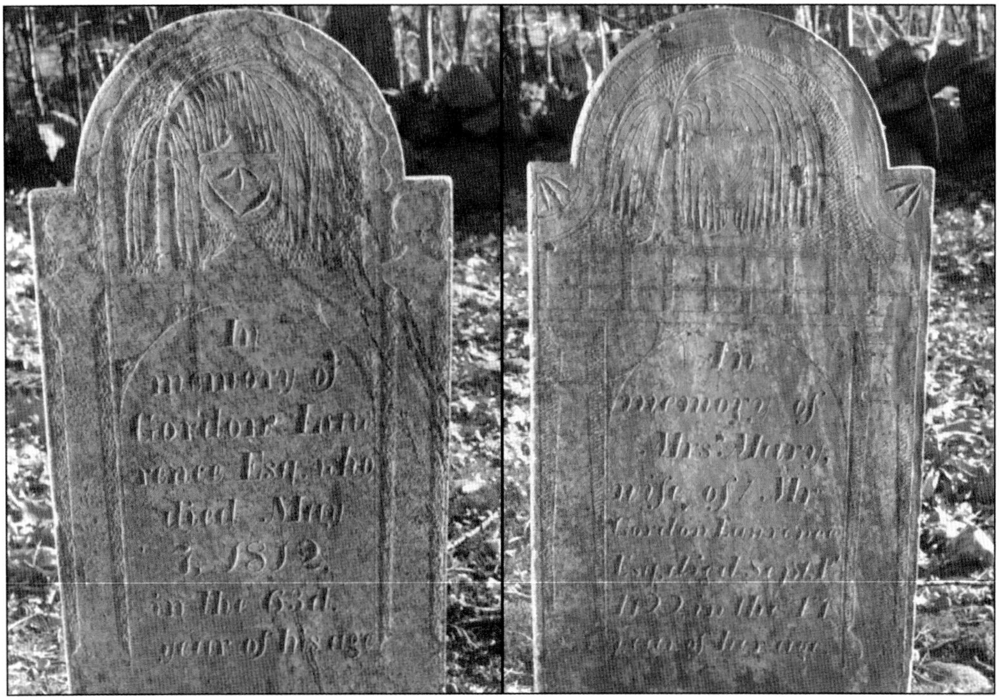

GORDON (1812) AND MARY (1822) LAWRENCE, LAWRENCE CEMETERY. These elaborate gravestones, likely the work of Matthias Weeks, were likely erected at the same time, around 1822–1823. Gordon Lawrence came early to the part of Meredith that is now in Laconia and was no doubt related to David Lawrence, who, with Ebenezer Smith, petitioned for Meredith's incorporation in 1768. Gordon was one of the town's legal voters in 1777 when it voted on matters pertaining to the American Revolution.

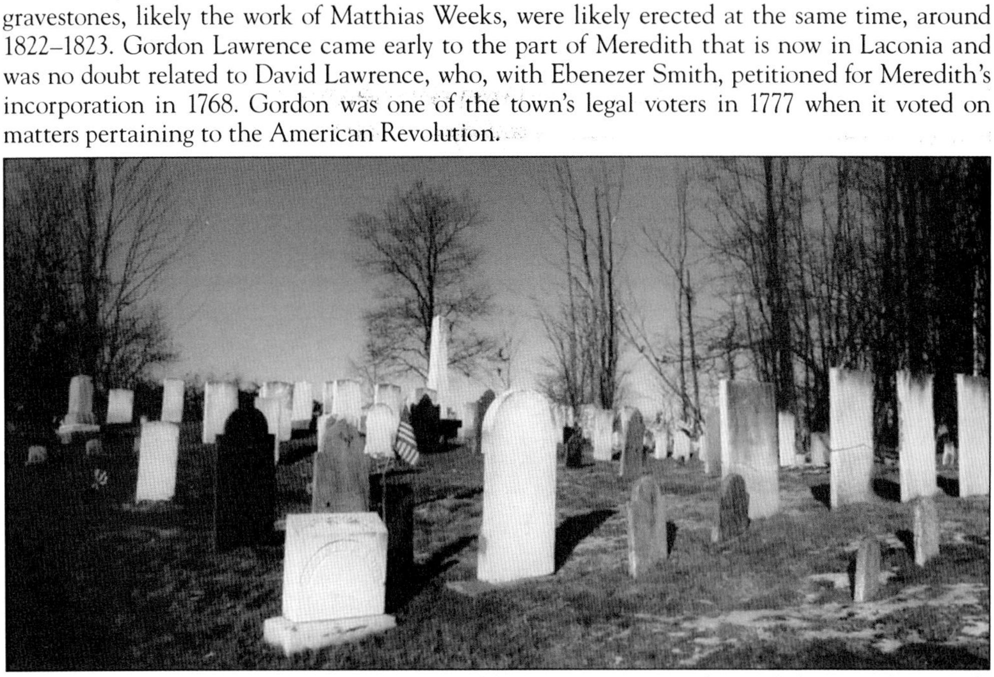

ROUND BAY CEMETERY. This picturesque and historic cemetery is located close to where early settler Ebenezer Smith built his homestead and is dominated by Smith family descendants. Members of his immediate family are buried here close to him, including his son Washington Smith. He died in 1855 when, on March 13, 1855, the floor of the unfinished town meeting hall collapsed when over 600 men rushed to vote by ballot.

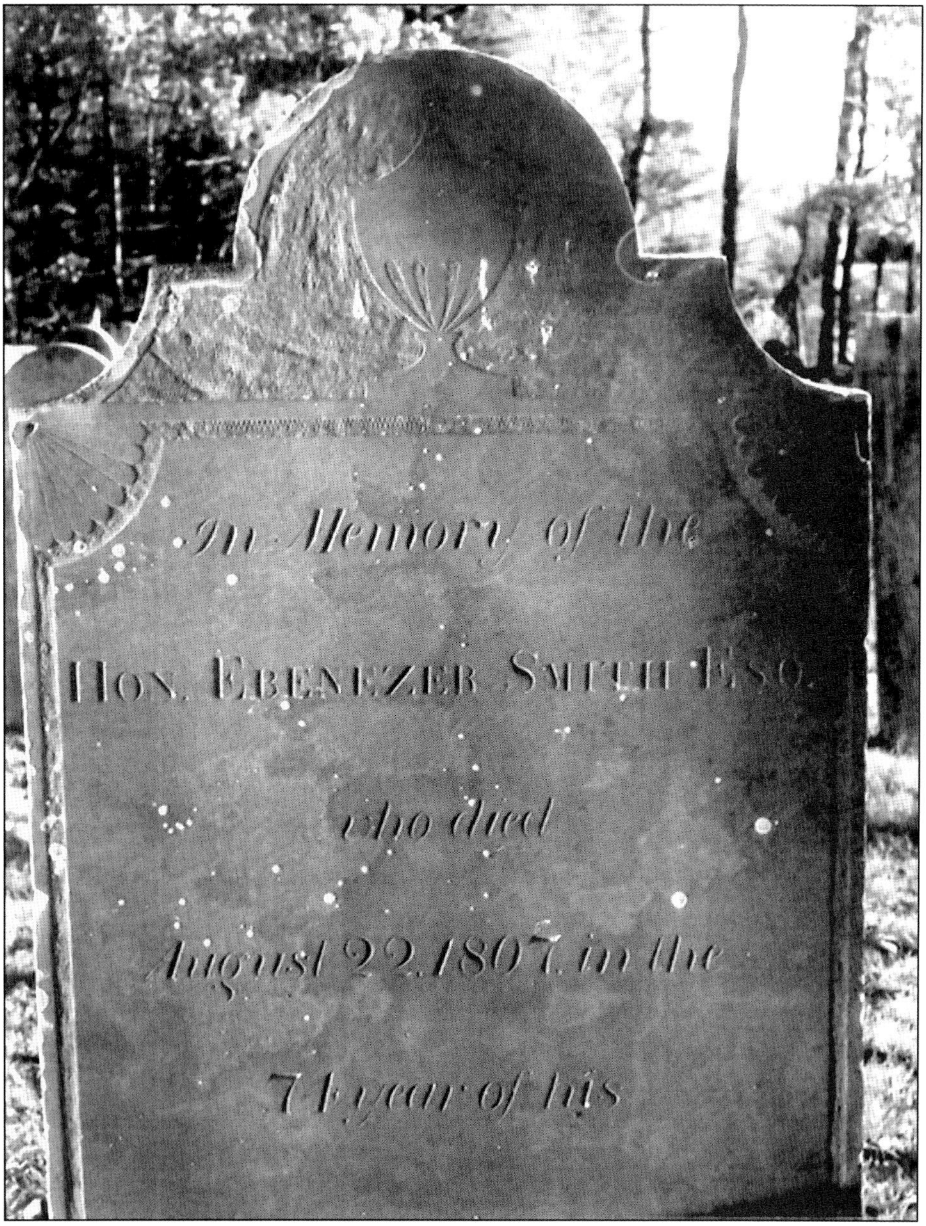

EBENEZER SMITH (1807), ROUND BAY CEMETERY. Without a doubt, Ebenezer Smith was the leading businessman and civic leader of his day in the Lakes Region. Though not a proprietor of Meredith, he arrived in the area early after purchasing his land at the head of Round Bay from proprietor John Purmort and moved here by the spring of 1766, less than five years after the first permanent settlers had come to the region. Prior to this, he had contributed to the area's settling by his work in cutting roads, building a bridge, and helping to build a sawmill at the Weirs. Smith would subsequently serve in Meredith government as a longtime town clerk and selectman and also served as a justice of the peace and a colonel of the local militia regiment. Though "autocratic," Smith was a fair and honest man. When helping to assess local taxes, he took into account those who had amassed a larger fortune and could afford to pay more taxes, while sparing those of lesser means due to crop failure, livestock loss, or illness.

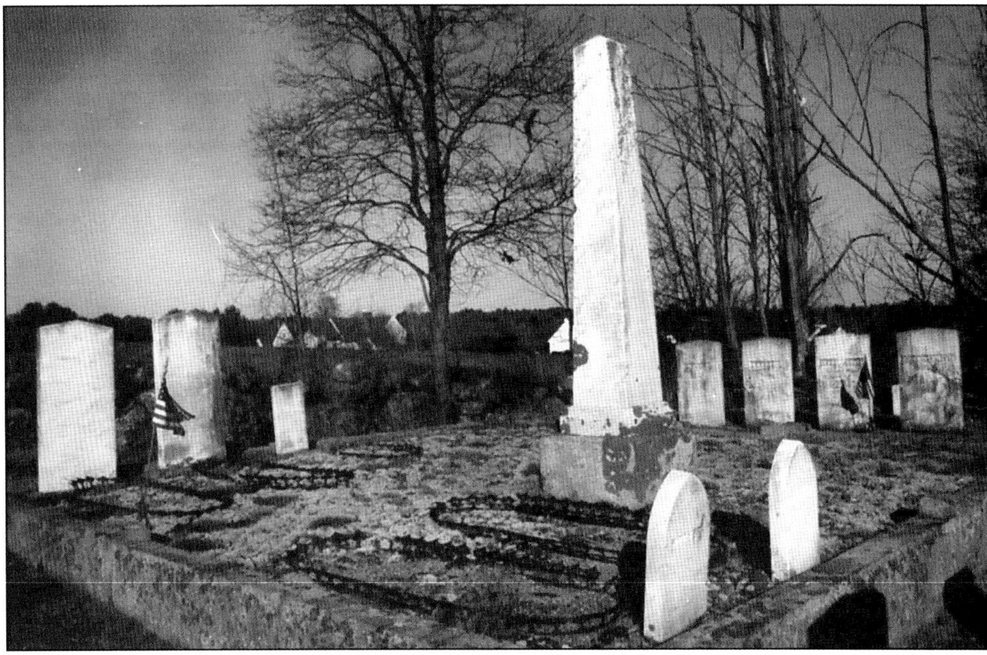

CROCKETT FAMILY PLOT, ROUND BAY CEMETERY. One of the most unusual highlights of this cemetery is the Victorian-style decorations that are found on the graves of the Crockett family. The oval-shaped devices depicted here were fashioned out of wrought iron and define the area where the deceased was laid to rest. Decorations like this were common in the mid-1800s, but few have survived intact such as these.

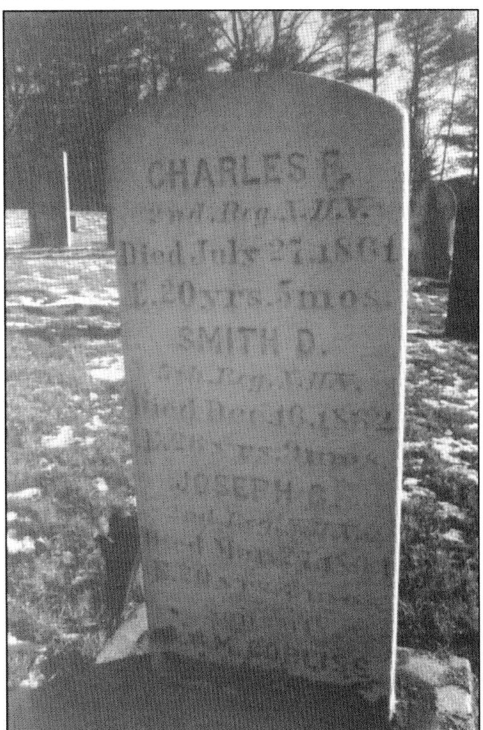

THE CORLISS BROTHERS (1861–1863), ROUND BAY CEMETERY. The family tragedies endured during the Civil War are demonstrated on this gravestone. Charles enlisted in May 1861 and died from disease in Washington, D.C., months later. Smith died of disease at Falmouth, Virginia, four months after his 1862 enlistment. Joseph, wounded at the second Battle of Bull Run, died of disease, like his brothers, in Concord seven months after he enlisted.

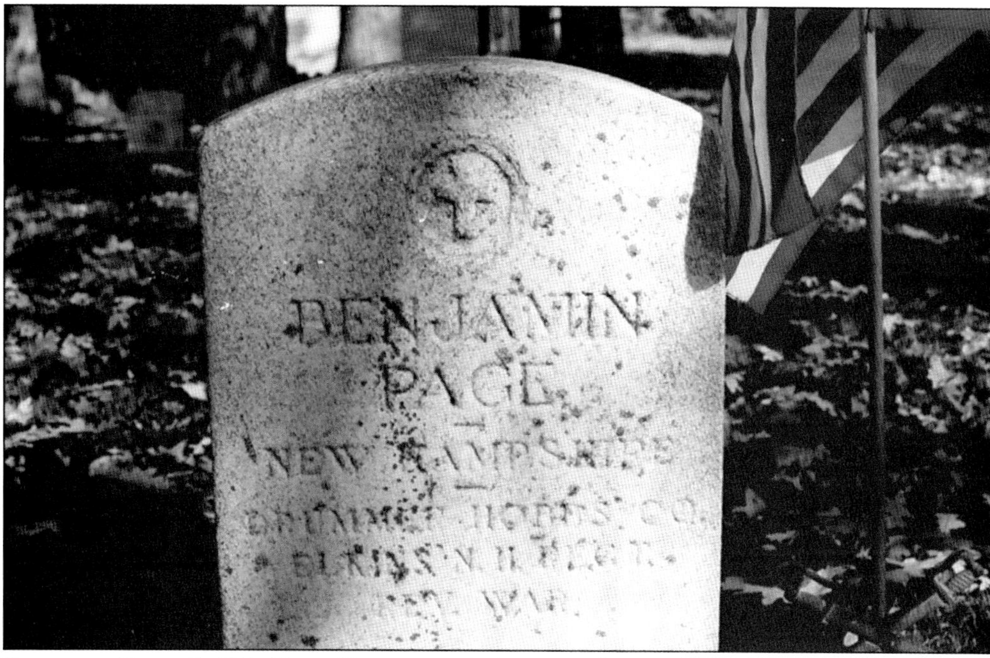

BENJAMIN PAGE (1850), PAGE CEMETERY. A drummer during the Revolution, Benjamin Page enlisted from Chichester in January 1777 for three years of service in Scammell's 3rd New Hampshire Regiment in the Continental Line. Serving in the company of Capt. Richard Weare, Page fought "against the common enemy" at such places as Saratoga, Monmouth, and Newtown before his discharge at Camp Danbury, Connecticut. He died in Meredith on June 24, 1850.

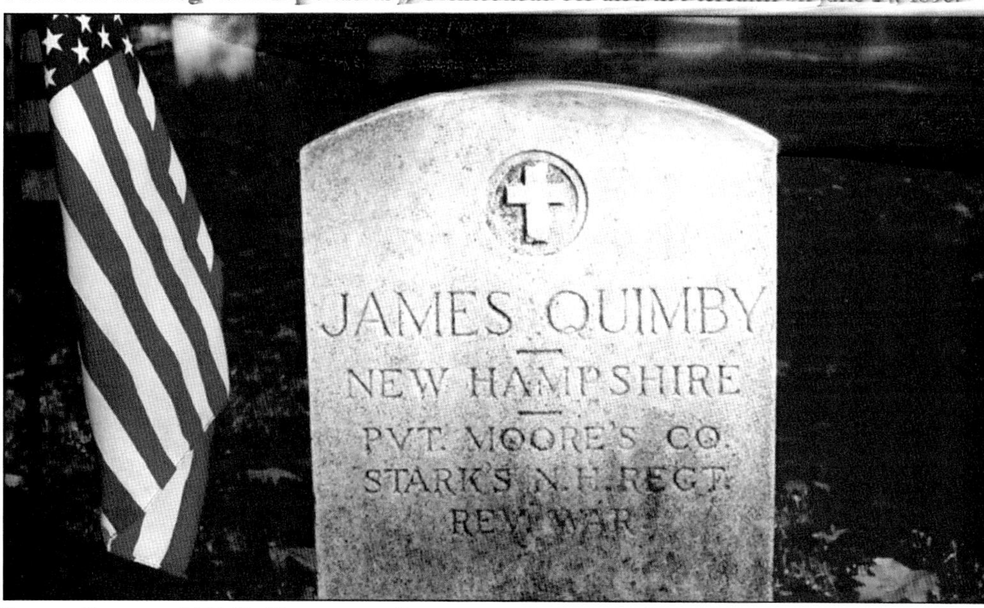

JAMES QUIMBY (1835), BLAISDELL CEMETERY. A native of Brentwood, James Quimby saw extensive battle action during the Revolution and afterward practiced the trade of a shoemaker. Serving for nearly five years during the war, Quimby fought in the 1st New Hampshire Regiment under Col. John Stark at Bunker Hill in 1775. From 1776 to 1780, he fought in Poor and Hale's 2nd New Hampshire Regiment at the battles of Hubbardton, Saratoga, and Monmouth.

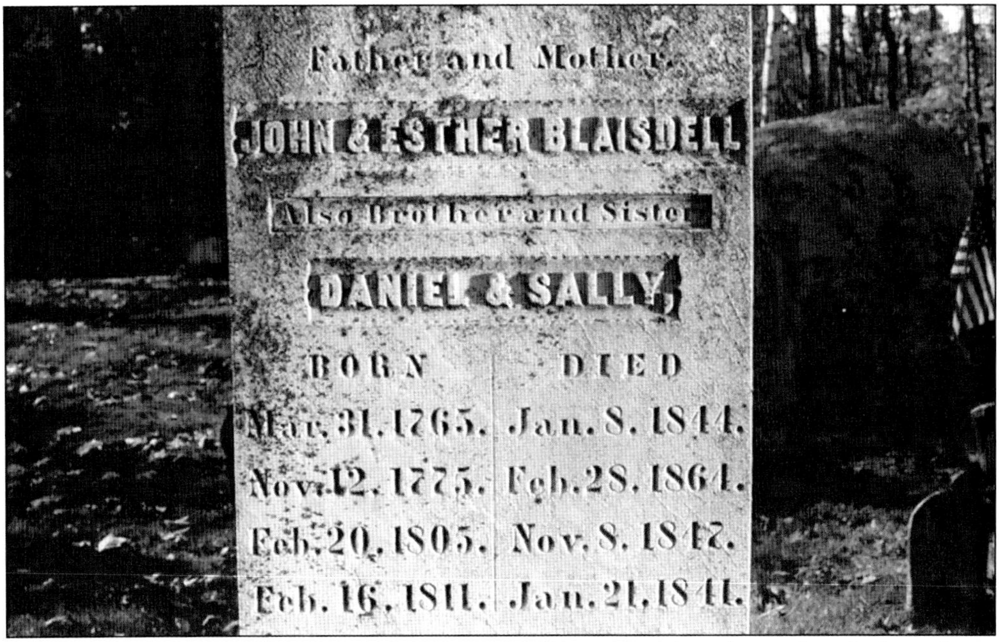

THE BLAISDELL FAMILY (1841–1864), BLAISDELL CEMETERY. Once located in the boundaries of Meredith, and situated adjacent to the Meredith town pound, this Laconia cemetery is also interesting because of the Revolutionary War soldiers buried here. One member of the Blaisdell family, appropriately enough, served as the pound keeper for a time, in charge of the stray cattle and horses confined within its granite walls.

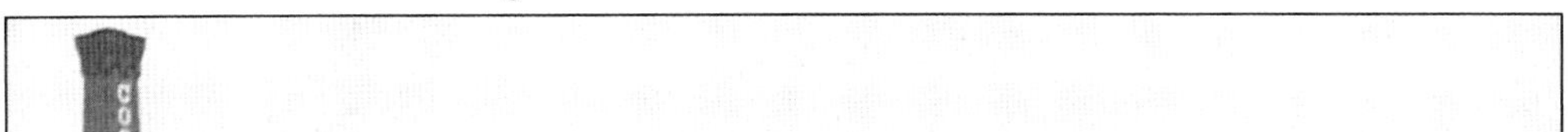

VIEW OF MEREDITH BRIDGE CEMETERY, C. 1910. This interesting view shows the commercial development that occurred around this cemetery and along the Winnipesaukee River in Laconia. Shown in the foreground is the Cook Lumber Yard, while at the right rear is shown a portion of the Meredith Bridge Cemetery. The cemetery is still in a commercial area today but is well preserved and maintained. (Courtesy Laconia Public Library.)

MARK PIPER (1821), MEREDITH BRIDGE CEMETERY. This simple slate stone is one of the oldest found in this cemetery. Mark Piper was likely the son of Elisha or Daniel Piper, members of the original Baptist Society in Meredith in 1797.

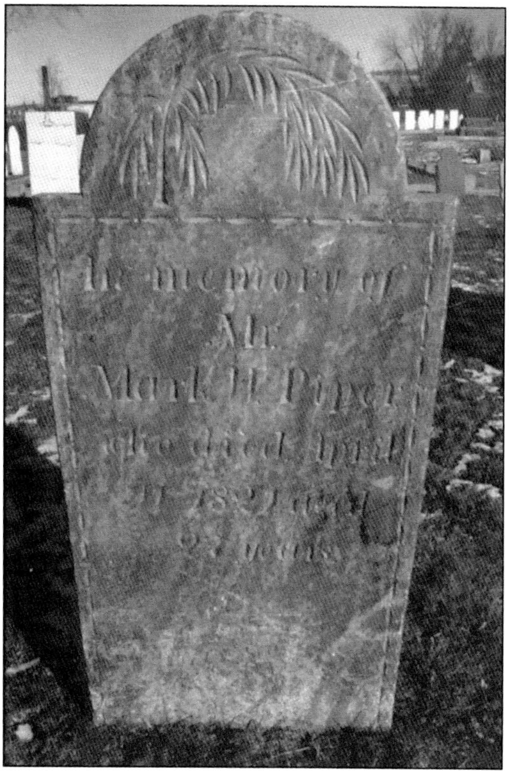

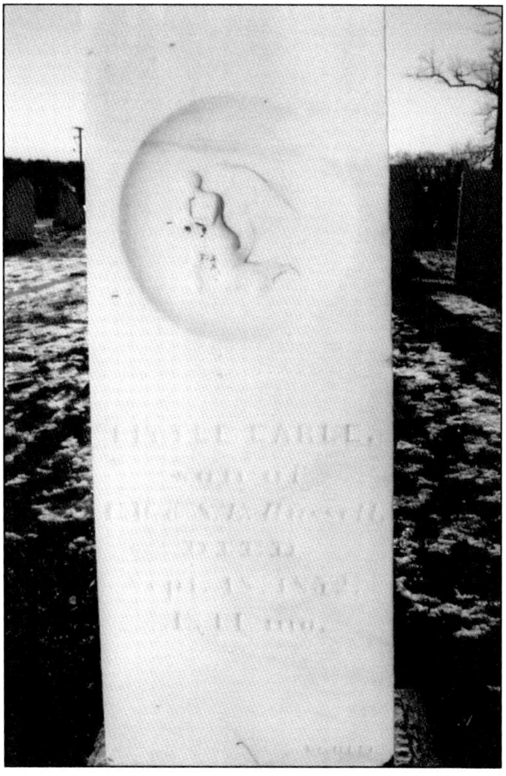

EARLE RUSSELL (1852), MEREDITH BRIDGE CEMETERY. This small marble shaft, adorned with an image of what is likely the Archangel Gabriel, is one of the most exquisite examples of the stonecutters' art found here. It was crafted by Albert Hull, a native of Moultonborough who practiced his trade in Meredith Bridge beginning around 1849. Note Hull's signature at the bottom of the stone.

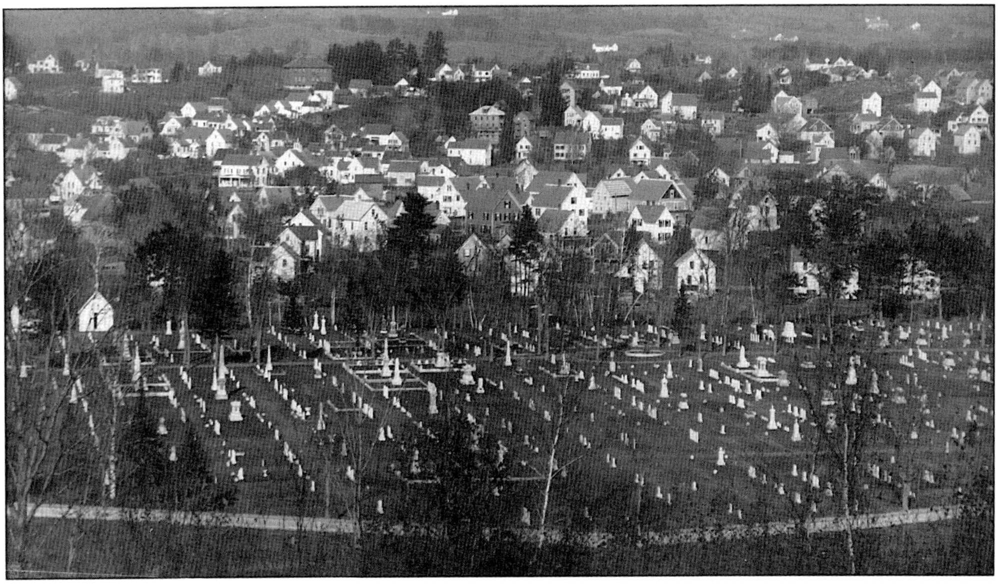

Aerial View of Union Cemetery. This interesting aerial view shows how Union Cemetery appeared around 1940. Established nearly 100 years before, Union Cemetery has grown to be the largest cemetery in Laconia. It is also the best known and has buried here some of the town's most distinguished citizens from its early beginnings to the present day. (Courtesy Laconia Public Library.)

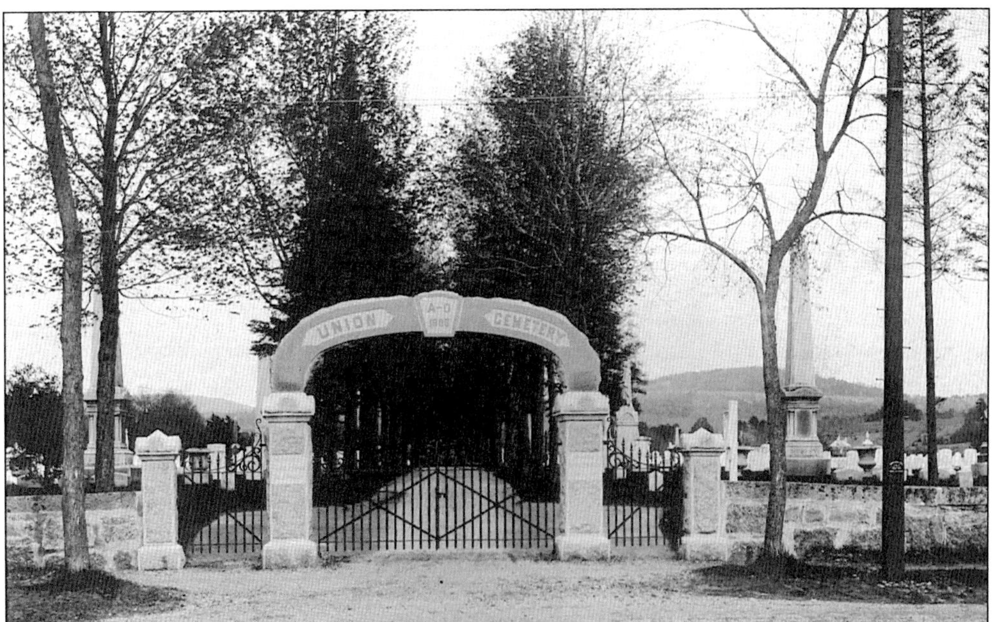

View of Union Cemetery. This view of Union Cemetery shows the massive granite arch and wrought-iron gate that were added to the cemetery in 1908. (Courtesy Laconia Public Library.)

ORIN COLE (1838), HILLSIDE CEMETERY, LAKEPORT VILLAGE. The slate stone shown here for the young son of Rev. Timothy Cole is signed at the bottom by Benjamin Day, a well-known stonecutter from Lowell, Massachusetts. Little is known about Reverend Cole; born in New Hampshire and by 1860 preaching in Haverhill, Massachusetts, he may have been an early preacher in the Methodist Episcopal church, formed here in 1838.

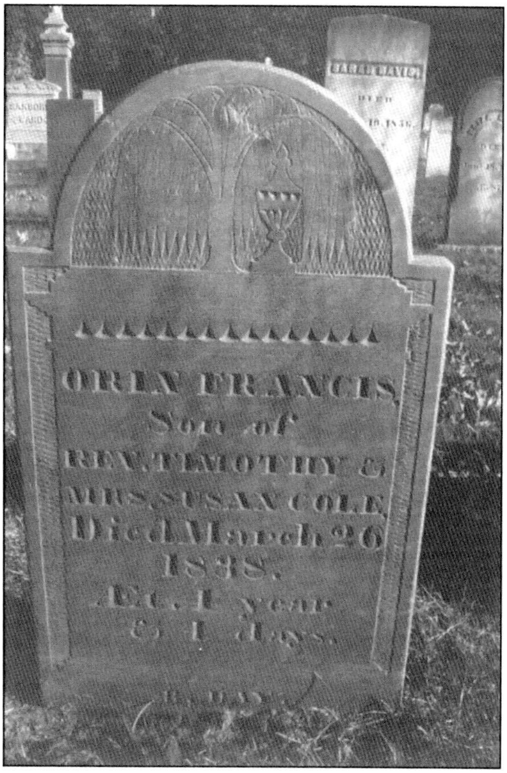

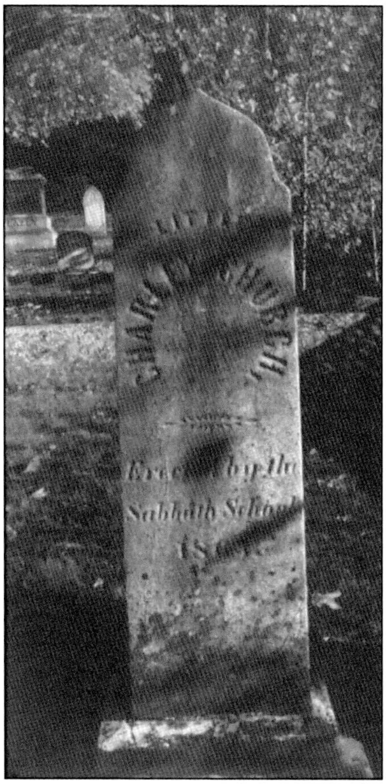

CHARLEY CHURCH (1863), HILLSIDE CEMETERY, LAKEPORT VILLAGE. "Little Charley" was the son of Rev. Samuel Church, a Baptist preacher from Ohio. The Sabbath school Charley attended had been in operation in town since 1818. After Charley's death, Samuel and his family moved to Bangor, Maine, and later back to New Hampshire. Though they died elsewhere, both of Charley's parents were brought back to Laconia to be buried next to their son.

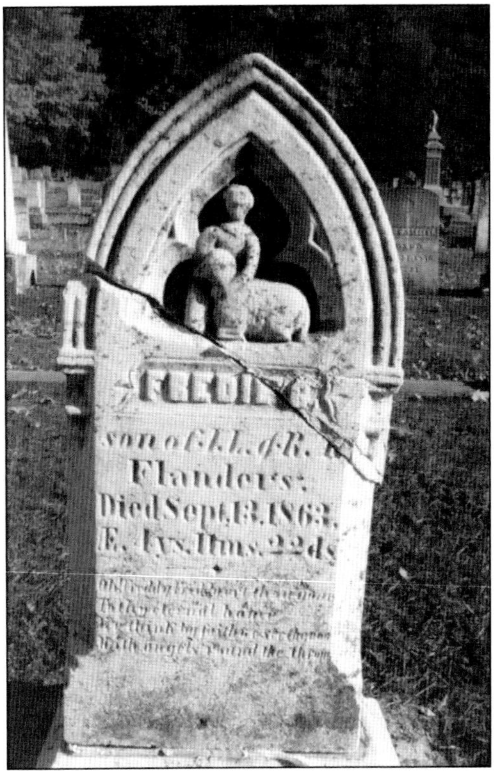

FREDIE FLANDERS (1863), HILLSIDE CEMETERY, LAKEPORT VILLAGE. Fredie was the young son of carpenter John Flanders and his wife Ruth and was their only child. His stone, depicting a boy petting a lamb, is one of the most poignant to be found here and is very appropriate; the lamb has long been a Christian symbol of innocence and resurrection and is often found on children's gravestones.

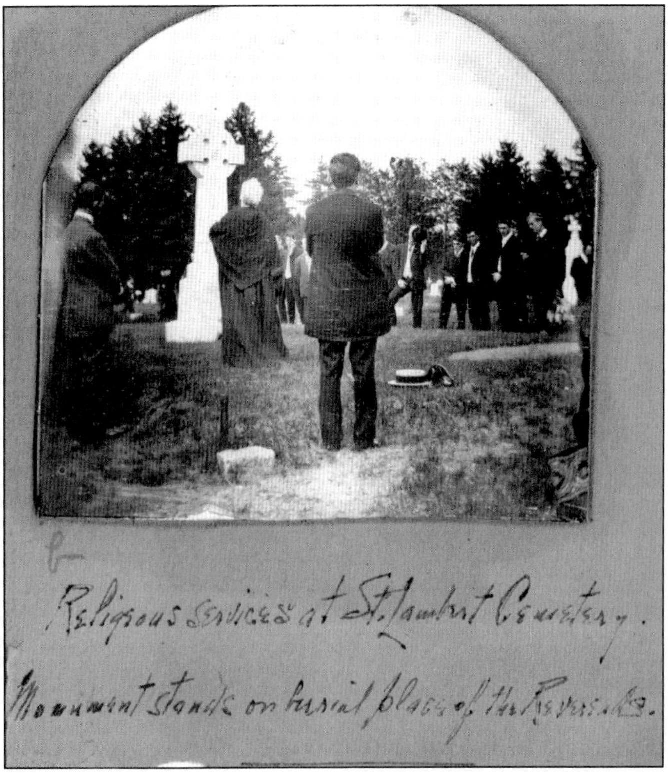

ST. LAMBERT CEMETERY VIEW, 1908. The Catholic faith has been strong in what is now Laconia since the 1830s. St. Lambert Cemetery was established and consecrated in 1881 and was no doubt named to honor Rev. John Lambert. This view shows a service being conducted at the monument in the reverend's plot where some of Laconia's earliest Catholic ministers are buried. (Courtesy Laconia Public Library.)

Nine

Gilford and Belmont

The towns featured in this chapter were originally part of Gilmanton, granted in 1727 and first settled in 1761. The territory comprising Gilford was originally part of Gilmanton's Upper Parish and went by the name of Gunstock Parish. The parish was set off as a town in 1812, taking its present name on the suggestion of a resident who fought during the Revolution at the Battle of Guilford Courthouse. It was not until 1776–1777 that the first settlers came to Gunstock Parish and built permanent homesteads. Prior to the building of the Gunstock meetinghouse in 1794, townsmen attended church at the Tioga meetinghouse, in present-day Belmont, or made the long journey to Gilmanton Lower Parish. The first church in Gilford was the First Free Will Baptist Church, headed by Elder Richard Martin and begun in 1797. Family or small neighborhood cemeteries predominated in Gilford. McCoy Cemetery is located just down the hill from the site of the old meetinghouse. This is the oldest cemetery in town, established around 1822. Here will be found the final resting place of Elder Martin and his wife. Hoyt Cemetery, another important cemetery, is located close to the site of John Edgerly's 1778 homestead and has buried here John Knowles, a well-known Free Will Baptist preacher who worked throughout the Lakes Region. The first town cemetery in Gilford was Pine Grove Cemetery, established in 1860, and the story of how the pine trees that mark its side boundary came to be planted there is a fascinating one. Finally there is the Davis Cemetery on Governors Island, owned by the Davis family from 1799 to 1857. Here is buried the near-legendary Nathaniel Davis.

The town of Belmont, part of Gilmanton's Upper Parish, was usually referred to as Tioga Parish until the separation of Gilford. It then became more common to refer to it as Upper Parish once again. As historian Allan Hackett states, "the site of the present village of Belmont remained an unbroken forest for many years." The first church in the parish was that on Province Road, built in 1792 and still standing today. The parish separated from Gilmanton in 1859 and took the name of Upper Gilmanton but changed it to Belmont in 1869. Because Belmont was only sparsely settled early on, neighborhood and family cemeteries are found throughout the town. Two of the most interesting are the Perkins Road Cemetery, which is the final resting place of some of the earliest settlers in town and their descendants. The Judkins and Hunt Cemetery on Hurricane Road is also notable not only for some older gravestones but also for 1908 automobile accident victim Synder Wallace, perhaps the earliest such fatality in New Hampshire. There is also one church-related cemetery in Belmont—Highland Cemetery. A modern Baptist church occupies the site today where the original Christian Baptist Church in town was built, and the old cemetery, with gravestones dating back to 1797, is well maintained.

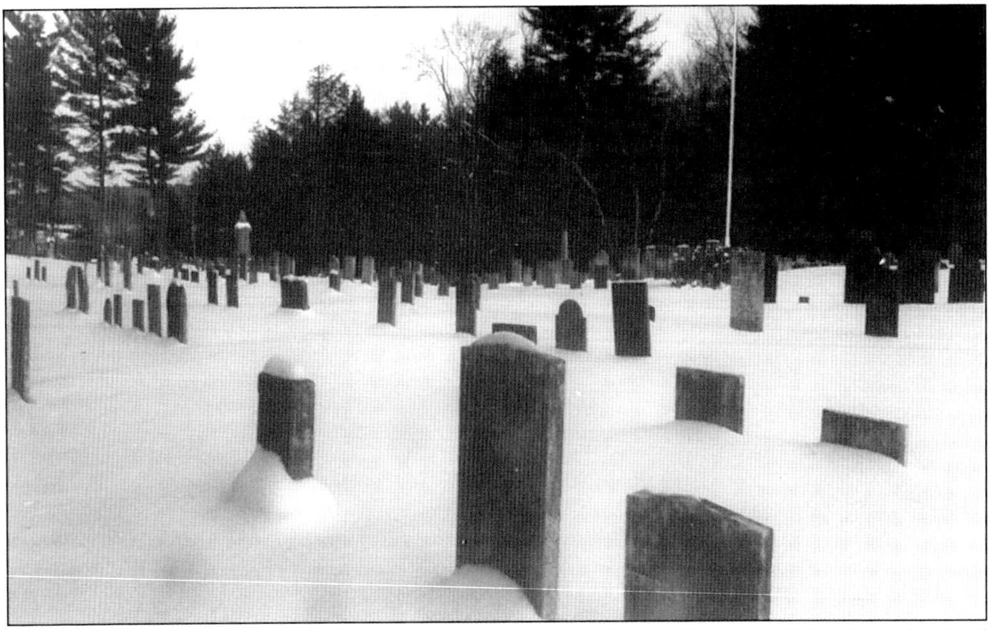

McCoy Cemetery, Gilford. This cemetery was formally established in 1822 when the land was purchased of James McCoy. However, it was certainly in use at an earlier date, as evidenced by the older gravestones found here. Interestingly, the town also arranged for the purchase of a communal burial shroud, which was rented to those in need for 17¢. Of the first 10 people buried here, 6 were children.

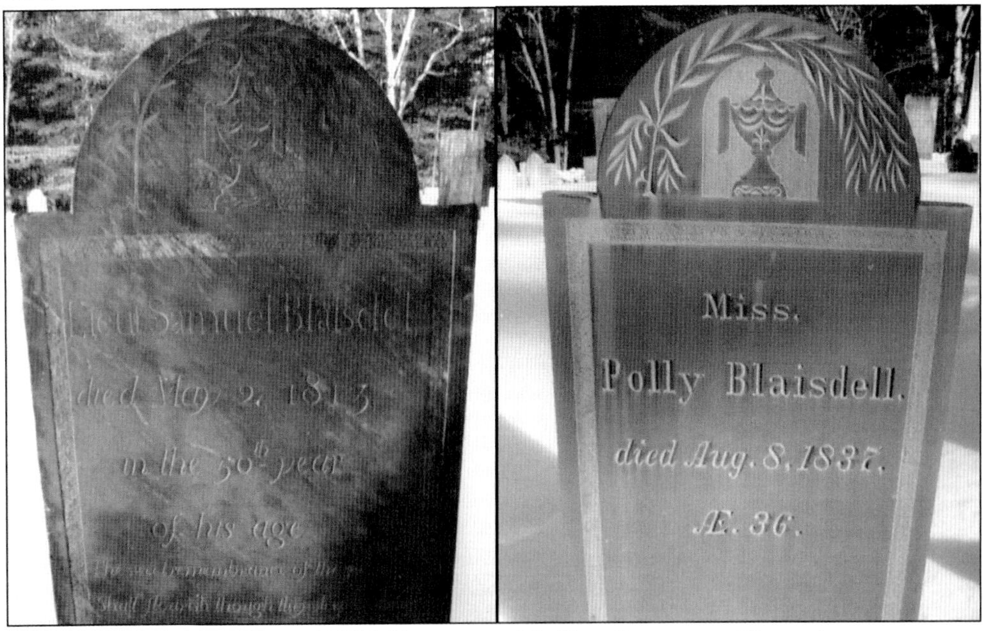

Samuel (1813) and Polly (1837) Blaisdell, McCoy Cemetery. These slate gravestones are some of the finest to be found in Gilford. Samuel Blaisdell was a blacksmith who set up his shop near Lilly Pond in 1789 and held religious meetings at his home before the Gunstock meetinghouse was built. His daughter Polly, apparently never married, may have helped out at her father's shop or may have been a schoolteacher.

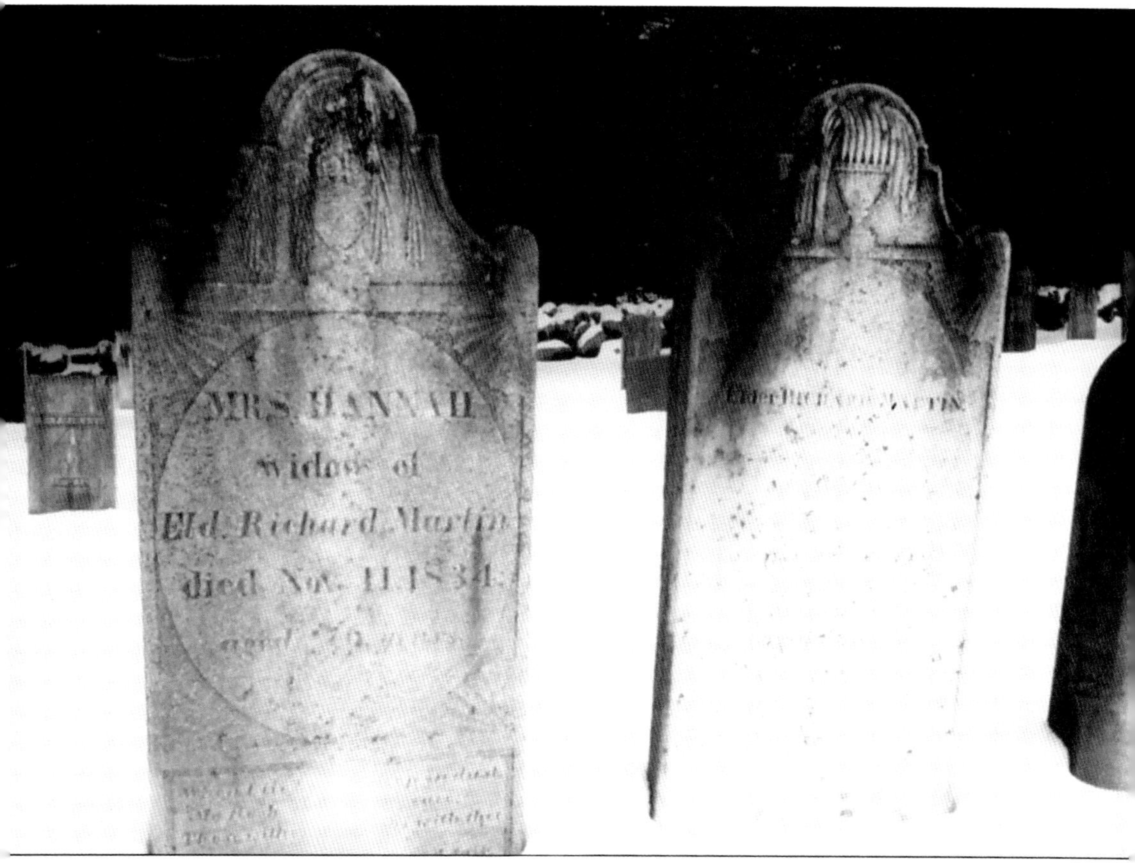

HANNAH (1834) AND RICHARD (1824) MARTIN, MCCOY CEMETERY. Richard Martin was one of the most influential men of his day in Gilford. A native of Lee, New Hampshire, he worked as a rope maker and ship's cook and served in the Revolution. Martin likely saw action on the high seas as a crewman on a privateer. Later Martin worked as a shoemaker and was ordained as a Baptist minister in 1795. He and his wife Hannah came to Gunstock Parish in 1796 and settled on a 70-acre farm. A well-known Free Will Baptist, Elder Martin traveled extensively throughout the Lakes Region, helping to establish at least six congregations. Because Free Will Baptist ministers received no salary, Martin worked as a tanner to support his family. His wife Hannah helped, too: "she earned herself something of a reputation as a land trader." Richard Martin preached to the end of his life, dying in October 1824 while on his way to conduct services. Hannah, no doubt supported by some of the income she earned as a land trader, survived 10 years as his widow.

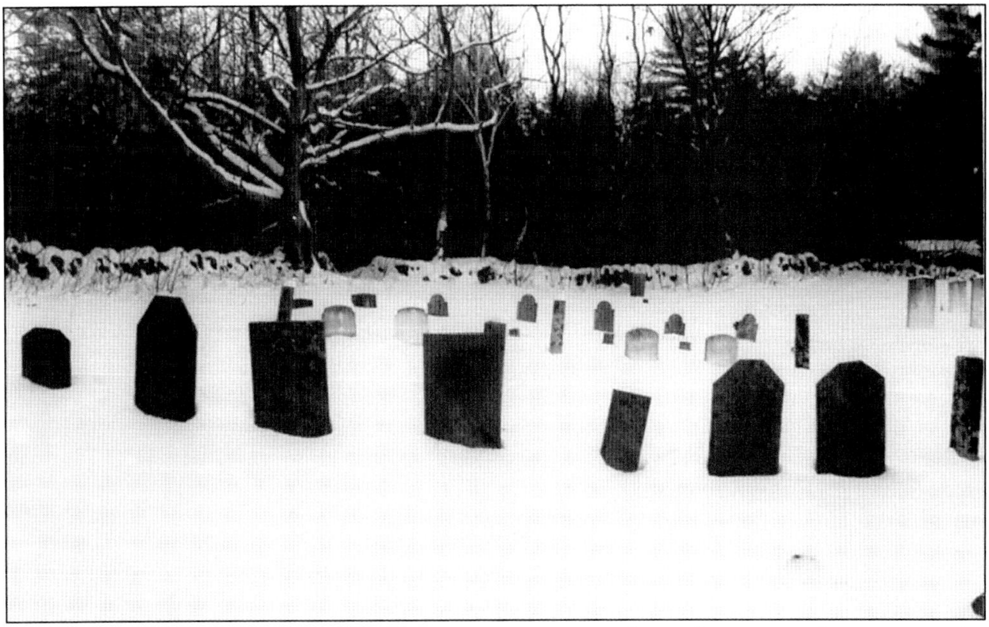

Hoyt Cemetery, Gilford. This picturesque cemetery, located in a rural setting at the junction of Hoyt and Wild Acres Roads, is an example of a family cemetery that evolved into a neighborhood cemetery over the years. Prominent among those buried here are members of the Hoyt family, who first arrived here around 1785, and the members of the Thing family.

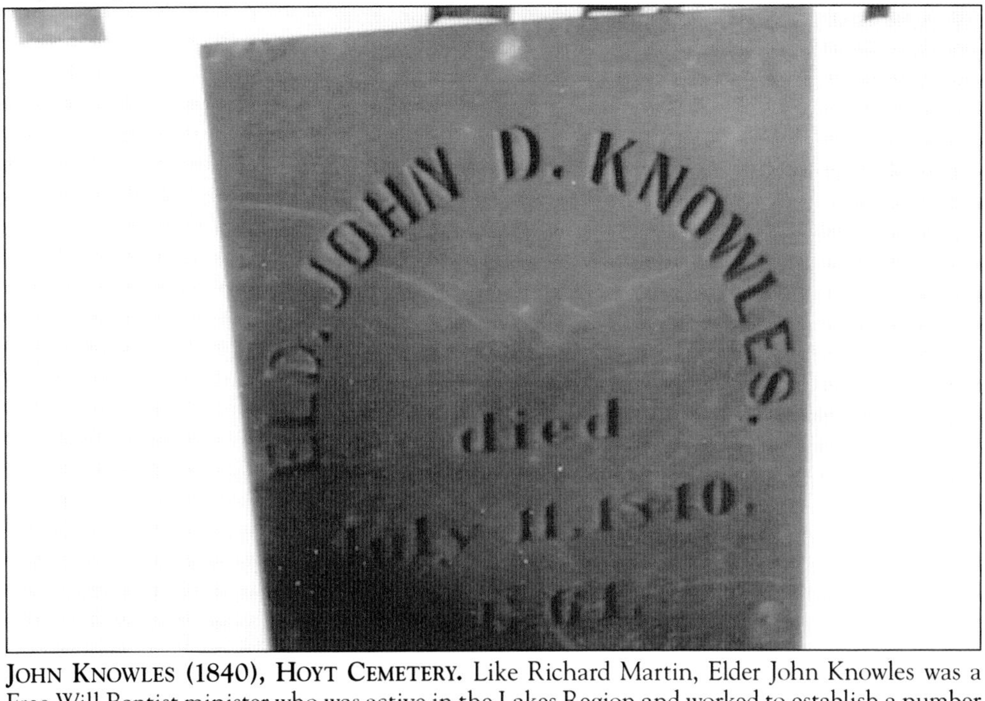

John Knowles (1840), Hoyt Cemetery. Like Richard Martin, Elder John Knowles was a Free Will Baptist minister who was active in the Lakes Region and worked to establish a number of churches nearby. Knowles lived on Liberty Hill and was the elder for a Free Will Baptist church that was gathered in that locale in 1816 and met at the Province Road meetinghouse (see page 116) in Tioga Parish (later Belmont).

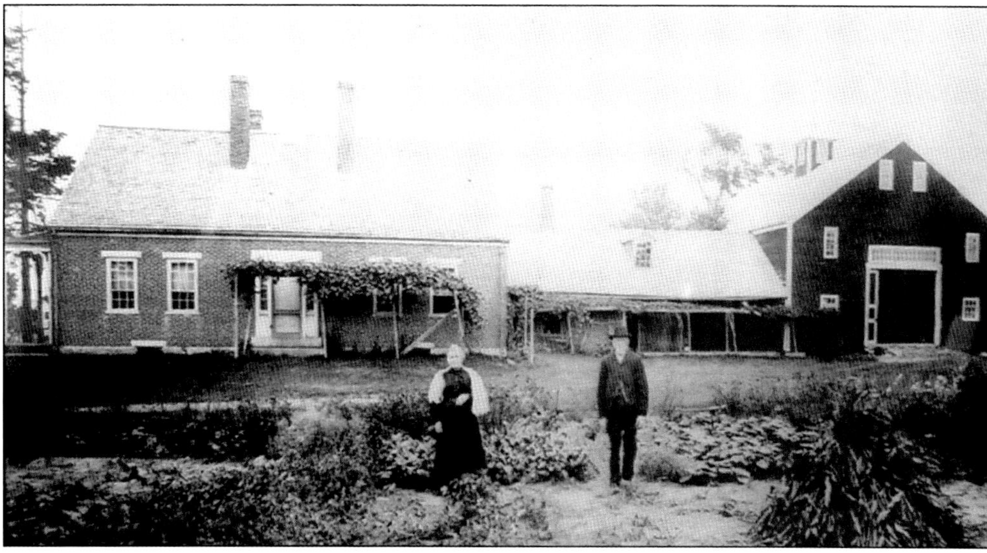

The Benjamin Rowe House, Gilford, Built around 1838. Benjamin Rowe arrived in Gilford from Brentwood in 1815. The cape farmhouse he built, constructed of bricks he made himself and still standing today, is the only house of its kind in New Hampshire. The land for neighboring Pine Grove Cemetery, established in 1860, was once owned by Rowe before he sold it to David Gould in 1838. (Courtesy Thompson-Ames Historical Society.)

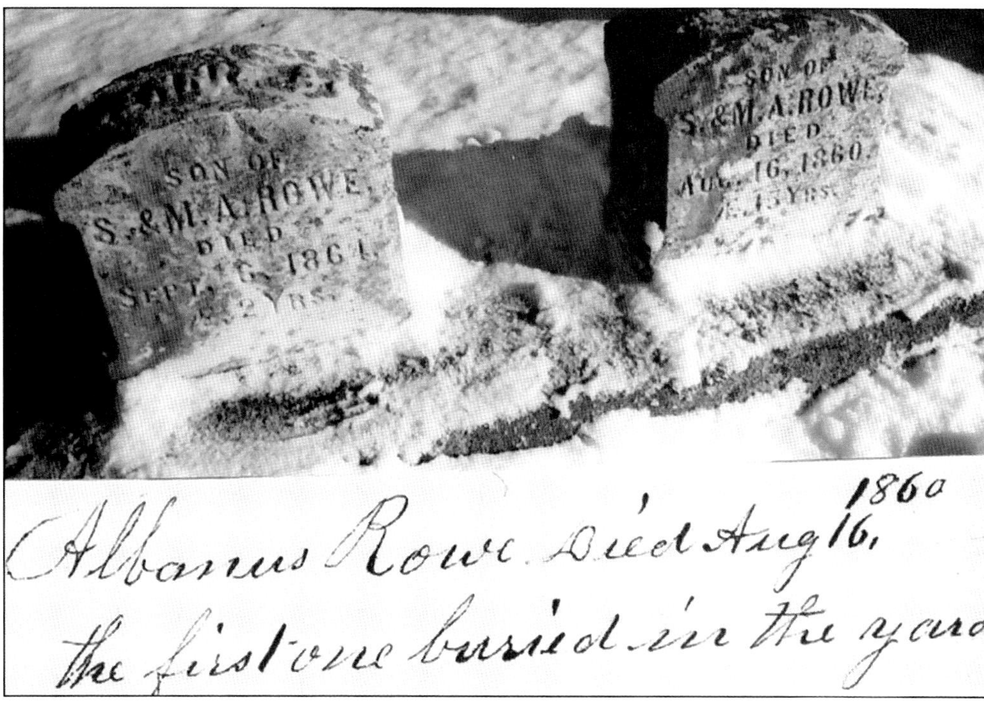

Bennie (1864) and Albanus (1860) Rowe, Pine Grove Cemetery. Bennie and Albanus Rowe were the sons of Simon Rowe and the grandsons of Benjamin Rowe. As is noted in town records, Albanus was the first to be buried here. Lore states that Simon Rowe planted the row of pine trees that are still standing today so that his wife Mary could not see the graves of her sons from her kitchen window. (Record courtesy Thompson-Ames Historical Society.)

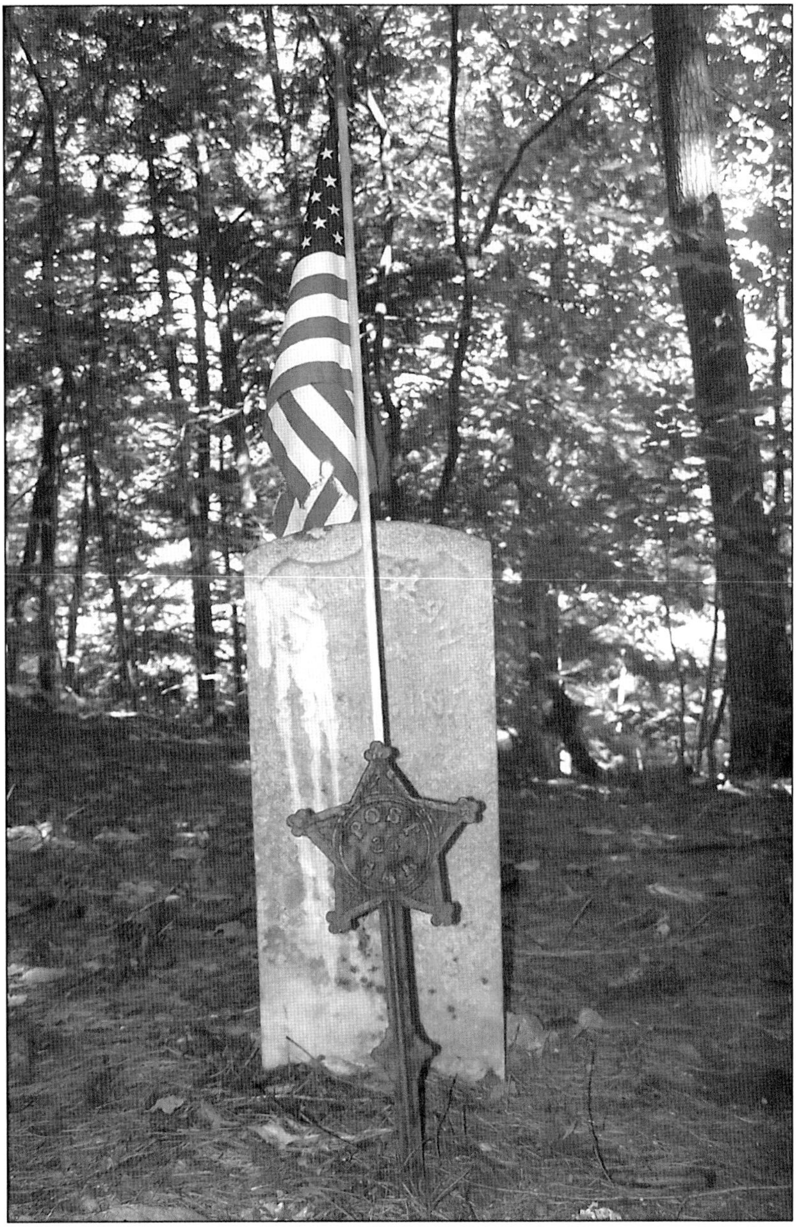

George Bean (1864), Bean Cemetery. George W. M. Bean is the sole person buried at this site near Ellacoya State Park. A native of Meredith, he was an early enlistee in the Civil War, joining the Laconia Volunteers in April 1861 at the age of 26. Discharged in May due to illness, Bean joined the 3rd New Hampshire Regiment in August 1861. He saw most of his battle action in South Carolina at such places as Port Royal, James Island, and possibly in the assault on Fort Wagner. Contracting smallpox, whether at home on leave or while in camp down south is unknown, Bean was placed in Gilford's town poor farm, cared for in an area designated for "pest cases." Bean subsequently died on February 20, 1864, probably spending his last days in isolation. Due to local fears of the smallpox disease, he was buried in isolation to prevent contagion. Though alone in death, Bean was not forgotten; it being said that children who passed by always decorated his grave with wildflowers. (Courtesy David Perry.)

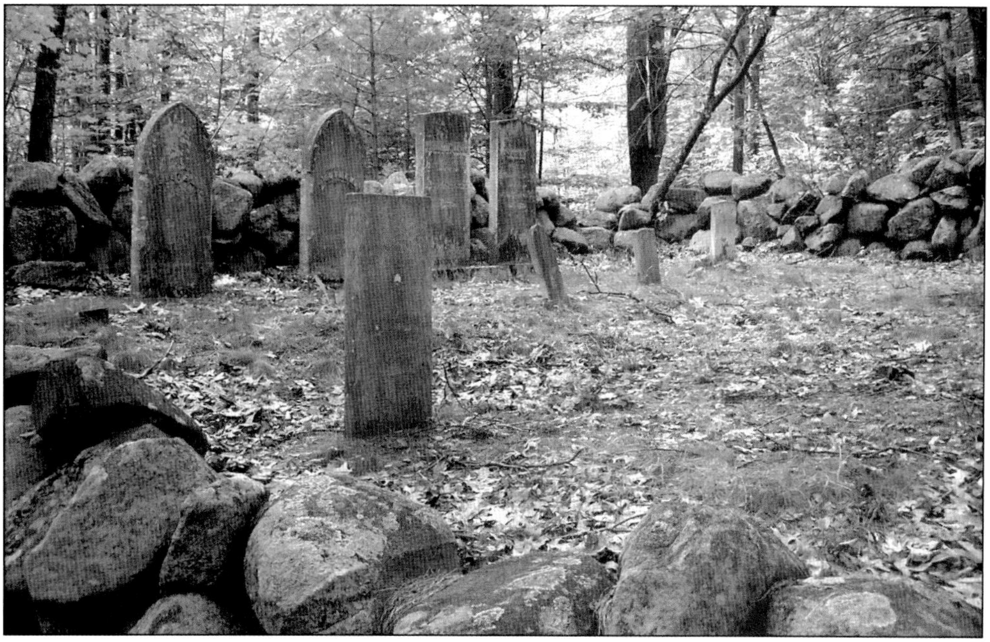

DAVIS CEMETERY, GOVERNORS ISLAND, GILFORD. The Davis family owned Governors Island from 1799 to 1857. Buried here is Nathaniel "Island" Davis. A "stalwart and commanding" person, he was a farmer who always sold his produce at a fair price. Davis was also a Millerite, believing that the end of the world would occur sometime in 1843–1844. Preacher William Miller held camp meetings on the island in 1840 and 1843. (Courtesy David Perry.)

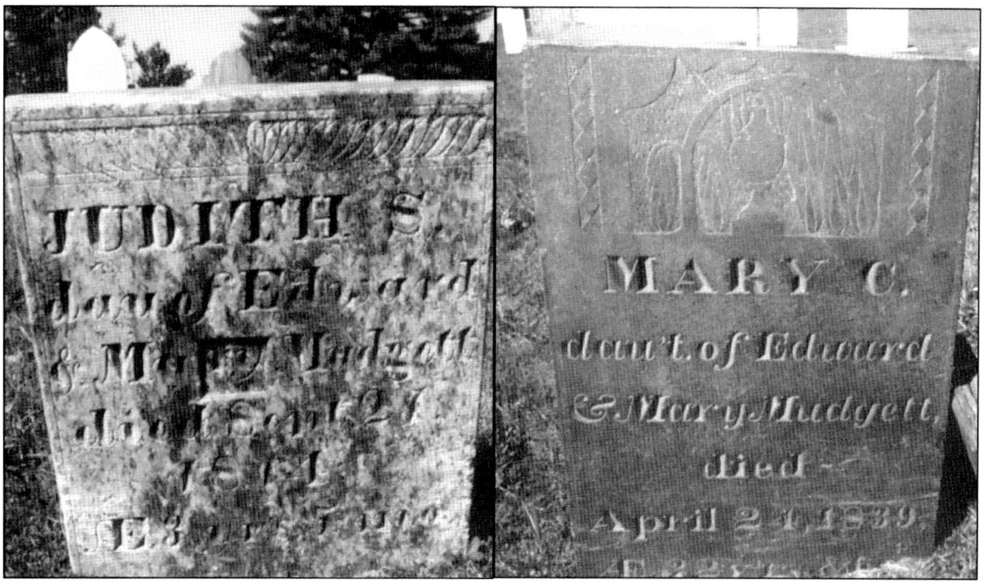

JUDITH (1814) AND MARY (1839) MUDGETT, PERKINS ROAD CEMETERY, BELMONT. Judith Mudgett, aged three, and her sister Mary, aged 32, were the daughters of Edward and Mary and are descended from the area's very first settlers. Judith's stone (left) was carved by a young Matthias Weeks. Note the chiseled out mistake in the name Mary. Mary's stone was probably carved by the Day family of stonecutters in Goffstown.

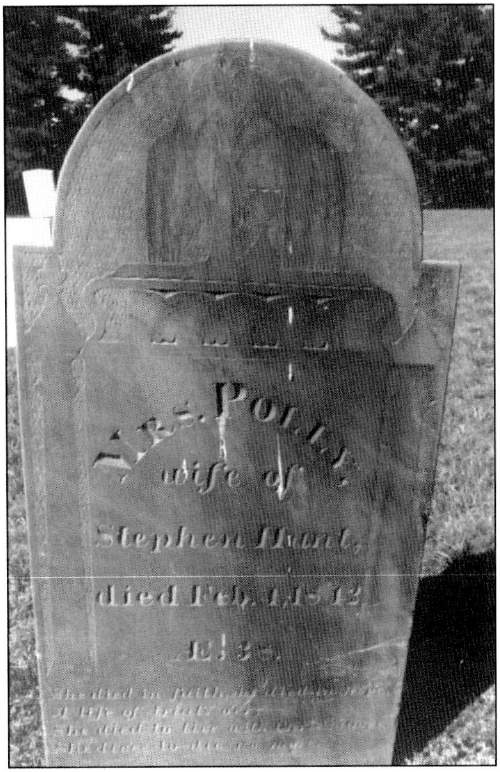

POLLY HUNT (1842), PERKINS ROAD CEMETERY. This interesting slate stone for the wife of Stephen Hunt was carved in Manchester by a member of the Day family. Elaborate for its time, it was likely expensive. Her epitaph at bottom reads, "She died in faith, she died in hope, A life of trial o'er; She died to live with Christ above, She lives to die no more."

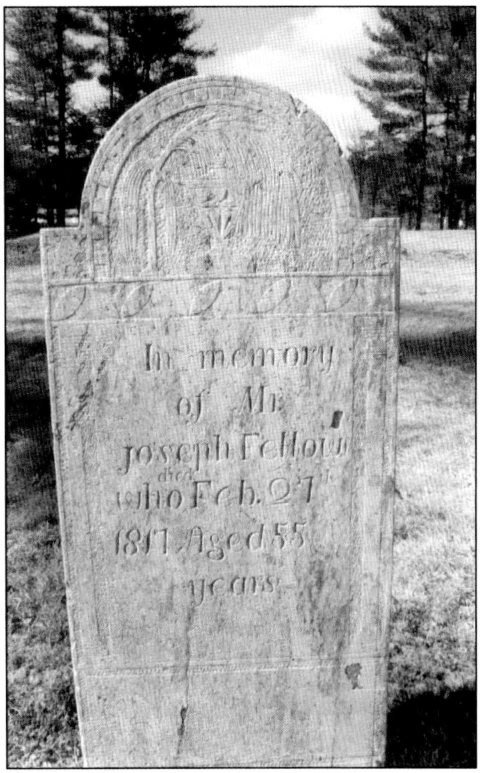

JOSEPH FELLOWS (1817), PERKINS ROAD CEMETERY. Fellows and his wife Mary, who died less than two months after he did and is buried beside him, came to Gilmanton's Upper Parish from Brentwood about 1790. On the nearby Tioga River, Fellows built the first sawmill and gristmill in town. Fellows's gravestone was carved by Matthias Weeks early in his career, as is clearly evident in its poorly arranged lettering.

JOHN SWETT (1794), HIGHLAND CEMETERY. This gravestone was carved by Matthias Weeks of Gilmanton and records the unusual manner of John Swett's death in 1794 in the epitaph at bottom, which reads, "His death was caused by the fall of a tree." Though this is the oldest dated burial at Highland Cemetery (once named Union Cemetery), this stone is backdated and was likely carved 20 or more years after Swett died.

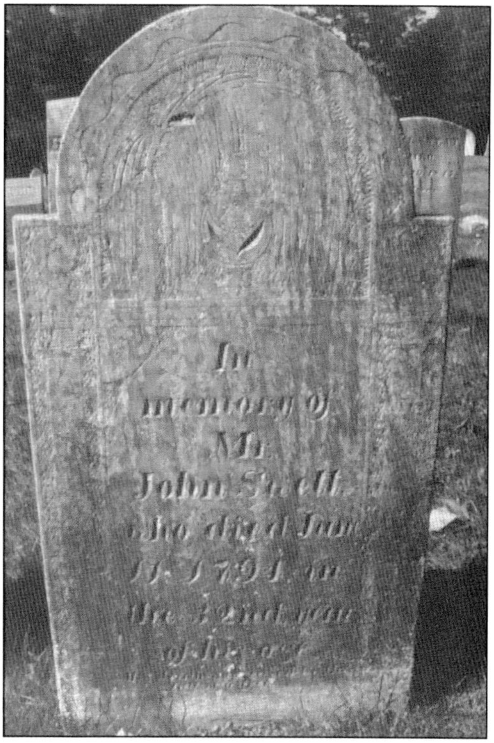

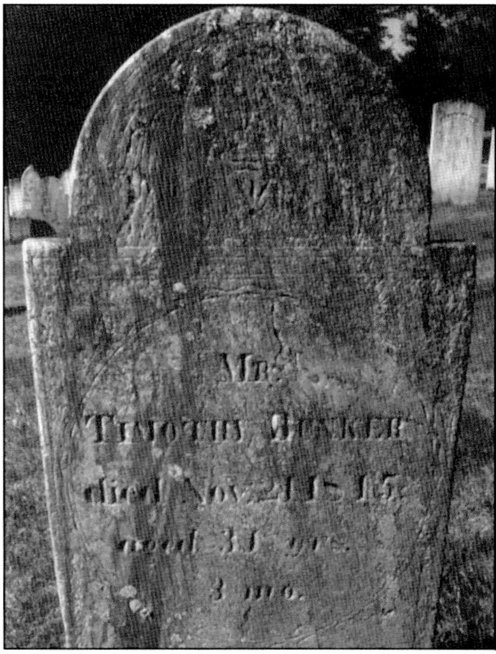

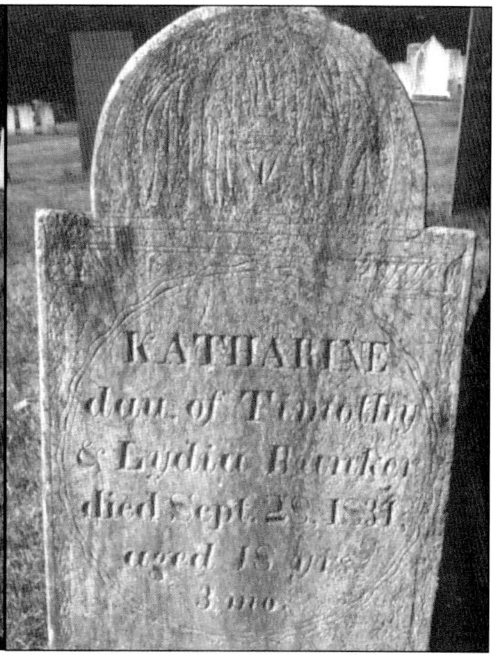

TIMOTHY (1815) AND KATHARINE (1831) BUNKER, HIGHLAND CEMETERY. Little is known of the Bunker family, including the father and daughter buried here. Timothy Bunker died while his daughter was just two years old, while Katharine died at age 18. Both stones, despite the difference in death dates, were likely created and erected at the same time by Matthias Weeks around 1832, after Katharine's death.

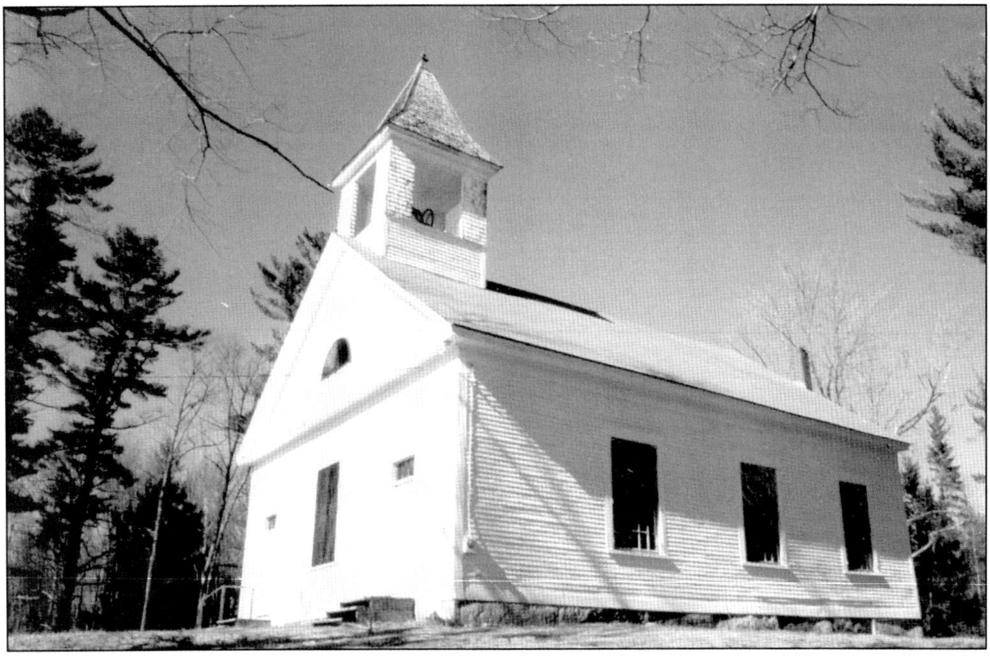

PROVINCE ROAD MEETINGHOUSE. This meetinghouse is the oldest church building found in the Lakes Region. Built in 1792, in what was then Tioga Parish in Upper Gilmanton, this church was used by several denominations until it became a Free Will Baptist church in 1816. Its first pastor was Elder John Knowles (see page 110), who preached here until his death in 1840.

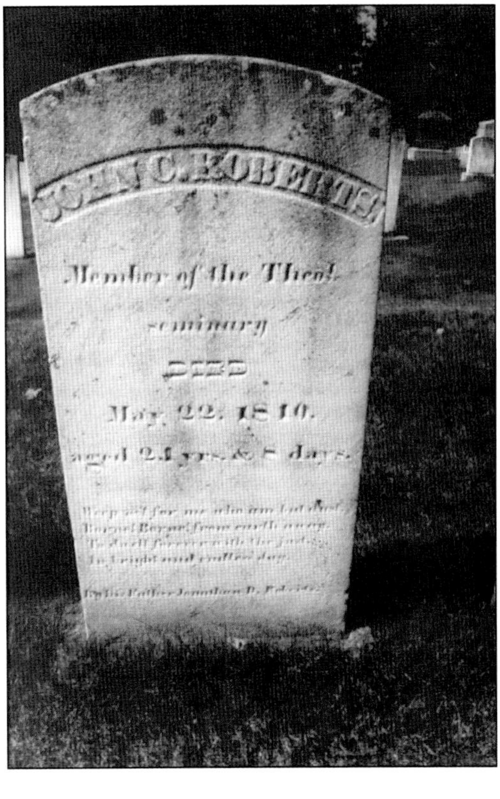

JOHN ROBERTS (1840), HIGHLAND CEMETERY. The stone for this young man, the son of Jonathan Roberts of Farmington, notes that he was a "member of the Theological seminary." The seminary Roberts attended was in Gilmanton and an offshoot of Gilmanton Academy, established in 1794. The divinity students here gained experience as preachers by supplying the pulpits for many area churches that had no established minister or regular services.

Ten

THE GILMANTONS

The last town in this study, consisting of Gilmanton ("the Centre Village"), Lower Gilmanton, and Gilmanton Ironworks, is the oldest around Lake Winnipesaukee. Originally called Gilmantown from the many proprietors and early settlers who bore the Gilman name, it was granted in 1727. While the area was not settled permanently until late 1761, this does not mean Gilmanton was a quiet wilderness; Native Americans, traders, and surveyors were active on a seasonal basis. Two small forts were even built at each end of Gilmanton prior to the French and Indian War, the northern one located in what is now Gilford, and a road cut between them. Neither substantial in size nor permanently manned, these forts at least were an attempt to facilitate commerce and development in the area. The first settlers in Gilmanton were Benjamin Mudgett and his wife Hannah, newly married for three weeks, followed closely by the families of John Mudgett and Orlando Weed. These first settlers were indeed hardy; Hannah Mudgett lived until the ripe old age of 95, dying in Meredith in 1834, while the first child born in town was Orlando Weed's daughter, Dorothy, born in October 1762. The settling of Gilmanton, once begun, proceeded at a quick pace. By 1763, the first minister, Rev. William Parsons, arrived in town to become both preacher and schoolmaster. In 1774, two churches were built, one for the Congregationalists, and one for the Baptists, each supporting their own minister. The Congregationalist church, called the Smith Meeting House after its first pastor, Rev. Isaac Smith, was roofed in 1775 but was not completely finished for 16 years. The Smith Meeting House Cemetery was established in 1776, soon after the new church became usable. The first burial to take place here was that of Lt. Joseph Philbrick, selectman, militia officer, and member of the meetinghouse building committee, in 1776. By the 1830s, the church membership had declined, and the Smith Meeting House was in a bad way. It was torn down in 1838, and in 1839, the meetinghouse now present was built as a replacement. The decline of the church continued and by the end of the Civil War was little used and virtually abandoned. The same held true for the Smith Meeting House Cemetery until civic leaders in the 1890s took matters into their own hands and raised funds to restore the meetinghouse and reclaim the cemetery. Today, Smith Meeting House Cemetery is one of the most beautiful and historic cemeteries in the state and offers the best collection of gravestone art found in the Lakes Region. Modern burials here include Grace Metalious, the author of the controversial book *Peyton Place*, who died in 1964.

Other interesting historical cemeteries abound in Gilmanton, including secluded Beech Grove Cemetery where is found the burial of an African American Civil War veteran; Copp Cemetery, the resting place for several generations of Copp military men; the Friends Cemetery for the Quakers that lived in town; and Tibbetts Cemetery, located on a hillside site with a fine collection of slate gravestones.

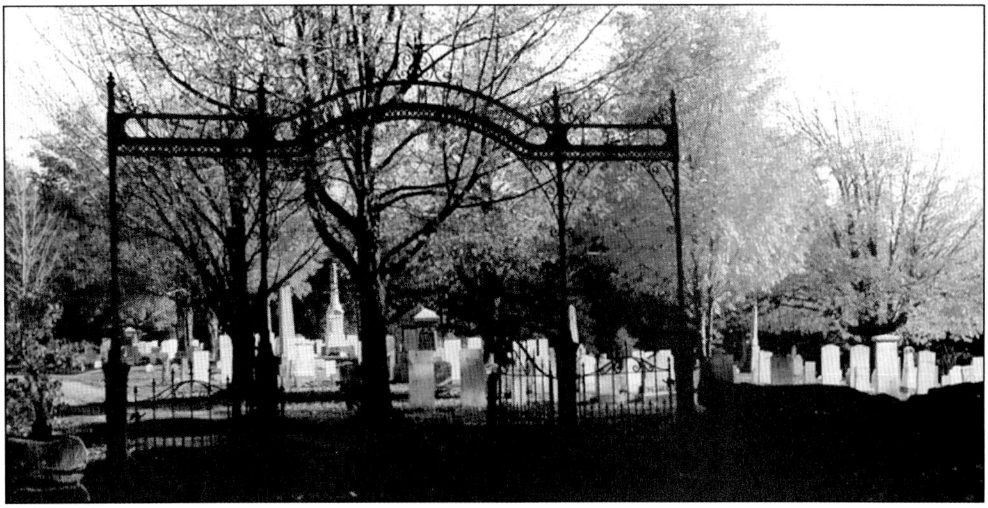

SMITH MEETING HOUSE CEMETERY. Now located on a quiet country road, the area around Smith Meeting House was at one time the center of early town affairs. Once the meetinghouse fell in disuse and disrepair, the same thing happened to the cemetery. However, town folk restored the cemetery over 100 years ago and erected this fine wrought-iron gate in 1911, restoring the cemetery to its former beauty in exemplary fashion.

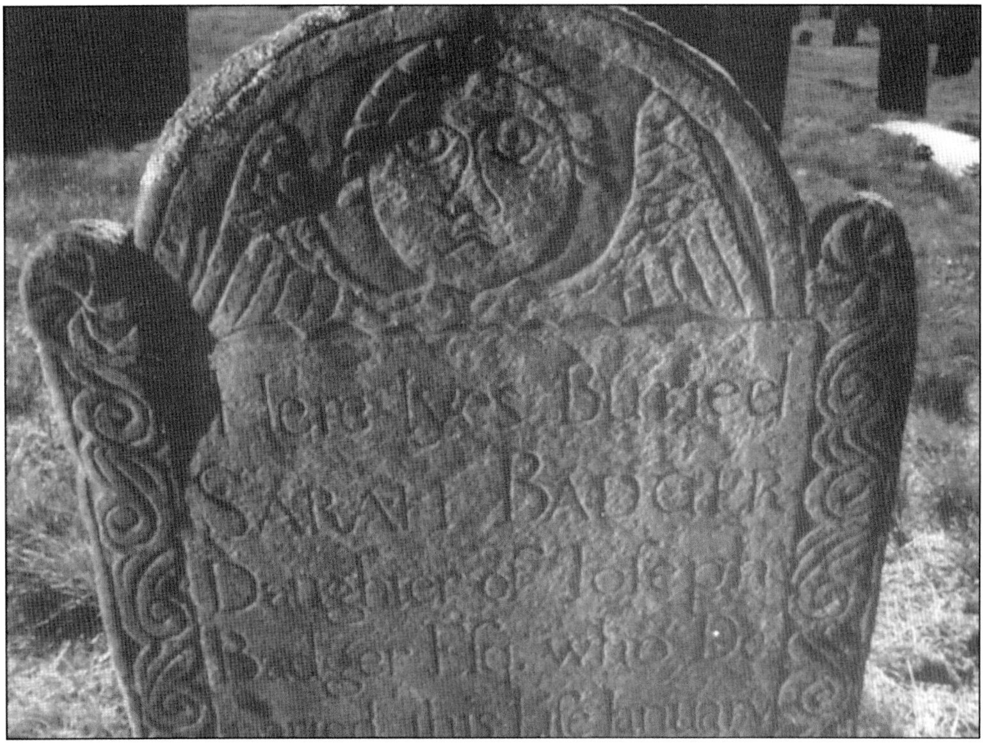

SARAH BADGER (1784), SMITH MEETING HOUSE CEMETERY. This gravestone, carved by Jeremiah Lane of distant Hampton Falls, is one of the oldest dated stones to be found here. Sarah Badger's father, Joseph Badger, was one of the town's most prominent settlers and served the town in many capacities, including many terms as treasurer, moderator of town meetings, selectman, and town clerk. He was also a trustee of Gilmanton Academy.

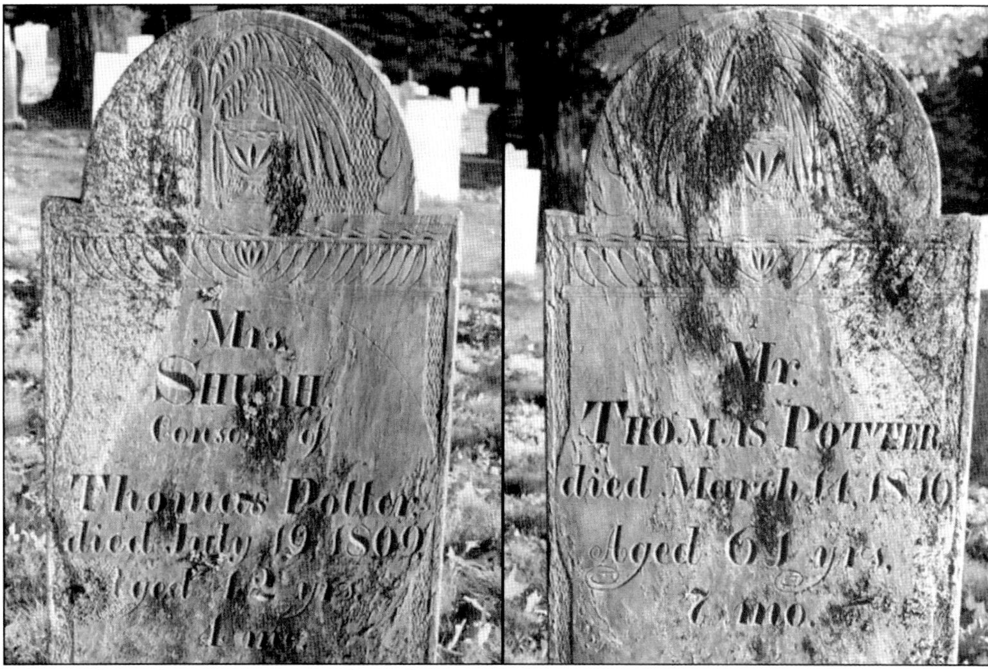

SHUAH (1809) AND THOMAS (1816) POTTER, SMITH MEETING HOUSE CEMETERY. The gravestones for this couple were carved by Gilmanton native Matthias Weeks. Hallmarks of his work include the circle around the epitaph area and the flower petal border above the names of the deceased. Little is known about Thomas Potter, but his wife, with the unusual name of Shuah, was born in Kingston, New Hampshire, the daughter of Daniel Gale.

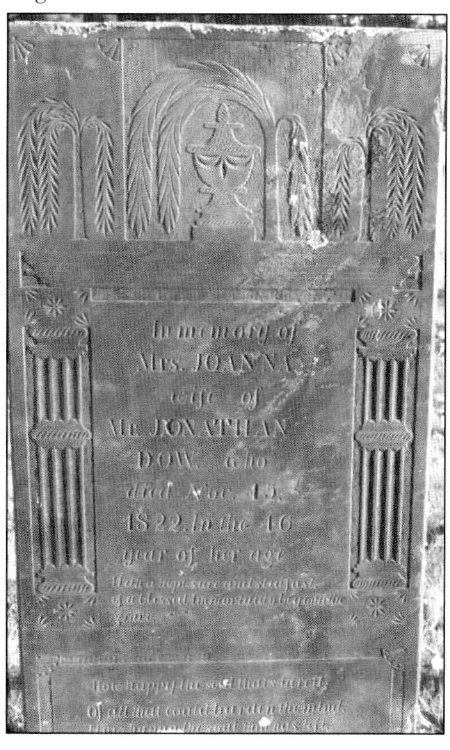

JOANNA DOW (1822), SMITH MEETING HOUSE CEMETERY. Joanna Dow's husband is probably the man that arrived here in 1774. If so, she was younger than him by 18 years or more. This attractive stone was carved by Matthias Weeks. Note the error in Jonathan's name. Dow was likely a Quaker; though he supported the American Revolution and "approved of the Declaration of Independence," he would not take part in the fighting.

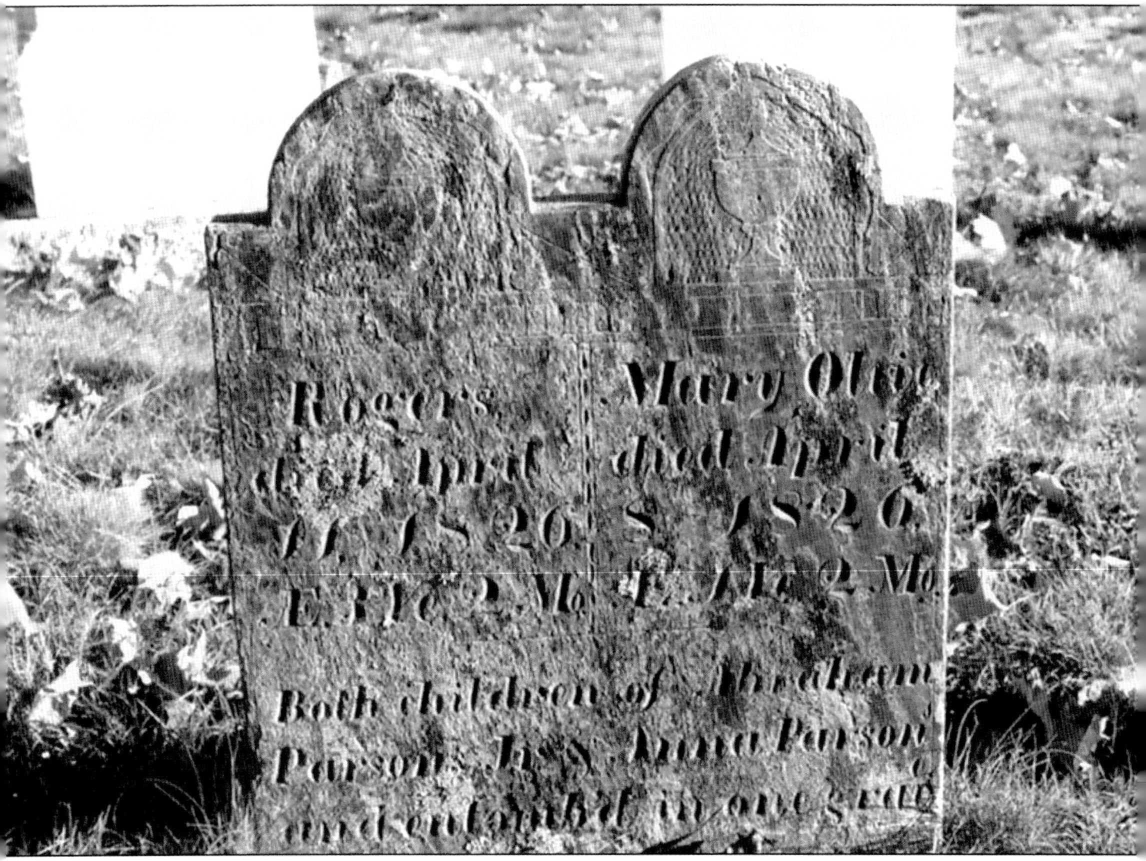

ROGERS AND MARY OLIVE PARSONS (1826), SMITH MEETING HOUSE CEMETERY. As the bottom of this Matthias Weeks–carved gravestone states, both of these children were "entombed in one grave." Ages three and one, respectively, Rogers and Mary were the children of Abraham and Anna Parsons. They tragically died within three days of each other, possibly due to one of the many spotted fever epidemics that hit the area at various intervals.

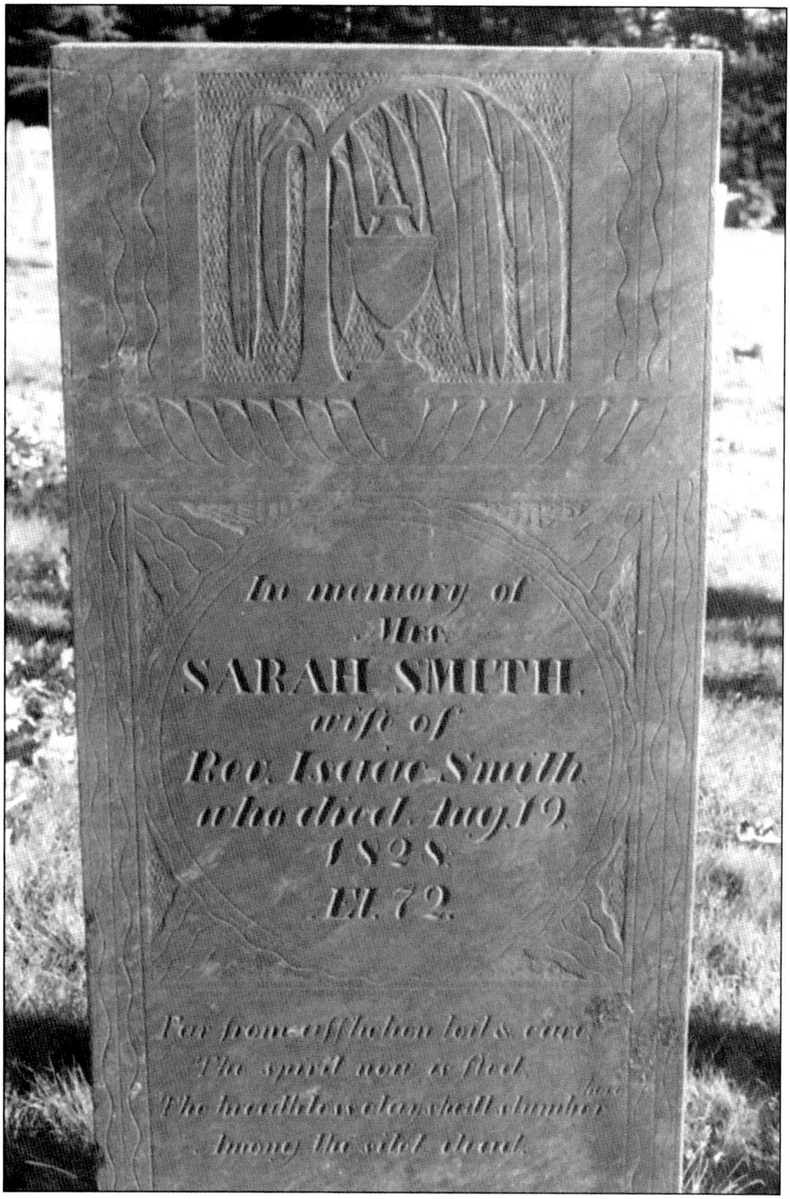

SARAH SMITH (1828), SMITH MEETING HOUSE CEMETERY. Sarah Smith was the daughter of Deacon Joseph Eaton of Haverhill, Massachusetts. She was the second wife of Rev. Isaac Smith, Gilmanton's first settled minister, marrying him on November 10, 1791. Isaac was a native of Sterling, Connecticut. He learned the trade of a shoemaker but later attended Princeton University with his brother and graduated from there in 1770. Isaac soon after came to the Lakes Region and was well received in his pastoral duties, accepting the call to preach from a group of Gilmanton citizens in 1774. Called an "animated and pointed preacher and a discriminating theologian" by historian Daniel Lancaster, Isaac Smith was beloved by his congregation and preached here for the rest of his life, despite problems with the town regarding his salary and taxation issues. Described as a "tall and slender" man, "rather bony," he caught a cold during a trip to Rochester and died on March 25, 1817, at the age of 72. Sarah, whose gravestone was carved by Matthias Weeks, lived for another 11 years.

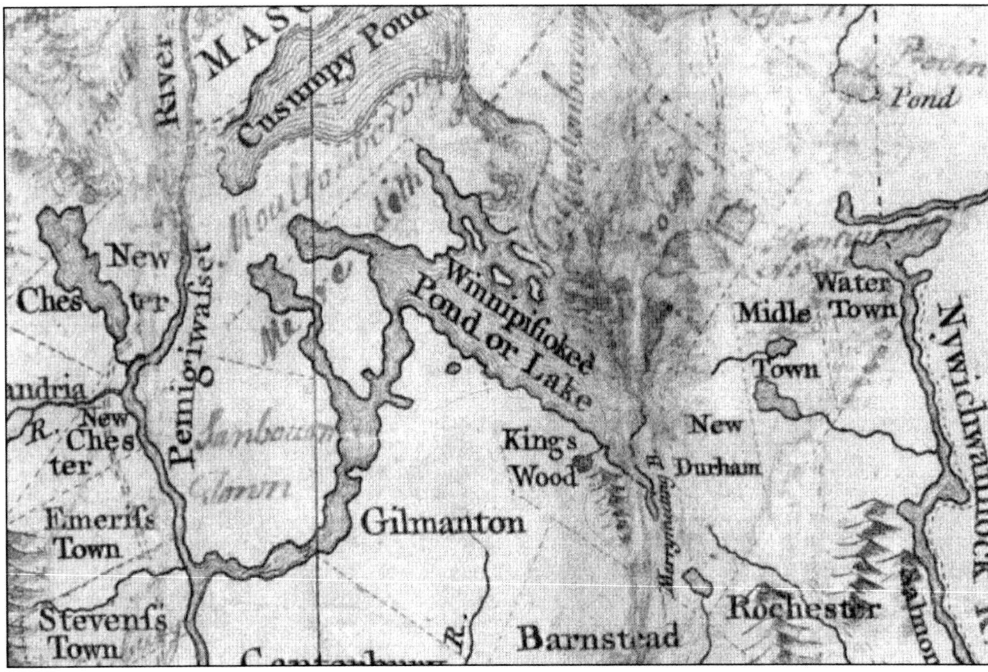

DETAIL, MAP OF THE PROVINCE OF NEW HAMPSHIRE, 1761, ENGRAVED BY THOMAS JEFFERY. This early map, engraved in the same year that Gilmanton was first settled, shows how the geography of the Lakes Region was viewed early on. Note that many of the townships granted around the lake, Gilmanton excepted, have their borders lightly sketched on this map, indicating a lack of actual settlement. (Courtesy Library of Congress.)

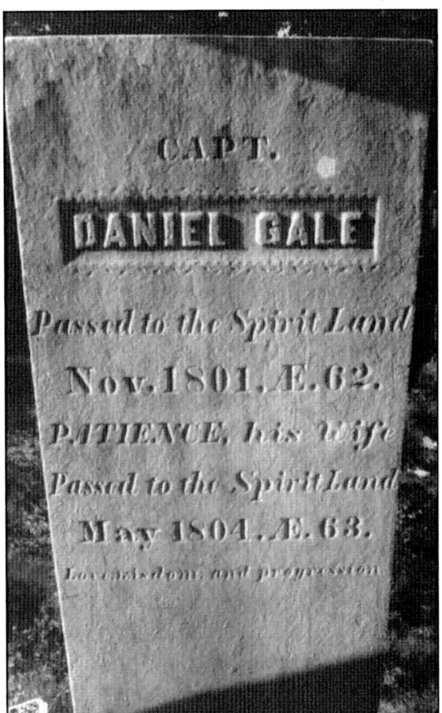

DANIEL (1801) AND PATIENCE (1804) GALE, SMITH MEETING HOUSE CEMETERY. Daniel Gale, the son of Jacob Gale of Kingston, arrived in Gilmanton in 1780. He served during the Revolution in 1775 in Poor's 2nd New Hampshire Regiment under Capt. Jeremiah Clough as a private and likely gained his title of captain from subsequent militia service. Though dated 1804, this stone was likely not carved until the 1830s, perhaps as a replacement.

WILLIAM SANBORN (1847), SMITH MEETING HOUSE CEMETERY. This marble stone is unusual for its depiction of an angel, carved in a style reminiscent of 18th-century slate gravestones. William Sanborn may be a descendant of one of Gilmanton's early settlers, John Sanborn, who arrived here in 1764.

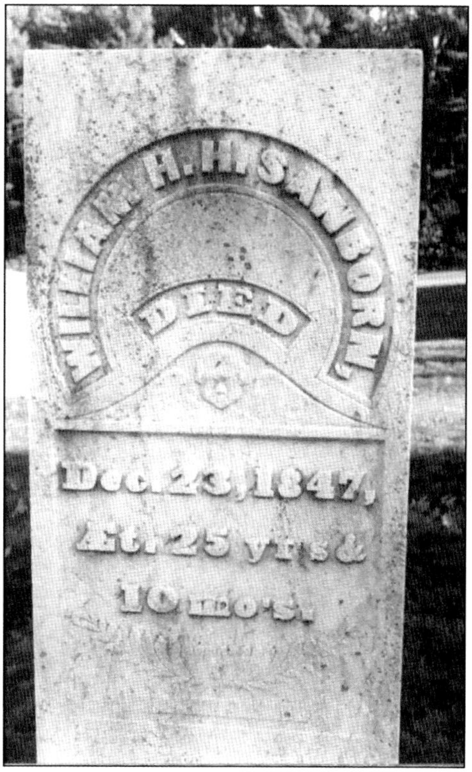

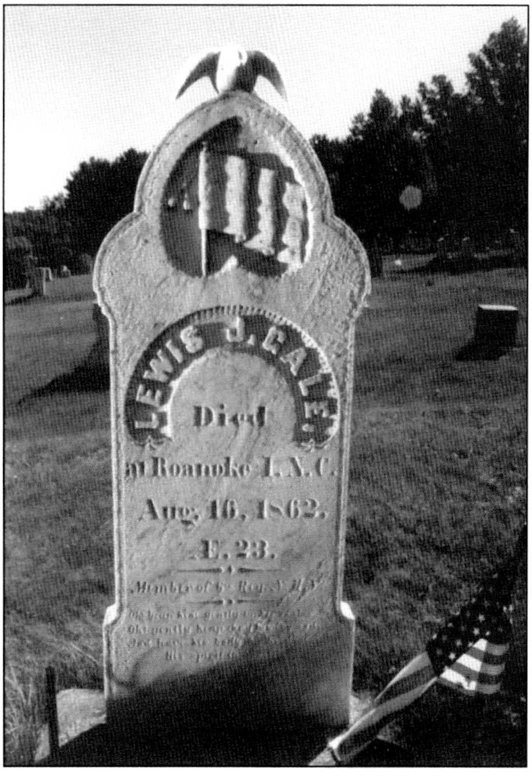

LEWIS GALE (1862), SMITH MEETING HOUSE CEMETERY. Continuing in the military tradition of the Gale family, Lewis enlisted in the 6th New Hampshire Regiment during the Civil War in November 1861. After seeing action in coastal North Carolina, Gale contracted a fever and died at Roanoke Island in August 1862. His unusual stone, with a sculpted dove perched on top, was carved by the Cummings stonecutters of Franklin, New Hampshire.

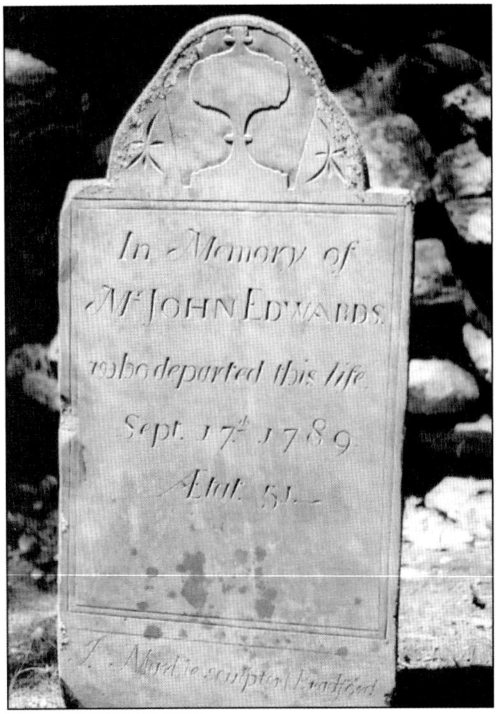

JOHN EDWARDS (1789), COPP CEMETERY. John Edwards's fine slate gravestone is the oldest in this yard and one of the oldest in the region. As is prominently noted at its base, this stone was carved by John Marble of Bradford, Massachusetts (and later Portsmouth, New Hampshire). A stone such as this, finely crafted and "imported" this far north into the wilderness, is a sure sign of Edwards's wealth and standing.

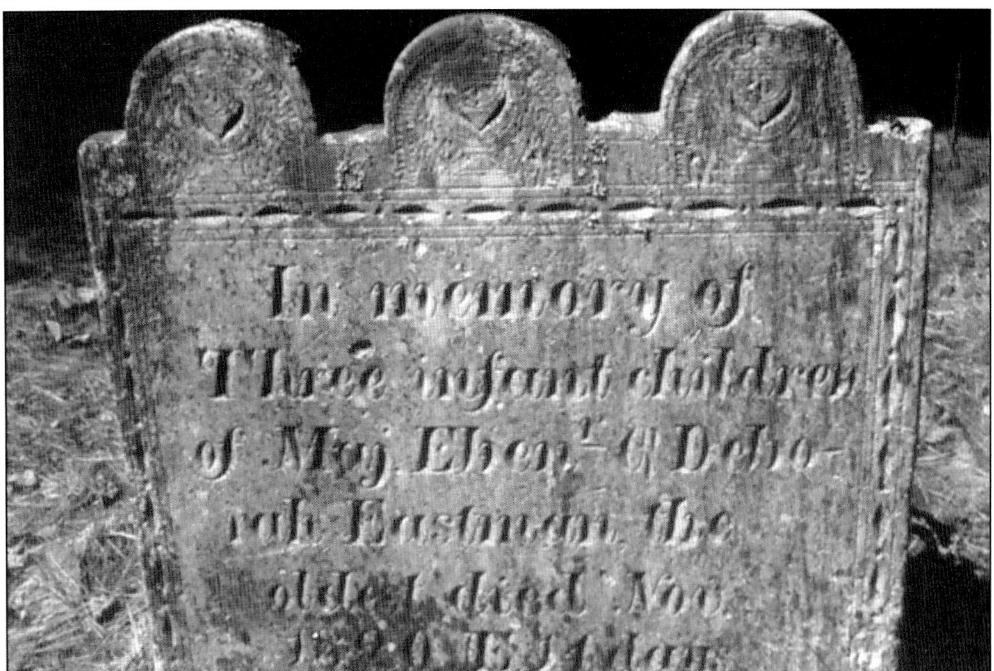

THE EASTMAN CHILDREN (1820), COPP CEMETERY. This gravestone is one of the most poignant in Gilmanton. Ebenezer Eastman moved to Gilmanton prior to the Revolution. During the war, he served in the Battle of Bunker Hill and was a capable officer. His wife Deborah, local lore states, had a strong premonition that her husband was killed at Bunker Hill and became quite distraught before finally learning that he had survived.

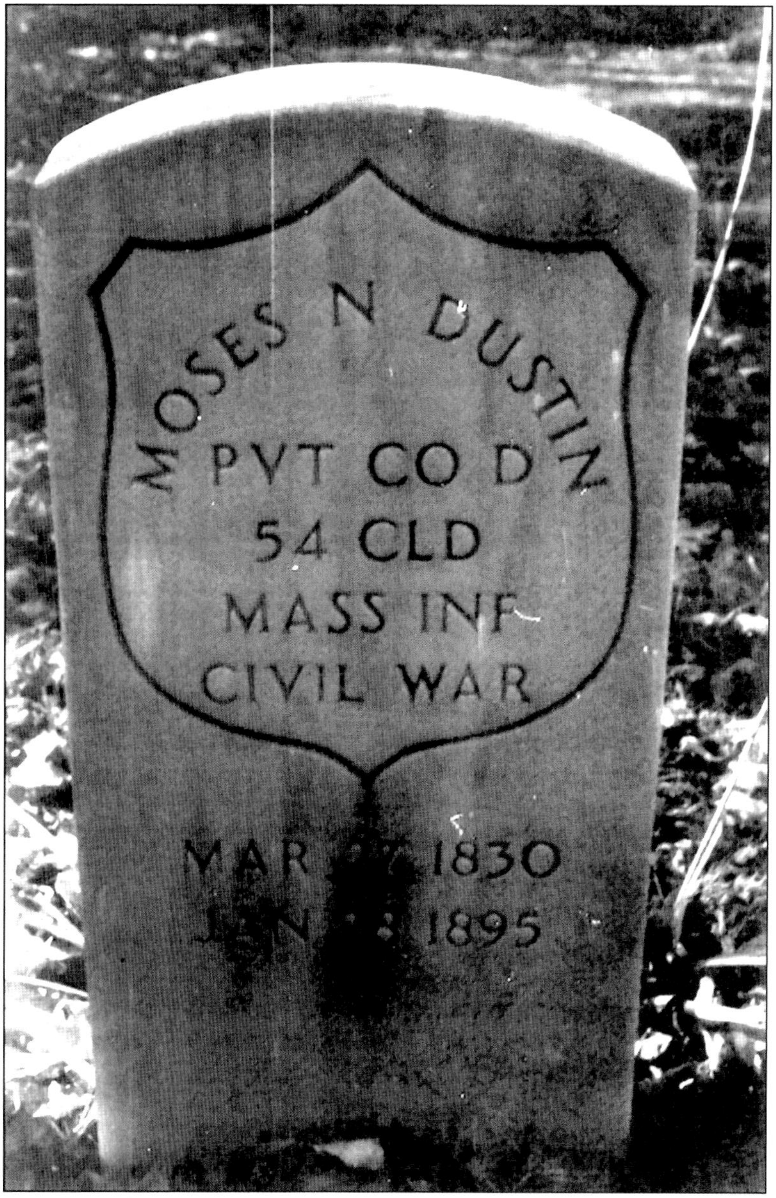

MOSES DUSTIN (1895), BEECH GROVE CEMETERY. Evidence of African American life in the area is scarce, but not so here. Moses Dustin was a free black who originated from Canterbury. He was drafted for Civil War service in the 54th Massachusetts Regiment in August 1863. Dustin saw service at the Siege of Fort Wagner, joining his unit as a replacement for the men of the 54th who had died in the assault on the fort (made famous in the movie *Glory*). Later stationed at Morris Island, Dustin became ill and was discharged. Soon after, in October 1864, he enlisted in the 3rd U.S. Colored Troops and saw duty in Florida before his service ended in October 1865. After the war, Dustin settled in Gilmanton as a farm laborer. Dustin was buried outside Beech Grove's boundaries, legend stating that no one wanted to be around him while he was alive and felt the same after he died. This likely reflects not on Dustin's character but on the prejudice of the times when it was still common for African Americans to be buried apart from whites.

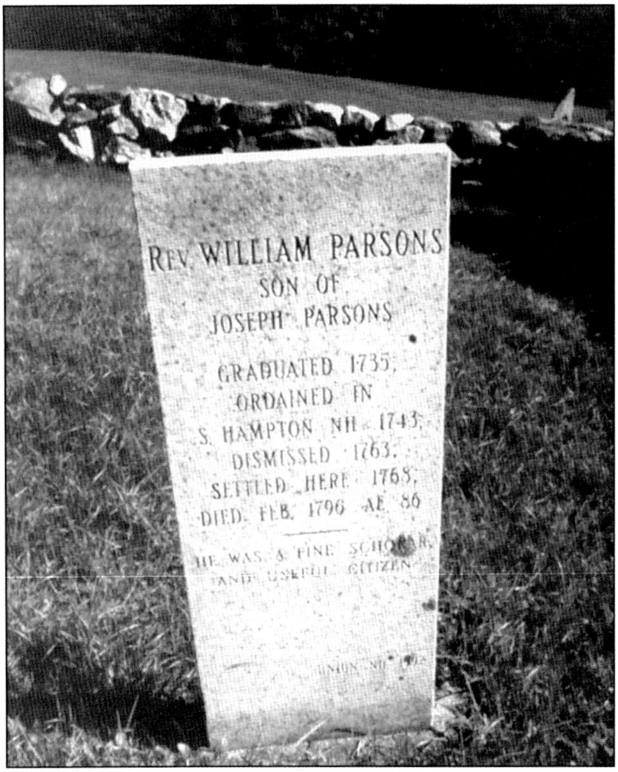

WILLIAM PARSONS (1796), PARSONS CEMETERY. This preacher-settler was a Boston native and Harvard graduate. The area was such a wilderness when he arrived that William Parsons had to cut a trail for his ox team with an ax to reach his homestead and on the night he arrived fell asleep, exhausted, beside his oxen. Parsons was a major influence; he taught school for years and was town minister before Isaac Smith's arrival.

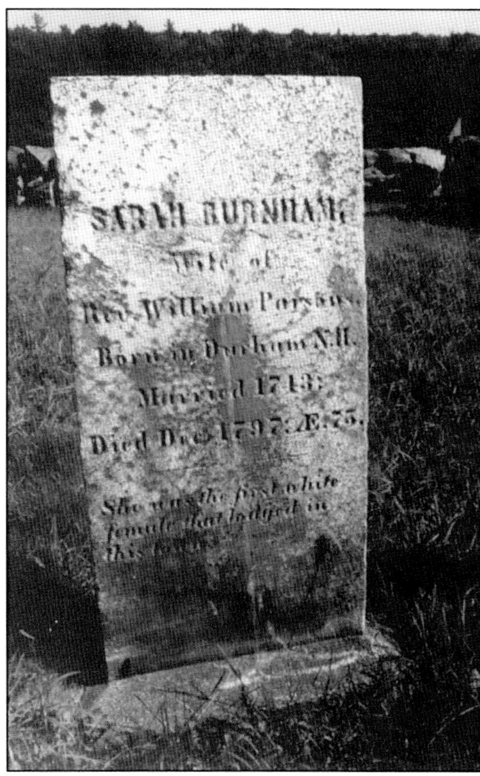

SARAH BURNHAM (1797), PARSONS CEMETERY. This stone, likely erected around 1840, years after Sarah Burnham's death, offers a rival claimant to the title of the first white female settler in Gilmanton, stating that Sarah "was the first white female that lodged in this town." That honor is usually accorded to Hannah Mudgett, who arrived here in 1761, but is disputed by this gravestone erected by Sarah's descendants.

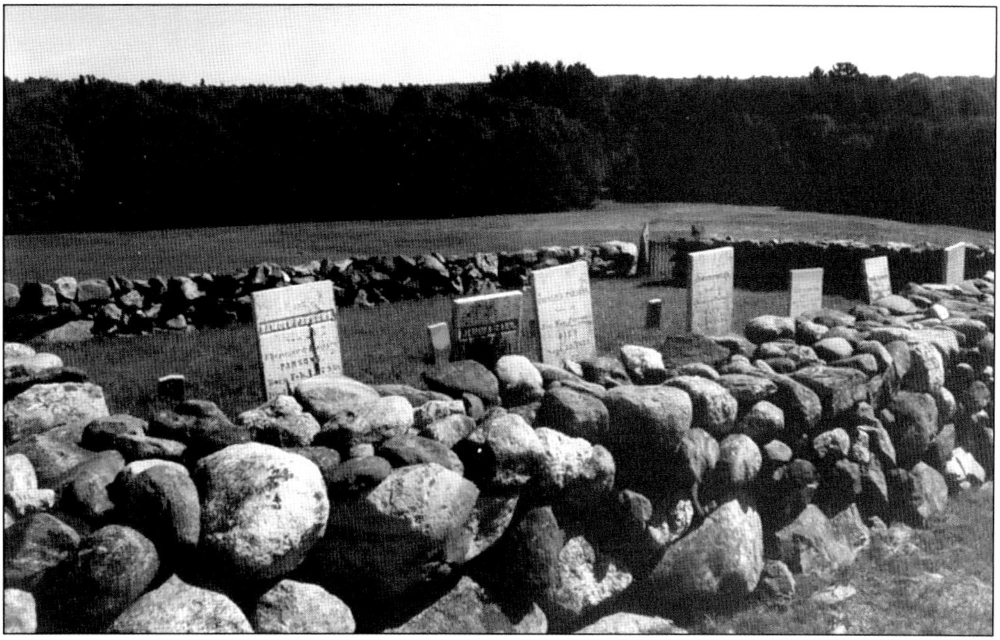

Parsons Cemetery. This rural cemetery is one of the most picturesque of the family cemeteries in Gilmanton. Located on a hill next to open farmland, it is surrounded by a neat stone wall and is well maintained. It is also located along the route by which most of Gilmanton's early settlers, William Parsons included, arrived in town from such places distant as Brentwood, Exeter, Kingston, and beyond.

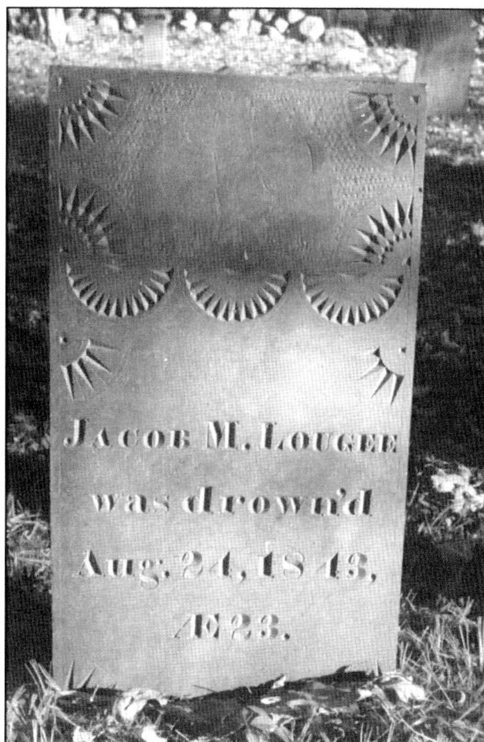

Jacob Lougee (1843), Tibbetts Cemetery. The Lougee family first arrived in town in 1766, Gilman Lougee settling here on 100 acres of land. The area they lived in, the western side of today's Crystal Lake, was known as Lougee Town. It was perhaps in this "pond" that young Jacob was drowned in 1843. His slate gravestone, with a weeping willow tree and many sunburst designs, is by an unknown carver.

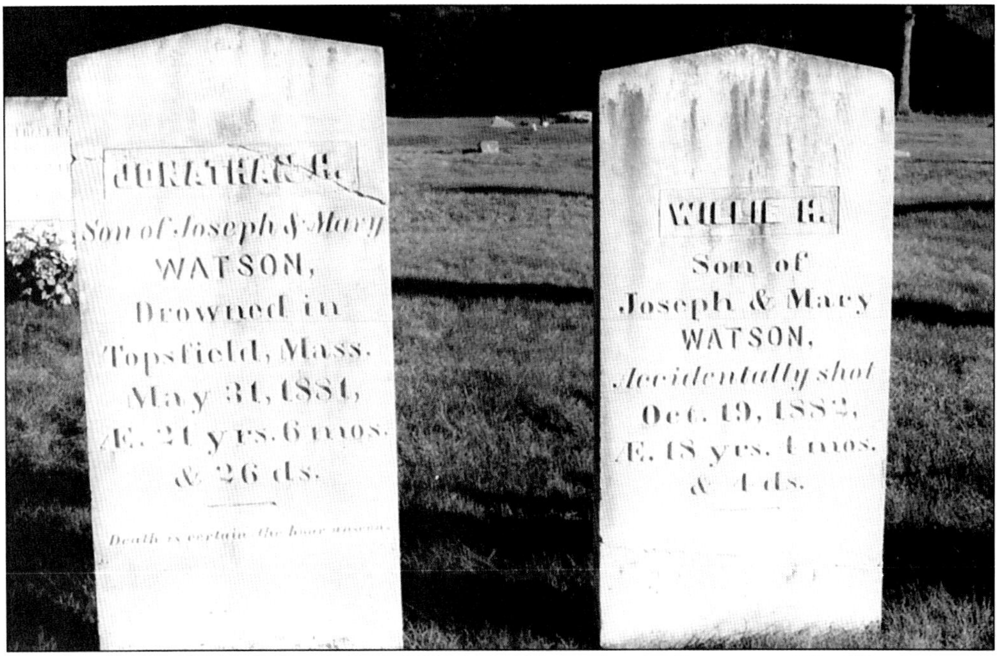

JONATHAN (1881) AND WILLIE (1882) WATSON, PINE GROVE CEMETERY. The Watson family gravestones found here graphically illustrate an ill-fated and unlucky family. Within a year and a half, two of Joseph and Mary's adult sons died in accidental circumstances. Nearby is the gravestone for their oldest son, Joseph, who died of disease in 1864 at Point Lookout, Maryland, while serving in the 12th New Hampshire Regiment during the Civil War.

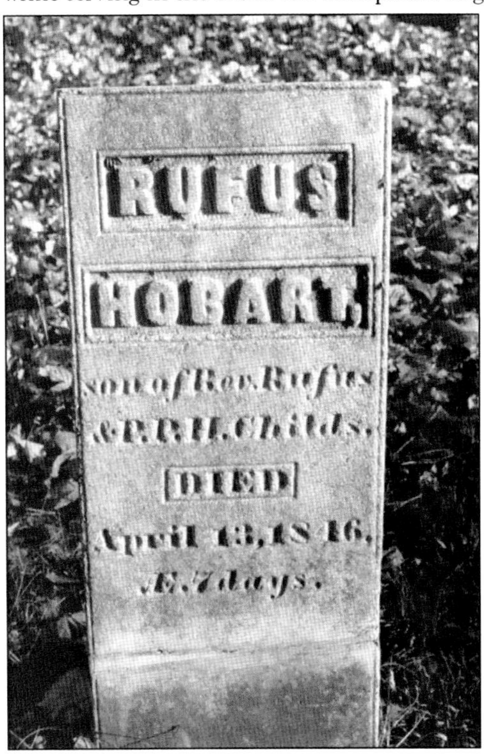

RUFUS HOBART CHILDS (1846), TIBBETTS CEMETERY. This infant was the son of Rev. Rufus Childs, a graduate of the Theological Seminary at Gilmanton in 1844. He accepted a call to preach at Gilmanton Ironworks in November 1844, continuing his ministry there for many years, and wrote that "there have been seasons of more than ordinary religious interest . . . but there has been no general revival in religion since the year 1838."